The Battle
For
Empire

The Battle
For
Empire
A Century of Anglo-
French Conflict

Jock Haswell

CASSELL · LONDON

CASSELL & COMPANY LTD
an imprint of
Cassell & Collier Macmillan Publishers Ltd
35 Red Lion Square, London WC1R 4SG
and at Sydney, Auckland, Toronto, Johannesburg

and an affiliate of The Macmillan Publishing Company Inc, New York

First published 1976

ISBN 0 304 29518 3

*Printed in Great Britain by
The Camelot Press Ltd, Southampton*
F475

Contents

Maps and Plans

Acknowledgements

I am greatly in debt to Mr Potts of the Ministry of Defence
Central Library, Miss Stephanie Glover of the Royal United
Services Institute for Defence Studies, Mr Tompsett of the
Folkestone Public Library and Mrs Grace of the Sir John
Moore Library at Shorncliffe not only for all their help and
advice over sources of information but for their patience
and understanding in not nagging me to return them. I am
also most grateful to Mr Robert Proctor for giving me so
many of his history books when he came down from University;
they have been of the greatest value. To Pam and Jamie
Williams I owe much more than I can ever repay. The Williams family have owned land in Jamaica, father to son, since
1671, and all of them seem to have been collectors of the
island's history. Unfortunately there was not enough time to
examine it all in detail but I was shown much that was fascinating, and unbounded hospitality and generosity enabled me
to see the country. To Mr Ian Cook, a neighbour of the Wil-
liamses, I am indebted for the story of the land crabs which
frightened Cromwell's soldiers. I would like to thank Mr
Roger Smith of Cassell's who has taken a great deal of trouble
in editing the manuscript and making helpful suggestions
for cuts, though we may not be in complete agreement
over the spelling of certain names—Tadusac, for example,
and Montmorenci. When drawing the maps I took the names
as I found them, and my sources were all eighteenth- or
nineteenth-century. I do realize how maddening it is to find
a misspelt name, particularly if it happens to be one's own,
or one's home town, and I must apologize if I offend any reader
with this fault—all I can say is that if my spelling is wrong, it
is the way it used to be spelt. Pepperrell, for instance: the
historian Francis Parkman actually wrote part of his account
of the Louisbourg affair in Sir William Pepperrell's study in

Massachusetts, and I feel his version must be right. Isabeau of Bavaria appears in history books as Isabelle and Isabel; I have taken the spelling from the effigy of her in Saint-Denis and the inscription on the marble bust in the Château de Vincennes. Indian names are always subject to error since they were usually an Anglicized version of a local word that was originally spoken and not written down; Mahratta and Maratha are typical examples—the former being the spelling used in the old Indian Army.

Finally, I am extremely grateful to my wife who accompanies me on research trips, who brings a clear and logical mind to the muddle of my indexing, and whose research work on my behalf is invaluable.

Lyminge 1975   J. H.

1 The Roots of Enmity

In the afternoon of 28 September 1066, William the Bastard, subsequently known as the Conqueror, sprang from his splendidly decorated ship on to the pebbly beach at Bulverhithe near Pevensey in Sussex. A fortnight later, on Saturday, 14 October, his invasion force met the Saxon army in pitched battle on Senlac ridge, where Battle Abbey now stands. Harold the Saxon king was killed, not, so the experts say, by an arrow in the eye, but by the sword of a Norman knight who had broken through the protective ring of housecarls.

This victory enabled William to establish himself in southern England and so create a Norman empire. The encounter was also the first of a long series of battles fought between England and France during the next four hundred years. At first it was the Normans—just as restless and acquisitive as their forebears the Norsemen—who were successful, for after seven years of war they conquered England, although they had no success against the Scots or Welsh.

The Norman knights and barons, having slain or driven out most of the Saxon landowners, took Saxon wives and mistresses, and in a comparatively short space of time were absorbed into the life and structure of the country. The effect of this in battle was far-reaching.

At Senlac the Norman chivalry—or cavalry—had looked with contempt upon the English infantry because on the Continent infantry were regarded as the lowest form of military life, being unable to stand up to the line of levelled lances bearing down with the full weight of lumbering war-horses behind them. But these Saxons stood firm behind their shields and brought down their mounted enemies with mighty swings of their double-headed axes. Senlac, decided only by Harold's death at the end of a fight which lasted practically all day, established the tradition and the reputation of the British infantry, best summed up perhaps by the French Marshal Soult after he had lost the battle of Albuera in the Peninsular War: 'I always thought they were bad soldiers; now I am sure of it. I had turned their right, pierced their centre and everywhere victory was mine, but they did not know how to run.'

The military marriage of Norman cavalry and Saxon infantry produced a formidable force, and when the Norman and Plantagenet kings of England went back to France to hold and expand their possessions on the Continent, they took with them small armies in which Horse and Foot fought together as a team, interdependent and linked by a bond of mutual respect for each other's prowess. Then, in the middle of the fourteenth century, the appearance of the 'English' archers (many of whom were Welsh), armed with the longbow of Gwent, completely revolutionized warfare and, particularly in the three great battles of Crécy, Poitiers and Agincourt, killed the flower of French chivalry in fearful arrow storms. The English dominated the battlefields of France and, as Sir Winston Churchill wrote, 'throughout the medieval history of England war with France was the interminable and often the dominant theme'.

In the latter half of the twelfth century Henry II, surnamed Plantagenet, created the Angevin Empire, ruling from the Pyrenees to the north of Scotland and owning more than half France. Englishmen, selling their wool in Flanders in order to buy their wine from Bordeaux, began to look upon the country across the Channel as a province of England, and for more than a hundred years, in what became known as the Hundred Years' War, they devoted their energies to the conquest of France, seeking to establish the Frenchmen who ruled them—the Plantagenets—on the French throne. Although they won battles they could not win wars, and they never really had any chance of complete success because the people of France were determined not to be dominated by the people of England. The years passed, the tides of warfare ebbed and flowed but one factor remained constant: the deep-rooted antipathy between the peoples of each nation who regarded one another as ancient and traditional enemies.

It was the ambition of many a French king to unite all

France against her great enemy, but their power had been weakened by the unfortunate system of appanages—the apportioning of great dukedoms to the younger sons of the kings. These royal dukes, such as Burgundy, Berry and Orléans, were fiercely independent of any central authority, and reduced the influence of the kings of France to little more than that of princelings who had no real sovereignty outside the boundaries of the province of l'Île de France, the region around Paris. Under that unhappy lunatic Charles VI, whose reign was torn by the civil war between the Burgundians led by John the Fearless and the Armagnacs under the Duke of Orléans, France and her monarchy reached their nadir.

In October 1415 Henry V of England destroyed the huge French army on the muddy battlefield of Agincourt and, being a skilful politician as well as an inspiring general, took every advantage of the mortal struggle between the Dukes of Orléans and Burgundy. In May 1420 Charles was made to sign the Treaty of Troyes which his Queen, the notorious Isabeau of Bavaria, and his Burgundian enemies had made with Henry V. By its provisions Henry was to become Regent of France immediately, and King of France when Charles died. He also obtained Charles's daughter, Princess Catherine, as his wife, and so it seemed as if the long battle for France was over; that what Henry had described as 'this good land' was to become a province under the English crown.

Henry V was only thirty-four when he died suddenly at the great fortress of Vincennes on the last day of August 1422, leaving his beautiful young wife with a son, Henry, only nine months old. Seven weeks later, on 21 October, Charles VI died (at the age of fifty-three) and at Saint-Denis the Herald of France cried, 'God grant long life to Henry VI, by the grace of God, King of France and of England.'

From the French point of view, things could not have been worse. The Dauphin, Charles VI's son, weak in body and lacking moral strength, had been led by his faithless mother to believe he was illegitimate and therefore had no unassailable right to the French throne. With no money and very few soldiers he was, to all intents and purposes, confined within a small area between the Seine and the Loire, and his people referred to him contemptuously as 'the little King of Bourges'.

3

He made no attempt to claim his inheritance, and the Duke of Bedford, as Regent for his nephew, ruled in Paris.

But then there arose one of the greatest figures in French history: Joan of Arc, shepherdess, saviour of France and, at only nineteen, martyr; a maid in whom all that is good and valiant, wise and tender in the human race was embodied. She gave to her king his self-confidence and his crown, and in creating a king and a tradition she re-created her country and its national pride.

The English failed altogether to realize the fundamental change wrought by the Maid of Orléans—Bedford attached so little importance to the 'incident' that he did not even bother to report her death to the King's Council at home. But in pursuing her primary aim of French unity Joan had placed the symbol of it, the crowned king, under the protection of the people, thus joining them all in a common purpose.

Thereafter, from the English point of view, nothing went right. After the defeat of gallant old Lord Talbot, Earl of Shrewsbury—he was eighty-six—at the battle of Castillon in July 1453, the English possessions in France were reduced to the town of Calais and a little strip of marshy ground beneath its walls. Vast areas of land in France, such as Gascony which had acknowledged English rule for three hundred years, changed hands for ever, and the anger and resentment of the English people at their losses found expression in the terrible Wars of the Roses.

For the next thirty years, while the English aristocracy destroyed each other, Charles VII reorganized France in a reign which was an unqualified success. Fearing his own 'ruling class' he governed through an efficient and energetic King's Council of ministers chosen from the middle class, and there was practically no field of national activity—trade, religion, foreign policy or defence—in which the hand of this king was not felt. Charles died on 22 July 1461 and his son, Louis XI, succeeded him. Neither of the two men had ever had any illusions about the other. Louis despised his father for his lechery, and Charles deeply distrusted his son.

Louis continued his father's policy of uniting and strengthening France, and to him these ends justified any means. Lying, deceit and double-dealing came naturally to him and he explained his conduct as a diplomat and politician by the cynical apophthegm, 'He who has success also has honour.' But he was greedy and impetuous, and he made one major error which was to have a profound effect both on the future of France and on her long contest with England. It stemmed from his conflict with Charles the Bold, who had inherited the dukedom of Burgundy on the death of his father, Philip the Good.

Charles the Bold did his best to persuade Edward IV of England, who had emerged victorious from the carnage of the Wars of the Roses, to join him in his quarrel with Louis XI. In this he was forestalled by Louis who, with justification, firmly believed that every man has his price. He met Edward on the bridge at Picquigny, not far from Amiens, in 1475, and offered him a pension. Edward, short of money and tired of fighting, accepted it with enthusiasm and signed the treaty which kept England out of France's civil war and brought the Hundred Years' War to an end.

Charles the Bold, looking elsewhere for support, tried to join Alsace and Lorraine to his possessions in Burgundy and Flanders, but in 1477 he was killed in an attack on Nancy, capital of the Dukes of Lorraine. His only heir was his daughter, Marie of Burgundy. For lack of a male heir the provinces of Burgundy and Picardy, formerly an appanage, automatically reverted to the crown. Louis, over-hasty, tried without success to marry the twenty-year-old Marie to his son, the Dauphin, later Charles VIII, who was only seven, and followed this up by annexing the Burgundian holdings of the county of Artois and also Franche-Comté, which was a fief of the Holy Roman Empire (Austria).

Finding herself thus dispossessed, Marie of Burgundy sought and found refuge in Flanders and then in 1477 married the Emperor Maximilian of Austria. She took to him as her dowry the Burgundian capital of Brussels and a large area of Flanders lying along the northern boundary of France.

This marriage altered the whole concept of allies and adversaries in Europe and began two hundred years of war between France and Austria, because Marie's dowry created a zone of extreme vulnerability, since described as the cockpit of Europe. The Germans coveted these border lands because

5

the Rhine flows down towards them, and the English have long been sensitive about the port of Antwerp on the Scheldt. Napoleon summed up this sensitivity with his remark that whoever held Antwerp held a loaded pistol at Britain's head; but the converse was also true—an enemy in Flanders was a direct threat to Paris.

In 1482 Marie was thrown from her horse and, too modest to allow any doctor to examine her injuries, died soon afterwards. She left one son, Philip the Fair, and a daughter, Margaret of Austria, aged two. Louis XI, quick to seize what he thought might be an advantage, arranged for the little girl to be betrothed to the Dauphin, and it was agreed that her dowry would be Artois and the Franche-Comté. This was a great diplomatic success, for with no question of annexation the two disputed provinces came back legally and properly to the French crown. At the same time, Austria (and the Empire) through her Austrian princess, Margaret, maintained a strong interest in them. It was particularly unfortunate that in this one vital region, giving the only easy access to France, such a tangle of conflicting interests should have arisen, because in 1496 Marie's son Philip the Fair married Joanna of Spain, and their child, later Emperor Charles V, was to unite Austria and Spain. This encircling menace supplanted the age-old threat of England which, because of the obstacle of the Channel, was nothing like so intimate and alarming.

Hostilities between France and England were suspended during the Wars of the Roses which at last came to an end when Richard III was slain in the battle of Bosworth Field in 1485. Henry VII, grandson of Catherine of France who first married Henry V, came to the throne, and the red emblem of Lancaster and the white of York were united in the Tudor rose.

The battle of Bosworth marked in England the end not merely of the Wars of the Roses but of the Middle Ages and of feudalism. In Europe, feudalism was engulfed by the forces of the Renaissance and the Reformation, changing the whole course of man's progress—but not his attitude to his neighbours. The scars of generations of war puckered the surface of diplomatic relations between France and England, and deep down in the body of both nations lay an incurable, mutual antagonism. The terrible defeats of Crécy, Poitiers and Agincourt were not forgotten by Frenchmen, and the English brooded on their eviction, by means they could not understand, from those provinces of France they had come to regard as English territory.

Under the dark shadow of enmity the differences between the two nations had become irreconcilable, and the struggle for domination, which in Europe for the time being was no longer to be so direct a confrontation, had in fact been carried into a far wider field by a handful of adventurers who were neither French nor British.

2 The Areas of Conflict

The French monarchy was now set fair on the road to absolutism, with the willing connivance of the French people who had come to the same conclusion as that reached by their hereditary adversaries across the Channel. The only protection for the rights of the ordinary people was a strong monarchy, synonymous with centralized control, the maintenance of law and order and the subjugation of the nobility. Neither the aristocracy nor the States General were able to oppose or check the growth of royal authority whose political platform was built of three firm planks: personal power, national acceptance of that power, and the unquestioned religious foundation for the monarchy as a system of government.

This government was stable, and under it the country prospered. Prosperity created leisure and from a combination of the two stemmed a growing awareness and deeper appreciation of ideas and the arts. This rebirth began more or less in the reign of François I in 1515, and the period of the Renaissance lasted until the death of Henri III in 1589. At this time the mariners of the Channel ports and Atlantic seaboard, becoming less preoccupied with inshore fishing and coastal trading, looked out across the ocean and began to think seriously of setting forth on those unknown waters to discover what was on the other side.

In England, so many members of the so-called ruling class had been either slain or executed in the Wars of the Roses that the whole basis of regional government and 'local authority' had been undermined. The war, and the economic and administrative chaos which accompanied it, had been a blood-stained blanket, stifling men's minds and making it almost impossible for them to see or think about anything but their immediate problems.

Since the reign of Henry II, first of the Plantagenets, the

English had devoted their energies to material affairs, such as the conquest of France, neglecting matters of the mind, and it was largely their indifference to metaphysics which enabled Henry VIII to bring about so painless a schism with the Church of Rome. There was no religious war in England, whose people were prepared to compromise and regard their sovereign as the temporal Head of the Church of England.

The principal effect of the Reformation in England was that men realized that the infallible could be questioned, the unassailable could be attacked; and this added immeasurably to the force of the Renaissance when it came. Almost everything which for centuries had been regarded, without any real analysis, as part of the unalterable system of life, now came under careful examination, and the stability of the Tudor dynasty created the right conditions for such scrutiny. Practically every field of thought and endeavour was affected: geography, religion, commerce and the whole social structure.

The great resources of mental and moral energy latent in the island race broke the bounds imposed by the struggle between the Houses of York and Lancaster and found expression in literature, the reorganization of agriculture and industry and, above all, in a quest for expansion which drove the merchants and mariners of England out across the distant oceans of the world. This sudden release of energy was the mystery and the glory of the Elizabethan Age, and although the exploits of the great adventurers have, by legend and tradition, been invested with romanticism, this is, with minor exceptions, unjustified. The adventurers were hard-headed, extremely practical men who undertook incredibly hazardous journeys with the primary object of making a profit. One may perhaps like to think of the early explorers—Corte Real, Vasco da Gama, the Cabots, Samuel Champlain and all the other men of exceptional courage and endurance—as inspired by the pure spirit of adventure and an urge to discover, just for the sake of discovery. No doubt some of them were, but in fact the initial voyages which revealed the oceans of the world and led in due course to the development of colonial empires, were prompted by nothing more uplifting than pepper.

Pepper came from the Spice Islands, the Moluccas, between the Celebes and New Guinea on the western edge of the

Pacific Ocean. Bales of pepper and other spices such as cin-
namon and cloves went first to the Malay peninsula and were
carried by Indian traders across the Bay of Bengal and then
across India. On the west coast of the sub-continent Arab
merchants shipped them in their dhows to the ports of Massawa
and Jiddah in the Red Sea and to the harbours of the Persian
Gulf, whence they travelled by camel caravans along the
great trade routes to the markets of Alexandria. From here the
merchants of Venice and Genoa, always menaced by pirates,
conveyed them across the Mediterranean to the markets of
Western Europe. On this long journey the bales changed hands
as many as twenty times, incurring countless levies from local
rulers, and so a bale of peppercorns, bought in an island such
as Halmahera or Buru for one ducat (about 50 pence), was
sold in England or Flanders for 105 ducats—a considerable
percentage increase and a classic example of passing on costs
to the consumer.

In the Middle Ages, and for long after, spices were a vital
factor in the economy of Europe and directly related to two
apparently insoluble problems. One was the difficulty of
feeding cattle and sheep in the winter and the other was the
need to provide a continual supply of meat. There was always
a shortage of fodder and so it became the custom to slaughter
animals in the autumn and to use spices, if not to preserve the
carcases, at least to disguise the smell of putrefaction when the
meat was eaten.

So essential a trade brought immense riches to all who were
involved in it, especially to the ports of Venice and Genoa.
Their customers, particularly those on the Atlantic seaboard,
began to think about breaking the monopoly of the overland
trade by sailing to the Spice Islands and bringing home their
own cargoes. Venice and Genoa looked on the idea as a
direct threat to their prosperity, and naturally enough showed
very little interest in finding a direct sea route to the Moluccas.
Thus it is not surprising that one of the best known of Genoese
seamen, Christopher Columbus, convinced that there was a
western route to the Indies, could find no sponsor in his home
city. Nor is it strange that Spain and Portugal, which could
have little or no share in the profits of the trade, became so
eager to find their own way to the riches of the East.

In the beginning, Portugal had one great asset, Prince Henry the Navigator. He was the third surviving son of King John I of Portugal, born in Oporto in March 1394, and it was his determination to find out what lay beyond the horizon which provided the impetus and the spur for his countrymen. His captains went out from his naval base at Sagres in the Algarve and, between them, discovered some four-fifths of what to them was the hitherto unknown world. Since in course of time France and England were to be the chief contenders in the acquisition of empires it is perhaps fitting that Prince Henry had both English and French blood in his veins. His mother was John of Gaunt's daughter Philippa, and on his father's side he was directly descended from Prince Henry of Burgundy who, at the beginning of the eleventh century, had been given the 'County of Portugal' when the Dukes of Burgundy allied themselves with the royal House of Castile.

The great age of discovery really began with the rounding of Cape Bojador by Gil Eannes, one of Henry's captains, in the summer of 1434. For two thousand years Bojador, on the edge of the Sahara desert, had been known to European seamen—including the inquisitive Normans—as the headland marking the edge of the world, and no one who had tried to sail beyond it had ever returned. This was because there was a reef running out to sea from the base of it for a distance of some fifteen miles so that if the mariner felt his way westwards to the end of this barrier he was then swept far out into the Atlantic by a combination of winds and currents. Long voyages against contrary winds and currents were not feasible until Henry the Navigator exploited the capabilities of the caravel. With a lateen rig copied exactly from the Arab dhow, its chief characteristic was an ability to sail close to the wind.

Gil Eannes pointed the way Bartholomew Diaz and Vasco da Gama were to take. He started them off on the route that led round the Cape of Good Hope and across the ocean beyond, to India.

Also aiming to find a sea route to the East, Joao Vaz Corte Real sailed westwards to America twenty years before Columbus. Neither of them actually discovered

America* because the Viking Leif Eriksson had landed in Massachusetts in A.D. 1003. Following Corte Real came Fernao de
Magalhaes—better known as Ferdinand Magellan—the first
leader of an expedition to circumnavigate the world, whose ship,
after his death, reached the goal of the Spice Islands. Almost
simultaneously in the East and in the West enormous new areas
of the world's surface became known to the seamen of Portugal
and Spain.

The voyages of Christopher Columbus, beginning in 1492,
enabled the Spanish to establish themselves in the West
Indies and Central America. Portugal was setting up her
trading stations in West Africa and pushing on towards
India—Bartholomew Diaz had rounded the Cape of Good
Hope in 1488. Both countries sent out more expeditions and
began to quarrel with each other over who had discovered
what, and when, and to whom it belonged. For example, the
Portuguese claimed that Columbus had not really crossed the
Atlantic at all on his first voyage and certainly had not discovered the Bahamas, Cuba and Hispaniola. They made out
that he had not in fact been any further than their own new
territory of Guinea, in West Africa. In 1493 Pope Alexander VI
intervened, intending to settle the dispute finally, and issued
two Bulls, dated May and September, which allotted specific
areas of exploration to each nation. In June 1494, by the
Treaty of Tordesillas, the Spanish and Portuguese agreed on a
line drawn north and south in the Atlantic, through a point
370 leagues (931 sea miles) west of the Cape Verde Islands.
Spain was to have all the lands she discovered to the west of
this line, and Portugal those to the east, 'provided they were
not already owned by a Christian ruler'.

Initially the Spaniards and the Portuguese both kept quiet

* In 1500, Cabral, a Portuguese sailor, discovered Brazil by accident
when he was on the way to India. Blown across the Atlantic by a storm, he
claimed the new land for Portugal. In the following year King Manoel sent
out an expedition to consolidate the claim. With it went a merchant, Amerigo
Vespucci, who wrote an attractive account of all he had seen. A German
scholar included this in a best-selling work of geography he was compiling,
and suggested the discovery be named America, after Amerigo, who was
not even a navigator. The name, applied at first only to a small strip of land
on the Gulf of Mexico, became popular in Europe and then was generally
accepted for the whole of the American continent.

about the achievements of their explorers, for they had no wish for other nations to share the spoils, but news of the Papal intervention and the treaty aroused considerable interest in the courts of England and France. Both Henry VII and Louis XII began to feel there was no reason why Portugal and Spain should have the monopoly of discovery, with its material benefits, and since neither the French nor the English had been consulted over this partitioning of the world they regarded the Treaty of Tordesillas as an arrangement which in no way concerned them.

At this time Henry VII had in his kingdom another Genoese, John Cabot, a naturalized Venetian. No one knows for certain what brought him to Bristol but it seems he shared with Columbus the dream of finding a sea route to Cathay. Much was known, if not altogether believed, of the mysteries and riches of the fabulous land of China after Marco Polo the Venetian had dictated the story of his adventures, the *Livre des Merveilles*, to the scribe Rusticiano of Pisa in the year 1298. But Marco Polo, his father Nicolo and his uncle Maffeo were not seamen, nor were they explorers in the true sense. Their long journey overland to the court of Kublai Khan, grandson of Genghis Khan, had been along the much-travelled caravan route and they went simply in search of trade. They spent about seventeen years in China, from 1275 until 1292, and brought back precious stones hidden in their clothing as evidence of the wonders they had seen.

Yet the fabled treasures of Cathay and the obvious advantages of direct trade with the Spice Islands together provided all the incentive the imaginative and commercially-inclined Italians, Portuguese and Spaniards needed. John Cabot was just as sure as Columbus that there was a way to these riches if only one sailed far enough towards the setting sun. He had, after all, travelled and traded in the Red Sea and the Levant, on the old spice route. He knew people who journeyed regularly to the Far East and so he knew, from other sources, that there was substance in Marco Polo's story. With his mind full of projects for a passage to the Indies by the north-west he spent several years looking for patrons to sponsor an expedition. He got no help from Venice or Genoa; Portugal and Spain had explorers of their own; the court in France was cautious, unwilling to invest in a dream, and it is said that Louis XII sent him to England to divert Henry's attention from Continental affairs.

Cabot's plan was based on the shape of the globe. It was obvious to him that anyone sailing through equatorial waters would have much further to go than if they kept as far to the north as possible. It was his intention to make what use he could of this geometrical fact, but he shared with Columbus the misconception that it was Asia that lay on the other side of the Atlantic, neither having any idea that the direct route to the Indies was barred by a vast, unknown continent.

Bristol was the obvious starting point for any transatlantic exploration. Seamen from that port had for years been exploiting the fishing grounds off Iceland, and in the West Country there was a pronounced spirit of adventure, born of strong commercial instincts and a lively curiosity, that was not so evident elsewhere in England. No doubt it was this general atmosphere which attracted John Cabot to the port, for he was there with his family in 1496, when the King came to the city. As the result of an audience with the King, Cabot received letters patent authorizing him to lead an expedition, at his own expense, consisting of five ships. He could sail wherever he wished and take possession of any lands he discovered, provided they had not already been claimed by other Christian people. He was to trade only from the port of Bristol, would not be liable for any customs duty and would possess a monopoly in his trading interests. In return for all these concessions which cost the King nothing, he was to pay Henry one-fifth of all profits.

In the late spring of the following year John Cabot managed at last to put to sea although, despite royal patronage, the support he received from the merchants and investors of Bristol was so meagre he was only able to fit out one tiny vessel, the *Matthew*, little more than a fishing boat, with a crew of eighteen men. On 24 June 1497 he sighted land but no one is quite sure whether it was the coast of Newfoundland, Labrador or as far south as Cape Breton Island. He went ashore, planted the flags of England and Venice, and then sailed southwards down the line of the coast as far, so it is said, as the shores of South Carolina. Being by then short of provisions he went home, absolutely confident he had found the lands of the Grand Cham. He was also sure that if he had been able to go on along the American coast he would have come to the island he called Cipango (Japan) which he thought was the source of all the spices and precious stones in the world. On his return he told Henry VII it would now be possible for London to become a far greater storehouse of spices than Alexandria had ever been.

Cabot was rewarded with the title of admiral and was lavishly entertained at court. In Bristol he promised the merchants not only a vastly increased trade in stock-fish, one of their main interests, but great cargoes of spices, jewels and silk which he would bring back from the rich cities of China and Japan. In 1499 he set out again, this time with five ships, and disappeared. Yet there was one immediate and tangible result of his voyages—the discovery, on England's behalf, of the Bank Fisheries off Newfoundland, already known to deep-sea fishermen from Normandy and Brittany, Spain and Portugal. Within a short time the seamen of the West Country no longer went to Iceland but took far larger catches and profits from the new fishing grounds.

There were other results, not immediately apparent. Cabot gave expression to the half-formed ideas of Englishmen who realized they had lost for ever any hope of possessing France, and yet felt the urge to reach beyond the narrow limits of their island, out into the wider world. He had the same effect on the mariners of England as Gil Eannes had had on Portuguese sailors: he pointed the way. The fact that he did not return underlined the dangers of his undertaking but deterred no one. Indeed, it is significant, and a testimony to the determination of these early explorers, that the awful hardships, dangers and disasters suffered by so many seem merely to have spurred others on.

Cabot also established that the Bulls of Alexander VI and the Treaty of Tordesillas were not just a formality. Before Cabot set out on his second journey the Spanish Ambassador protested vehemently to Henry VII on behalf of the Kings of Spain and Portugal that expeditions of this sort were bound to be to the prejudice of their Catholic Majesties. Thus, as the likelihood of war on land against France receded, so the probability of maritime conflict with the people of the Iberian peninsula increased.

Cabot's son, Sebastian, following where his father had led, made two voyages under the patronage of Henry VII. The dates of them are in dispute, but his object was to find the North-West Passage to the Indies. He passed through what was later named Hudson Strait into the open water of what he thought was a sea beyond, but is in fact Hudson Bay. Pushing on, sure that he was sailing round the north of America, he ran into such danger from ice that his crews forced him to turn back, and he went south, searching for a westward passage in warmer waters. When he came back from his second journey he learned that his patron had died—in 1509—and that the government under the new king, Henry VIII, was not prepared to follow up the discoveries he had made. Two years later, Sebastian went to Spain and stayed there, becoming a Pilot-Major under Charles V.

The English, led by Italians, had made contact with the North American continent, and the French were quick to follow. In 1506 Denis of Honfleur sailed into the Gulf of St Lawrence and in 1518 the Baron de Léry tried without success to establish a French colony on Sable Island. The Baron did, however, leave a memorial to his failure in the form of multiplying herds of cattle, bred from the few he had brought from France. In 1524 a Florentine navigator, Giovanni da Verrazzano—another adventurous Italian—hired by the French King François I, sailed north from the coast of North Carolina to Labrador and declared that all the land he had seen now belonged to France.

When Verrazzano returned to François I and announced his discoveries, he was making the first substantial claim laid by anyone who was not working for either Spain or Portugal, and the French seemed to grasp, far more quickly than the English, the idea of taking and holding land in the form of colonies. Most of the English seamen of the sixteenth century were interested only in making their fortunes; by lawful trading when conditions were favourable, and piracy when they were not. So, while the English were voyaging to Brazil and the West Coast of Africa, fishing off Newfoundland, lying in wait for the treasure fleets and fighting the galleons of

Spain in the Caribbean, or searching for the North-West Passage, the French were moving quietly into Canada and strengthening their grip on the northern half of the North American continent.

Although the Phoenicians had sailed round Africa in a clockwise direction, leaving Kosseir in the Red Sea in July 600 B.C. and arriving at Alexandria in February 597 B.C., no one, until Henry the Navigator put pressure on Gil Eannes, had been successful in the continual battle against contrary winds and currents on the anti-clockwise route. At length, in 1488 Bartholomew Diaz made his way round the Cape of Storms (Cape of Good Hope) into the Indian Ocean and in 1498 Vasco da Gama dropped anchor off Calicut on the Malabar Coast of India. For the next hundred years the Portuguese held fast to their monopoly of trade with India (throughout this book 'India' is the whole sub-continent as it was before Partition into India and Pakistan). They set up a factory— in its original sense of an establishment for traders conducting their business in a foreign country—at Calicut, but later their influence was centred at Goa and spread to Ceylon. Competition was inevitable, and in 1580 Portugal came under the sovereignty of Spain, so that attacks on her East Indian trade became a means of damaging the proud Spanish, whose acquisition of empire had made them so unpopular.

In 1582 Edward Fenton, an Englishman, in the galleon *Leicester* and with three other ships failed in an attempt to sail direct to India and challenge the Portuguese monopoly. Another venture by James Lancaster and George Raymond set off in 1591 with three ships. Raymond's ship sank with all hands off the Cape of Good Hope—one ship had already been sent back with all the scurvy cases—and Lancaster went on alone. He reached the Eastern Archipelago, captured two Portuguese ships and made his way back to Ceylon where he hoped to catch some rich convoy; but his men had had enough and insisted on going home. Many died on the long journey and Lancaster had to put in to the West Indies for fresh food. While he was ashore, mutineers stole his ship but he managed to get home in a French privateer after being away for nearly three years. By all standards his voyage had been a disaster but it had in no way blunted his enthusiasm to try again.

The capture in 1592 of a Portuguese carrack whose cargo was worth the then enormous sum of £150,000 had a profound effect on the merchants of London who were beginning to realize that up to now they had enjoyed little or no share in the immensely valuable and profitable trade with the East. In 1596 Captain Benjamin Wood was given command of another expedition, which again was a disaster. After two of his three ships had been lost he was wrecked on the coast of Burma and nothing more was heard of him. Yet, five years later, in 1601, one survivor of his expedition was picked up by a Dutch ship from the then uninhabited island of Mauritius. He had crossed the Bay of Bengal and the Indian Ocean, a distance of about 3,300 sea miles, in a small native boat.

The first European competitor to challenge the Portuguese-Spanish interests in the East was a Dutchman, James Houtmann, who left Texel Island in 1595 and set up a factory at Bantam in Java. Feeling that if the Dutch could do it, they could too, the English formed an Association of Merchant Adventurers in London in 1599. Since Queen Elizabeth was then going through one of her periodic attempts to come to some peaceful arrangement with Spain the project received no support until her negotiations broke down, and during the delay the Adventurers doubled their capital and applied for a grant of incorporation. They were given their charter on 31 December 1600, and it brought into being the greatest development and trading organization in the history of the British Empire, the East India Company.

Early in 1601 James Lancaster, now Sir James, set sail with four ships and had an extremely successful voyage.

In France, Henri IV's Grand Surveyor, the duc de Sully, had no doubt about the importance of flourishing overseas trade and colonies. In 1608, the same year in which the French naval captain Samuel Champlain founded Quebec as the capital of the French colony of Canada, the Company for Trade with the Indies was formed. Once in being, this French East India Company seems to have remained inactive for the next thirty years. In 1642 it tried to justify its existence by forming a colony in Madagascar. This was not a success, but that great minister, Jean-Baptiste Colbert, chief adviser to the young king Louis XIV, was just as alive as Sully had been to the advantages to be gained by trade with India. He allocated funds for the formation of a new company. After wasting much time and money on another failure in Madagascar the company sent an expedition to Surat and established the first French factory in India in the autumn of 1668.

Surat was hardly a suitable place in which to begin a venture of this sort. The English 'Supreme Presidency', as their main company headquarters was called, had been settled there for nearly forty years, and those of its staff who were not irritated by the arrival of the French were amused by their presumption. Yet this presumption was by no means as laughable as the English merchants thought at first. In 1674 François Martin set up a factory at Pondicherry and two years later a French fleet sailed up the Hooghli river and landed a party of settlers at Chandernagore. The contest between the French and the English for supremacy in India had begun.

Meanwhile the growing strength of the French in Canada was becoming a threat to the English colonies which had been planted between the Atlantic coast and the Allegheny mountains. In the West Indies the steady increase of French influence and the depredations of French privateers were causing much alarm and distress to the English settlers who were beginning to realize the commercial potential of the islands they occupied.

Both nations had been comparatively late in entering the competition for empires, and at first they had no real cause to fight one another; in fact there was a tendency to co-operate. For example, in 1565 Sir John Hawkins, on his way home from the West Indies, was glad to help starving Frenchmen in a colony planted on the coast of Carolina by Captain René Laudonnière. The operations of both nations were fiercely resented and contested by the Spanish and the Portuguese who had divided the world between them; yet, as time went on, neither could sustain or protect the huge areas they had claimed. Before long it became obvious to the English and the French that all competitors would have to be swept out of the way if they were to develop their own interests. Inevitably the development of their own interests brought them into direct opposition.

There were many places, in West and South Africa, the islands of the Indian Ocean, in what used to be called Indo-China, some of the Pacific Islands and even Tasmania, where there was competition—even the occasional hostilities—but no serious confrontation. Only for the vast spaces of the North American continent, for the wealth of the sugar islands of the Caribbean and for dominion over India was there war between the two nations.

The colonial contest between England and France was fought in these three areas, and it was a contest which lasted for a hundred years. Beginning in the middle of the seventeenth century it went on until the Peace of Paris in 1763, which brought to an end what Pitt, Lord Chatham, called the first world war. Better known in Europe as the Seven Years' War, and in America as the French and Indian War, this global struggle decided which of the two cultures, languages and influences would dominate the world, and the seeds of it were planted in the reigns of François I of France and Henry VIII of England when Jacques Cartier first went to North America.

3 North America

The fundamental differences in policies between the French and the English had a profound effect on their long contest for colonies and empires. Whereas the French tried to colonize the areas in which they hoped to trade, the English discovered, very early on, that the two functions were not compatible.

In France, during the administration of Louis XIV's great minister Jean-Baptiste Colbert from 1664 until 1683, their policy was sound enough: territorial expansion to increase trade, protected by naval power and supported by a strong economic structure and national wealth—all under centralized control which handled every detail. Unfortunately Colbert himself was the only man capable of putting it into practice, and when he died the men who took over the great offices of state for which he alone had been responsible—finance, trade, the navy and the colonies—allowed everything to decline. English policy had always been more resilient, being based on the idea that the man on the spot was the best judge of a local situation. Thus the death of a king or a minister, a change of government or a financial crisis was unlikely to have any immediate or short-term effect on overseas possessions.

The French explorers and adventurers of the seventeenth century were on the whole more successful than the English in their dealings with the inhabitants of America, India and the West Indies. With certain notable exceptions—for instance the comte de Lally in India—the French were courteous and accommodating, whereas the English were apt to conduct their affairs with a self-confidence which raised barriers between them and people whose co-operation was sometimes vital. The French had no inhibitions about adapting themselves to their surroundings, even to the extent, in some cases, of living naked among the cannibals of the West Indian islands or appearing in the paint and feathers of an Indian brave,

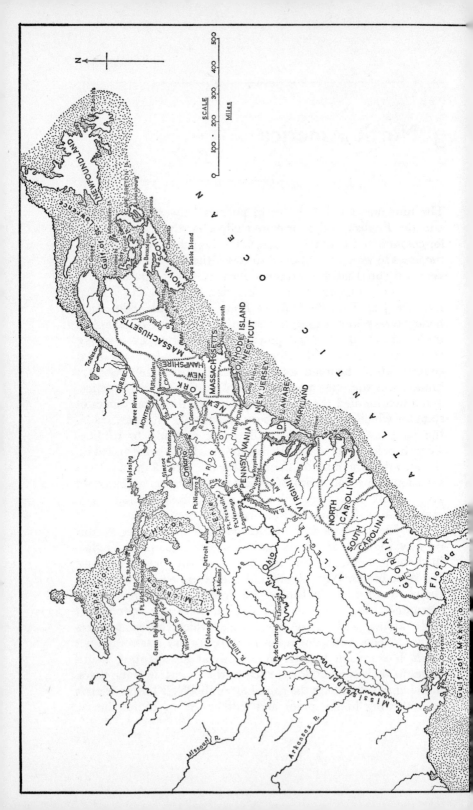

nor did they disapprove of mixed marriages—unthinkable to such people as the colonists of New England. Paradoxically, they went to such lengths to indicate their indifference to dissimilarity in colour, creed and culture, that sometimes they were despised for behaviour which showed how little they respected their own customs.

In commerical affairs the English system of joint-stock companies which initially sponsored factories, and sometimes colonies, for the profit of their shareholders, usually allowed them to operate in a free market. The French exploited their colonies mercilessly, buying their produce as cheaply as possible and forcing the colonists to buy French goods at an inflated rate. This policy rebounded with telling effect in the case of the French Company of the Isles of America, for the colonists in the West Indies ignored its monopoly, invited the Dutch to trade with them, and the company went bankrupt.

In religious matters the French had a distinct advantage. Their missionaries were mainly Jesuits whose doctrine, no matter where they went, was simple and uniform. An aura of bigotry and discord was generated by a multiplicity of Protestant sects in areas colonized by the English who, for this reason, were seldom able to make a lasting religious impact on the local inhabitants.

From the political point of view the differences were even more marked. The French deliberately involved themselves in the internal affairs of the people with whom they came in contact. They flattered, showed great deference to the authority of local chiefs or rulers and conformed to local customs. They gave sympathy and gained in return tolerance, friendship and influence.

Inevitably the English attitude to foreigners kept them somewhat aloof. If they became involved in local politics— as they did in India—it was usually for strictly military reasons or because there appeared to be no alternative. They were seldom obsequious. It does not seem to have occurred to any of the early explorers that they might not be welcome, and possessing a comfortable feeling of superiority they were quite fearless. One of the best examples of this was the visit paid by Richard Chancellor in 1553 to the court of the Tsar of Muscovy, Ivan the Terrible. Chancellor was chief pilot

Sketch Map of the North American Area

in an expedition led by Sir Hugh Willoughby to find the North-East Passage to Cathay. Separated from the other two ships in a storm, Chancellor sailed into the White Sea and was conducted by 'barbarians' to their village of Nenoksa, not far from Archangel. While the crew wintered in the village, Chancellor went south by sledge to Moscow to call on the Tsar, carrying with him letters of recommendation from Edward VI. Everyone at Ivan's court lived in abject terror of him, and the general atmosphere was one of cringing servility, but Chancellor, granted an audience in the midst of a magnificent assembly, strode forward with complete self-assurance and so impressed Ivan the Terrible that the Tsar wrote to Edward VI giving a friendly invitation to all Englishmen to trade in his kingdom.

Yet perhaps the greatest difference of all was that of temperament. The men who went out from France to build the French empire were adventurers, explorers, soldiers, merchants and missionaries. Few of them had the resolution of, for example, the Pilgrim Fathers, whose object was to construct a whole new life in a new world, severing if necessary the ties with the land of their birth. Not many French colonists were prepared to settle down and till the land for their descendants to inherit, most of them feeling that they were exiles and hoping that when they had made their fortunes, preferably by commercial enterprises, they would be able to lay their bones in France. They were glad enough to take what they could from the new lands, they were not willing enough to give back all that was needed to keep them when their authority was challenged.

The first Frenchman to land in Canada was the Norman, Denis of Honfleur, who sailed from Dieppe to the Gulf of St Lawrence in 1506. Starting out from St Malo in the early spring of 1534, Jacques Cartier, a Breton, was the first French explorer and colonist to make a serious attempt to ignore Cabot's claim of 1497 and establish a French claim to the territory of New France. It was he who gave the name St Lawrence to the great waterway, and Mount Royal to the hill where Montreal now stands.

His patron was a young nobleman, comte Philippe de

Brion-Chabot, a personal friend of François I, who shared the King's dream of a great empire in the New World. The expedition consisted of about 120 men in two small ships, and after an untroubled passage of only twenty days they reached the coast of Newfoundland on 10 May 1534. Sailing anti-clockwise round the island, Cartier passed through the straits of Belle Île and found the coast so uninviting that he turned back. Running south across the Gulf of St Lawrence he sailed through the group of Magdalen Islands, along the coast of Prince Edward Island and landed on the shore of New Brunswick, somewhere just to the south of Miramichi Bay, at the mouth of one of the many rivers in this area. Like the Vikings before him, he found a land of plenty. Forests full of maple, ash and pine, fields of purple vetch, wild straw-berries and innumerable fat wood-pigeons, as well as streams full of salmon led the travellers to believe they had found a country which would give substance to their King's hopes. There seemed to be remarkably few inhabitants and those they met were friendly. Cartier moved on, and below the promontory of Gaspé he erected a crucifix, thirty feet high, on which he placed a shield bearing the arms of France.

Avoiding the autumn storms he returned to St Malo on 5 September (1534) and announced that he had discovered the gateway to Cathay—in fact, the mouth of the St Lawrence. He aroused just as much enthusiasm and excitement in France as John Cabot had done in England. Here lay a splendid, ready-made empire full of riches to be collected and heathens to be converted. The King, the merchants and the Church were all delighted.

On 19 May 1535 Cartier set sail again with three ships, *l'Hermine*, *La Petite Hermine* and *Emerillon*. This time he went up the St Lawrence river as far as Montreal, but his explora-tion, much of it in birch-bark canoes, took so long that he realized he would have to spend the winter where he was. Coming back down the river he came to a green island where vines grew in such abundance that his men, perhaps a little wistfully, called it the Isle of Bacchus (it is now the Île d'Orléans). Above it the river narrowed between lofty walls of red-stained grey rock, and on the northern side where the heights levelled off into a mighty promontory, were the wigwams of Stadacona, the capital of the region. Here, on the plateau where Quebec was to be built, the local chief Donnacona offered them hospitality. The ships were moored in a safe anchorage and Cartier built a small fort nearby where he made his preparations for the winter. This Breton sailor had no conception of what was in store for him and his companions. The storms, the cold and the snow exceeded anything they had ever imagined. Out of his party of 110 men twenty-five died and practically all the remainder fell sick with scurvy. Fortunately for them, one of the Indians told Cartier of a cure—a decoction made from an evergreen tree which was probably a spruce or arbor-vitae—and it worked, after Cartier and his men had consumed all the leaves and bark of a large tree. On 16 May 1536 the expedition set sail for France and reached St Malo on 16 June.

For the next four or five years François I was too occupied with his war against the Emperor Charles V to sponsor another voyage, but in 1541, after peace had been signed, he sent Cartier off again, this time accompanied by François de Roque, Sieur de Roberval, of Picardy, who was appointed 'Governor of Canada'. With them went a large number of prospective colonists, livestock and stores for founding a colony. Cartier piloted the expedition to the St Lawrence and returned safely to his manor house of Limoileu near St Malo; ennobled for his services to France he died in peace many years later. Roberval founded his colony at Charlesbourg Royal, near Cap Rouge on the St Lawrence, but hunger, scurvy and a disastrous winter drove him and the few survivors home again in the spring. In 1549 he tried again, without success, and came back to Paris where, so the story goes, he was killed one night in a street brawl.

Nearly forty years passed before either France or England made any further attempt to plant a permanent settlement in Canada, and then in 1583 Sir Humphrey Gilbert, half-brother of Sir Walter Raleigh, led an expedition to the safe harbour of St John's, Newfoundland. In the name of Queen Elizabeth I he took possession of Newfoundland, thereafter called 'the oldest colony'. St John's was a popular place, full of French, Portuguese, Spanish and English fishing vessels from the Grand Banks, and Gilbert, armed only with a piece of paper signed by Elizabeth, set up his own form of government, enacted a large number of laws and by sheer force of personality compelled all foreign sailors to acknowledge his authority. His charter was as generous and impractical as charters usually were at that time, giving him an area extending 600 miles in every direction from St John's. He was thus responsible for (on today's map) New Brunswick, Nova Scotia, Prince Edward Island and parts of the provinces of Labrador and Quebec. In common with most Elizabethans his main object was profit, and he spent a great deal of time and energy searching, without success, for silver mines. On one of these trips his largest ship was lost, and since supplies were running very low and winter was approaching he resolved to return to England. He set out in the *Squirrel*, a vessel of only ten tons, which went down with all hands in a hurricane. Sir Humphrey is a noble figure in the history of North America, and he is chiefly famous for his encouraging remark, shouted to the crew of the companion vessel *Hind* at the height of the storm and quoted by Hakluyt in his *Voyages*: 'We are as near to Heaven by sea as by land.'

In 1598 the marquis de la Roche, a nobleman of Brittany who had been given the titles and privileges of the unfortunate Roberval, led a private venture to Canadian shores in one small ship. Unable to find volunteers for his project, he had toured French prisons, selecting what he hoped would be suitable material. Steering much farther south than Roberval, he came upon the bleak sandspits of Sable Island which seemed to him an ideal spot to park his convicts while he went on to choose a site for his colony on the mainland. He went off, and at first his colonists were perfectly happy—virtually anything was better than the inside of a French prison. There was a lake of sweet water in the middle of the island; for food they had the wild descendants of the cattle left behind by Baron de Léry, masses of wildfowl and plenty of edible berries of various sorts. It was not a very comfortable place; there were no trees on the island, only sand dunes, grass and bushes, and little shelter from the incessant wind.

The marquis sailed away towards the mainland but his ship, caught up in a succession of storms, was blown right back across the Atlantic and wrecked on the rocky coast of

Brittany where he fell into the hands of a powerful enemy, the duc de Mercoeur. For no recorded reason, other than enmity, de Mercoeur threw the marquis into prison and left him there. Meanwhile conditions on Sable Island had deteriorated, and the convicts were having a miserable time, although they did not have to resort to cannibalism, which happened in colonies elsewhere—particularly Virginia in the dreadful winter of 1609. They kept themselves alive on the raw meat of the cattle, clothed themselves with hides and built a crude shelter with timber from several wrecks on the shore. At length the marquis was able to get a message to the King, now Henri IV of France, and a ship was sent to the island. When it returned, the convicts it brought back were paraded in front of the King, with their matted hair and beards and still wearing their hides. The sight so upset Henri IV that he pardoned them all and sent them home. The marquis, broken in health and fortune, died soon afterwards.

While the marquis de la Roche was in prison a naval officer named Chauvin, of Rouen, went into partnership with a merchant of St Malo, called Pontgravé and, on the condition of founding a colony in the valley of the St Lawrence, the partners were given a monopoly of the fur trade in the St Lawrence region. They kept to the letter of the bargain and left sixteen men, badly housed, clothed and supplied, to endure the winter of 1599 in appalling conditions at Tadusac. A trading vessel which arrived in the following spring found that most of the sixteen had died and the remainder had gone native and were dispersed among the wigwams of the Indians. The colony was only another link in the chain of disasters, all similar, but the fur trade was an enormous success, opening the eyes of the merchants of France.

No attempt was made to repeat the experiment at Tadusac but the fur trade went from strength to strength. On a third voyage to Canada in 1600 Chauvin died, and the whole of his enterprise collapsed. Three years later Champlain, perhaps the greatest name in the early history of the country, came to Canada.

Born at Brouage in 1567, Champlain became a captain in the French navy and was well known to Henri de Navarre, Henri IV of France. Henri employed Champlain on the extremely delicate intelligence mission of exploring part of Spanish-held Mexico and visiting Spanish settlements in the West Indies.

In 1603 the elderly Governor of Dieppe, Aymar de Chastes, followed up earlier attempts to colonize Canada by sending Champlain to take another look at the St Lawrence. Champlain followed the track already clearly marked by Cartier and found that Indian wars had destroyed all traces of any European settlements. After Champlain's return to Dieppe, one of his companions, Pierre du Guast, le Sieur de Monts, a nobleman-adventurer, decided to return to Canada with Champlain and the Baron de Poutrincourt and, bearing in mind all they had learned of the terrible winters on the lower reaches of the St Lawrence, they sailed southward for what was known as Acadie or Acadia.

Acadia was never anything more than a vague geographical term embracing the enormous area between latitudes 40° N and 46° N, in other words, from Montreal in the north to Philadelphia in the south, with New York, Boston and the Bay of Fundy in between. They set out in 1604, with two ships and a mixed company of gentlemen, thieves and rascals, and came to a harbour in the Bay of Fundy which de Monts called Port Royal (and the English, later on, Annapolis Royal) and there established their colony.

Like all the previous attempts it failed, but in 1608 Champlain began all the work again by founding Quebec. He also established Montreal as the gateway for the Indian fur-trade and the defensive outpost against Indian attack on the young French settlements. It was he who explored and named the Richelieu river and the lake which bears his own name, as far as the headlands subsequently called Crown Point and Ticonderoga.

Jesuit missionaries followed in Champlain's footsteps, spreading the Gospel with their own brands of courage and endurance, but it was Champlain who settled the French firmly into Canada.

In the same year as the founding of Quebec the English 'Company of Adventurers for Virginia' at last succeeded in planting a settlement on the James river, under that dominant and quarrelsome character Captain John Smith. Edward Maria Wingfield was the first elected president of the small colony, but it was Smith's energy, resourcefulness and determination that rescued the undertaking from its difficult beginnings. Although the famous story of Smith being captured by the Indians and saved from a horrible death by Pocahontas, daughter of Chief Powhatan, has been questioned on the grounds of inconsistencies in the account Smith gives in his *History*, as well as the fact that Pocahontas was only twelve at the time, there is no way of actually disproving it.

This colony of James Fort or Jamestown was founded only twenty-two years after the birth of Virginia Dare, the first English child to be born in America, in the ill-fated colony on Roanoke Island. Her mother was the daughter of John White, the governor appointed by Sir Walter Raleigh in 1587 when he made a second attempt to plant a permanent colony on the island. The first attempt, made in 1584, had failed because of food shortages and continual trouble with hostile Indians. The colonists had been brought back to England in June 1586 by Sir Francis Drake, when he called at Roanoke with a large fleet on his way home from a successful raid on the Spaniards in the West Indies.

No one knows what happened to Virginia Dare and the second colony. All was well when her grandfather Governor White left the island in November 1587 to return to England on colonial business. When he managed to get back again in 1590 he found the site abandoned, without any trace of where the colonists had gone. Many years later other colonists in the area were told conflicting tales by the Indians, one was of slavery ending in massacre and another of absorption into a friendly Indian tribe.

The French had made similar attempts, but further to the south, some twenty years before Raleigh's ventures. In 1562, after reconnoitring the coasts of Florida and Carolina, Captain Jean Ribault chose what appeared to be a suitable site in Carolina and planted a Huguenot colony there under the leadership of Albert de la Pierria. Not long after Ribault had returned to France his colonists murdered de la Pierria and tried to follow him, but most of them died on the way. Two years later a fresh attempt was made by René Laudonnière, in the same place, and he was joined by Ribault. This time the colony was attacked by Spaniards seeking to extirpate all traces of heresy in the New World, who slaughtered Ribault and most of the colonists while only Laudonnière and a few companions managed to escape. The Spaniards then occupied the little fort and took over the remains of the colony. In 1567 a French expedition led by Dominique de Gourges swept down upon them and in revenge hanged every Spaniard they could find. No further attempt was made to colonize this blood-soaked spot.

Thus, by the year 1609, six years after James I of England had succeeded Elizabeth I, the French were well established at Port Royal in Acadia and at Montreal and Quebec in Canada. The English had a firm footing in Virginia. Only a year after Elizabeth's death James had announced that he did not consider himself to be at war with Spain, and after brief negotiations peace had been arranged in a treaty which made no mention of England's rights to trade or colonize in the West. Philip II of Spain, dying in despair in 1598 after seeing the ruin of his empire and all his hopes to subjugate England with the combined force of the Armada and the Duke of Parma's Netherlands army, had warned his son that Spanish trading interests in the West Indies could no longer be protected. Philip knew only too well, as death approached, that the great days of Spain and Portugal as colonial powers were over. At the time of Elizabeth's accession in 1558 he and many others in Europe had shared the opinion that England, a little Protestant island in the great sea of Spanish and French Catholicism, could not survive except as a vassal state of one of these great powers. Since then she had defeated Spain, the greatest world power, and become a world power herself.

James I did not at first realize the position. In any case he was so inconsistent it is doubtful whether a proper understanding would have been of much benefit to him. In 1606 he laid claim to all that part of the North American continent between the latitudes of 34° N and 45° N, and published this through the medium of a patent which brought into being the Royal Council for Virginia. In effect he had announced his sovereignty, based on the discoveries of John Cabot, over an area stretching from just north of the French colony at Port

Royal, south to the scene of Raleigh's failure at Roanoke.

Such claims and pronouncements were of no interest to the French. For the next six years they went peacefully about their business in Acadia and Canada while the English in Virginia, after a succession of troubles caused largely by their initial choice of a very unhealthy site, shortage of supplies —the winter of 1609-10 became known as the 'starving time'— and a collapse of organization, morale and discipline, solved their problems and began to prosper. Both nations appeared to be content in their respective areas and there was no sign of conflict.

Then, in March 1613, the Society of Jesus in France sent out a new expedition to Canada in the charge of a courtier named Saussaye, who took his ships to Lahave and, following Cartier's example, there set up a large crucifix. This one bore the arms of Madame de Guercheville, a wealthy Lady-in-Waiting who had financed the venture. After a brief pause at Port Royal, Saussaye sailed down the Atlantic coast until he reached Mount Desert where, after a lot of argument, it was decided to plant the new colony and call it St Sauveur.

It was unfortunate for Saussaye that soon after his landing at St Sauveur a Captain Samuel Argall, an extremely dubious person from Virginia, came sailing up the coast of what is now Maine in a well-armed privateer. He heard of the new French colony, and on the ground that it was a deliberate infringement of the sovereign rights of King James I, attacked it.

His raid was no more than the unlawful act of a pirate, but it began a new chapter in the story of the battle for empire between England and France. It opened the contest for possession of the North American continent.

Argall seized all the colony's stores, turned a number of Frenchmen adrift in an open boat and took the rest away to a lenient captivity in Virginia. The men in the boat were rescued by Indians, and meeting a trading ship were taken safely back to France. Their compatriots, when they reached Virginia, spoke of the French settlement at Port Royal, and Argall was sent to destroy it. This offensive attitude was incomprehensible to the French who, by virtue of Verrazzano's 'discoveries' in the reign of François I, claimed rather more of the continent than was in James I's patent for the Royal

Council for Virginia; but it was an academic argument of no concern to Argall, or indeed to any Englishman.

Argall descended on the open town of Port Royal while the Governor, Biencourt, and most of his men were away hunting or trapping or working in outlying fields. Buildings were sacked and burned, and the standing crops were destroyed. The wretched colonists had to keep themselves alive throughout a bad winter on wild roots and anything they could get from Indians who had little enough to spare, but despite this they managed to survive the winter and to rebuild a large part of Port Royal.

Although for more than twenty-five years after the failure of Sir Humphrey Gilbert's colony the English seemed to have lost interest in the cold and stormy north, their fishermen went in large numbers to the fishing grounds off Newfoundland. Colonization was not easy anywhere, but it was less difficult further south, and it was for this reason that all the available effort, and it was not very great, had been devoted to Virginia. By 1620 the population had risen to about 1,200, and in that year the Puritan emigration to New England began.

Sailing from Plymouth on 6 September the *Mayflower*, with 100 Pilgrims aboard, crossed the Atlantic and arrived at Cape Cod on 11 November. They established their first settlement at the harbour of Plymouth, named by John Smith six years previously when he was charting the coasts of Maine, New Hampshire and Massachusetts—which he called New England. After a dreadful first winter in which fifty of the colonists died and only four out of eighteen wives survived, progress, under the wise and inspiring leadership of William Bradford, thereafter was steady. Within seven years they had repaid the loan of £1,800 made to them by a London syndicate of financiers, of whom Thomas Weston was the head. This gave the colony its independence and the freedom they had come to seek. As they said themselves, to them freedom was liberty of conscience, but with a great deal of truth Fortescue points out that 'the majority understood by this phrase no more than a licence to coerce the consciences of others, and the few that really sought religious liberty wandered far before they found it'.

The influx of Puritans to the new colony increased considerably when it became apparent in England that Charles I intended to make himself as absolute as any French monarch. The flow continued until 1640 and then ceased for the time being when Parliament was recalled and the great revolutionary, John Pym, began his own war against the King, the bishops and all forms of arbitrary power. It began again when Charles II came back from exile in 1660 and the Stuart monarchy was restored.

The Puritans were in many ways quite different from the other colonists trying to establish themselves along the Atlantic coast between Penobscot in the north to Savannah in South Carolina. The others were sponsored by commercial interests and most of them were volunteers hoping to make their fortune. The Pilgrim Fathers and those who followed them went to America because of disagreements with the Church and State in England so fundamental that life under the Stuarts had become intolerable. There was a passion and a bitterness in their feelings which distance did nothing to assuage. They regarded themselves as a shamefully persecuted minority and they never forgave England for what they considered she had done to them. Thus it is not in the least surprising that when there was serious trouble between the American colonies and the Mother Country a hundred years later, the core of rebellion lay in Boston, the heart of Massachusetts and New England.

The bitterness, the divisions and the differences remained for generations and were certainly apparent to George Washington, the father of his country, who disliked New Englanders and said so, plainly. Yet it must be remembered that in the struggle against the French in North America the New Englanders were the only colonists who invariably showed real spirit and determination. This background of resolution, and of faction and discord, is the key to the history of New England, and to much of the history of the United States.

In 1625 James I gave to the first Puritan settlement in New England a charter of incorporation and, no doubt feeling he was doing the Pilgrim Fathers a favour, proclaimed that henceforth the territories of Virginia and New England (the boundaries of New England being defined as 40° N and 45° N of latitude) would form part of his empire. Three years later the colony of Massachusetts Bay was founded by John Winthrop and then raised to a corporation in 1631. Emigrants from Massachusetts Bay formed another settlement, in Connecticut, in 1635, and in the same year Roger Williams of Massachusetts, driven almost to despair by the efforts of his fellow colonists to 'coerce his conscience', went off and planted his own colony of Rhode Island. Then, in 1638, further differences among the New Englanders led to a new settlement at New Haven. In fact much of the story of the early New England colonies is one of intolerance leading to schism, merely repeating the circumstances which brought about the initial emigration from the Old World.

Within a few years Massachusetts began to assume a dominant position among the northern colonies, absorbing the small scattered settlements of Maine and New Hampshire, and in 1644 became the head of the four federated colonies of New England—the others being New Haven, Plymouth and Connecticut.

At the end of the year 1620, only a few weeks after the *Mayflower* left Plymouth, Sir William Alexander obtained from James I a grant of territory which he called Nova Scotia, after his homeland, and another colony was planted in Acadia, not far from Port Royal whose inhabitants were just beginning to recover from the depredations of Argall. Alexander does not appear to have had any offensive designs against the French, either in Acadia or Canada, but the French were now on their guard. Cardinal Richelieu, having set Louis XIII firmly on the throne of France as an absolute monarch, then turned his attention to Canada and the problems confronting Champlain in Quebec.

Richelieu founded the 'New Company of the Hundred Associates' with himself at the head of it. He also published the company's charter which made the usual extravagant claims. Territorially the company now possessed Canada, Acadia, Newfoundland and Florida under the general title of New France. All New France was declared to be Roman Catholic and no Huguenot was allowed to set foot there. The company was given a perpetual monopoly of the fur trade and a fifteen years' monopoly of all other trades except that of the fisheries. To defend its rights the company received, as a personal gift from Louis XIII, two battleships, well armed and equipped. Yet in the year 1628, while all these decrees and plans were being made in France, Champlain and his little garrison in Quebec were starving. France and England were again at war, this time on a religious issue, and Charles I's favourite, 'Steenie' Buckingham, made his disastrous descent on La Rochelle with the object of bringing aid to the Huguenots.

In the early summer the French admiral de Roquemont left Dieppe for Quebec with a fleet of eighteen ships carrying troops and supplies, intending to relieve Champlain and strengthen the French hold on Canada. He was too late. An English fleet under Sir David Kirke was crossing the Atlantic ahead of him.

Kirke anchored off Tadusac and sent a boat up the St Lawrence. With the courtesy customary on such occasions, his messenger explained the situation to Champlain and suggested that he surrender. Champlain replied that 'he would abide the decision of combat' and assured Kirke that Quebec would not be easy to take. Kirke was deceived by this bold front, and withdrew, unaware that the small garrison had practically no food or ammunition and that the walls of the fortress had, in places, been reduced almost to rubble by winter frosts. Off Gaspé, Kirke met de Roquemont's fleet and after a fierce little battle he captured it, thus destroying all Champlain's hopes. Now in serious trouble, the garrison of Quebec somehow lived through the winter, but the situation became so bad that Champlain contemplated abandoning Quebec altogether and marching into the Iroquois country, taking one of their stockaded 'towns' and living on the large stores of grain he knew he would find. Before he could really make up his mind to do anything so drastic Kirke returned, in the spring of 1629, to be hailed as a deliverer by the starving garrison.

Kirke seems to have behaved very well. Champlain surrendered on honourable terms and the French settlers were allowed to remain on their holdings. An English settlement was established on Cape Breton Island, and Canada and Acadia passed into English hands. This did not apparently cause any distress to Louis XIII who had the idea that his

North American colonies were more trouble and expense than they were worth. Then Champlain returned to France and explained to Louis the enormous strategic importance of the St Lawrence river as being not only the gateway to North America but also a means for curbing any expansion of the New England colonies. Champlain had long planned to paddle up the Richelieu river, through Lakes Champlain and George, carry his canoes across to the headwaters of the Hudson river and go down it to the sea. This in fact was the highway of lakes, rivers and portages on which the main battles for possession of the New World were to be fought. Guarding the northern end of it was Quebec, while New York protected the south. Hitherto, France had held one and England the other. Whoever held both could hold the continent.

Like the majority of French kings, Louis XIII was loth to neglect any means of curbing the power of England. On the ground that the Convention of Susa had brought an end to the war shortly before Kirke's capture of Quebec, and therefore Kirke had had no right to continue the war on his own, Louis began to agitate for the return of his North American possessions.

Kirke's expedition had not been a proper naval one. It had been sponsored by a company of London merchants whose object was trade, not conquest. Quebec, to them, gave access to the immensely valuable fur trade which up to now had been monopolized by the French. When he saw Quebec for himself, Kirke recognized its strategic importance, and he and his sponsors were determined not to give it up. However, in 1632, at the time of the negotiations before signing the Treaty of Saint-Germain-en-Laye, Charles I of England was embarrassingly short of money. He was persuaded by the French that the honour of France demanded the return of Canada and Acadia, snatched illegally in time of peace; and to show there were no ill feelings France was prepared to pay £50,000 as compensation—even in those days a trivial amount to pay for a continent.

Kirke and the merchant-owners of the land pleaded their cause with passion, and Kirke's strategic appreciation is evident in their appeal: 'If the King keep Quebec we do not care what the French or any other can do, though they have an hundred sail of ships and ten thousand men.'

Charles signed the Treaty and Emery de Caen was sent from France to relieve Kirke of his command at Quebec. In 1633 Richelieu and his Company of the Hundred Associates once more took control and Champlain was made Governor of Quebec. He died two years later, on Christmas Day 1635, at the age of sixty-eight, in the colony of which he has been called the father.

Though Quebec and Canada were once again firmly under French control, Acadia was not permanently lost to England. In 1654 Oliver Cromwell, the Lord Protector, sent an expedition under Major Sedgwicke to attack Dutch settlements on the Hudson river. Sedgwicke went beyond the letter of his orders, for he attacked and captured the French ports of Port Royal, Penobscot and St John's and brought Acadia back under the English flag—where it remained until 1667. In that year, by the terms of the Treaty of Breda it was handed over to France, and the French dominion of Canada and Acadia became established.

Meanwhile much had been happening in the British colonies further to the south. The Civil War, which had really begun with the battle of Edgehill in October 1642, so disrupted life in England that it became impossible for the mother-country to exercise any control over territories on the other side of the Atlantic. The colonies were left to get on with their own affairs as best they could. This delighted the people of Massachusetts who took steps to create an independent State out of the confederacy of New England. They coined their own money, conducted their own foreign policy with the French in Acadia and did their best to cut themselves off from other colonies which were loyal to the King. During the First Dutch War of 1653 they indicated to Cromwell that they would support whichever side made their support most worthwhile, and Cromwell exempted them from the restrictions of the Navigation Acts.*

* Aimed at the world monopoly of the carrying trade which the Dutch were on their way to achieving, Cromwell's Navigation Act of 1651 laid down that no goods might enter an English port unless carried in English ships or the ships of the country the goods came from. Since the American Colonies had but few merchant ships this would have crippled their export trade.

When Charles II came into his own again in 1660 the New England confederacy fell apart. Connecticut was given a separate charter and, under the terms of it, absorbed New Haven. Rhode Island was also granted her own charter and thus Massachusetts was somewhat isolated. Many complaints had been made, particularly by London merchants, of violations of the terms of her original charter during the period of the Commonwealth. When Charles began to investigate them the first reaction of the colonists was to threaten armed resistance, using their local militia, but they changed their minds and fell back upon procrastination which was both skilful and evasive. For nearly a quarter of a century they managed to fend off attempts to revise their charter and not until 1684 was Massachusetts brought back to a position of dependence on the mother country.

In this time the number of English settlements in North America had increased greatly. Lord Baltimore obtained Maryland in 1632, and a colony was planted in Carolina in 1663. James, Duke of York, afterwards James II, was given a patent by his brother Charles II for Delaware, New Jersey and New Amsterdam in 1664, and William Penn received Pennsylvania in 1680.

When James, whose main interests at this time were England's trade and sea-power, received his patent, dated 12 March 1664, he appointed Colonel Richard Nicolls, 'an Old Officer and a Groom of His Bedchamber', as his Deputy-Governor and equipped him for his enterprise with three warships, a troop transport, 450 men and the sum of £4,000. The 'enterprise' was nothing less than a straightforward act of military aggression, for England was not at war with Holland although the Dutch, very sensibly and naturally, had taken advantage of England's internal problems, which had really begun when Charles I came to the throne, and their behaviour towards English factories, particularly in the East Indies and on the West Coast of Africa had, in the opinion of the English, given good grounds for reprisals.

Nicolls sailed from Portsmouth in May 1664 and reached Boston at the end of July. Here he collected a small addition to his force, a contingent from Connecticut under the command of John Winthrop, while a similar contingent collected in

Massachusetts assembled too late to accompany the expedition. The tough old Dutch Governor of New Amsterdam, Peter Stuyvesant, had ample warning of what was going to happen, but the Dutch West India Company had failed to maintain the fortifications of the port, and the apathy of the Dutch colonists prevented any serious resistance. On 18 August Nicolls arrived off Coney Island and asked politely for surrender on very reasonable terms. The Dutch settlers were to keep their lands, religion, laws and trading outlets with England. Stuyvesant's instinct was to fight but he had no support, so he dillied and dallied, praying without much hope for relief, until his own people forced his hand. On 29 August New Amsterdam capitulated without a shot being fired; Nicolls renamed it New York, after his patron, and its inhabitants became English citizens. Sir Robert Carr was sent to take over the Dutch settlements in Delaware and thus the whole coast, from Maine to Carolina, came into English hands.

At the time, the Dutch, realizing that New Amsterdam was virtually indefensible because it was so overshadowed by the powerful New England colonies, made no attempt, diplomatic or otherwise, to obtain restitution, but they recaptured New York in 1673, during the Third Dutch War. It was restored to England by the peace treaty signed on 9 February 1674.

The only people really affected by England's acquisition of New York were the French, because it meant that the contest for North America, in which the great waterways of the St Lawrence and the Hudson were such critical factors, took on a more definite shape. New York guarded the entrance to a navigable channel running deep inland from the Atlantic and linked by a brief march to the southern end of Lake Champlain. Just north of Albany, described by Nicolls who captured it as 'a fort up the river', the tributary Mohawk gave access to Lake Oneida and then Lake Ontario, explored by Champlain in 1615. Indian hunters and trappers of the north and west, bringing their canoe-loads of pelts into the trading factories of the east, had to come through Lake Ontario whose eastern shores were closer to New York than they were to Quebec. Strategically, both settlements were on an equal footing, for in a country without roads the waterways they commanded were practically the only lines of communication; but Quebec had the disadvantage of winter ice.

There was a major difference in motivation between the French and the English in their respective colonies. The English worked hard to make their settlements self-supporting by agriculture. This tended to make them intensely parochial in their outlook, preoccupied by the problems which beset those who grow things, and far more concerned with the weather and soil in their own valley than with what lay beyond the hills on either side.

The interests of the French lay in trading with the Indians, hunting, and in exploration. The spur behind most of the exploration was the saving of souls. The zeal of the Jesuits in seeking out and baptizing the savages, which led often enough to appalling hardships and sometimes an agonizing death, took them into the heart of the continent. They followed Champlain's trail up the Ottawa river, by Lake Nipissing and French river to Lake Huron, and back by Lake Simcoe and Lake Ontario. They spread out to Lake Michigan and Lake Superior, setting up their mission stations and claiming huge areas of land in the name of Louis XIV. Through all this endeavour, the French in Quebec and Montreal began to appreciate the vastness—and value—of the land they lived in, and to realize how sound had been Champlain's advice to Louis XIII on the need to keep the English out of it.

In 1664, while England was still preoccupied with the restoration of the Stuarts, the Intendant of Canada, Jean Talon, made his plans to secure French territory along the western boundaries of the English colonies and so pen the English between the Allegheny mountains and the Atlantic coast. The design was based on holding the rivers which were the north and south lines of communication in the interior, exploring, tracing and then fortifying them as far south as the Gulf of Mexico, if it was found that they flowed that way. In 1670 Talon sent out a man named Nicholas Perrot, an explorer who spoke many of the Indian dialects, to call the western tribes to a conference. Having issued the invitations Perrot went on through the Lake Superior region and down the flank of Lake Michigan to where Chicago now stands; the

centre, then, of the numerous Miami tribe. He then returned to
Sault-Sainte-Marie where the delegates of the tribes had
assembled, and he told them they could consider themselves
fortunate because they were all now under the royal protection
of King Louis XIV of France. Most of them had no idea what
he was talking about.

He then formally annexed to France the whole of the region
of the Great Lakes. While on this expedition Perrot was told
by the Indians of a great river which they called Méchasebé,
'The Father of Waters' (the Mississippi) which flowed south,
and this, from the sound of it, appeared to be the answer to
Talon's problem of containing the English.

Dreams of a waterway to Cathay were still much in the
minds of many explorers, and Talon, told of the Father of
Waters, felt that it might be the direct route to the Pacific.
One way or the other, exploration was bound to yield results
vastly important to Canada, and France. Early in 1673 a
Jesuit priest, Father Marquette, and a trader named Jolliet
were sent to find the Mississippi. From Quebec they made their
way to the north-western shore of Lake Michigan, paddled up
the Fox river to its source, carried their canoes across to the
headwaters of a tributary of the Wisconsin river and went
with the current. On 17 June 1673 they came to the broad
Mississippi and travelled down it for a month, passing the
mouths of the Illinois, the Missouri and the Ohio. Everywhere
along the banks the Indians were friendly and hospitable;
and those at the mouth of the Ohio were dressed in cloth and
carried muskets which proved their contact with English
settlements on the eastern seaboard.

Marquette and Jolliet went on as far as the junction with the
Arkansas river, and here the natives, who had had some
experience of Spanish settlers, were frighteningly hostile. By
force of personality the two Frenchmen turned a moment of
grave peril into one of cordial welcome, so that instead of
being murdered they were feasted and everyone smoked the
pipe of peace. At this point the explorers decide to turn back.
They now had good reason to believe the huge river flowed
into the Gulf of Mexico and not into the Pacific; they were
warned that the tribes further down were dangerous and they
had no wish to visit the Spanish settlements said to be at the

mouth of the river. They returned along the Mississippi and the Illinois, crossed over to Lake Michigan and at the end of September reached the Green Bay Mission, on Lake Michigan. Soon afterwards Father Marquette died, away in the wilderness, worn out by years of travel, toil, self-sacrifice, danger and devotion to his faith.

Immensely heartened by the information brought back by Marquette and Jolliet, Talon now looked for others to carry his great project further, and found Robert la Salle.

La Salle was an adventurer who really believed there was a north-west passage to Cathay, and he was determined to find it. He had come to Canada some years before Nicholas Perrot set off on his journey to Chicago, and in order to make enough money to pay for his proposed expedition, by trading in furs, and to make himself familiar with the language and customs of the tribes whose help he would need, he disappeared for several years and lived among the Indians. Persuaded by Talon to go south instead of north he made a number of comparatively short journeys before setting out on the main venture. He discovered the Ohio river. In 1678, while exploring the waterway between Lake Ontario and Lake Erie he came upon the Niagara Falls where, with a proper appreciation of strategic values, he built a fort. In the following year, on the shores of Lake Erie, he constructed a ship which he named *Griffin* and sailed her through the strait of Detroit and across Lake Huron. From the far shore he sent the ship back with a cargo of furs, but she did not arrive and no one knows what happened to her.

In January 1682 he carried his canoes overland from the southern shore of Lake Michigan to the headwaters of the Illinois and came out on the Mississippi early in February. Landing in places where the Indians were friendly, and keeping well out in the centre of the broad stream when they were not, his little party slipped swiftly down on the current, from winter into spring and then summer as they journeyed south, and on 19 March they came to the delta of the Mississippi. Paddling back, against the current and beset by many delays, la Salle did not return to Quebec until the spring of the following year (1683), but as soon as he arrived he laid formal claim, in the name of France, to all the land he had traversed, and a good deal more. All the vast area between the Allegheny mountains west to the Rockies, and from the Rio Grande north to where the Missouri was but a shallow stream, was annexed to the French Crown under the name of Louisiana, in honour of Louis XIV.

La Salle returned to France and the court greeted him as a triumphant hero. Soon afterwards, at the head of a large expedition, he set out from La Rochelle to sail direct to the mouths of the Mississippi and there found a colony, but he miscalculated the position of the river and overshot it by several hundred miles. He landed with a small party and started back eastwards. Finally, after trying hopelessly to thread their way through the pathless tangle of swamp and forest, his followers mutinied and, resenting his determination and ruthless discipline, murdered him.

He had done much to further Talon's great plan. The rivers Ohio and Mississippi could indeed be barriers to the expansion of the English colonies on the Atlantic coast, and if the more adventurous of the New Englanders crossed the Allegheny mountains they would soon be checked. Yet the mere annexation of uncharted territory was not enough. The French were resolved to cut off all New England contact with the fur trade, and so they began to construct forts and strengthen those which already existed. Fort Niagara was in good condition; the stockaded outpost known as Fort Frontenac, at the northern outlet of Lake Ontario, was replaced by a stone building. The Jesuit mission at Michillimackinac, between Lakes Michigan and Huron, was reinforced with troops and defences to guard the strait. Fort Miamis, built on the south-eastern shore of Lake Michigan, barred the way from the lake to the upper Illinois, and Fort St Louis protected French trading interests on the plains of the Illinois.

This slow tightening of the French grip on Indian trade was just as much of a threat to the Five Indian Nations, the Iroquois, as it was to the Dutch and English settlements, whose inhabitants had allied themselves with the Indians. The Iroquois did not grasp the significance of what was happening and the English, preoccupied with the problems of agriculture, their enthusiasm for religious disputes and their endless quarrels over boundaries, neither knew nor wanted to know what was going on on the other side of the mountains. Farming the good lands between these mountains and the sea they felt secure, not only geographically but in the strength of their population; that of New England exceeded 90,000, against only 12,000 in the whole of Canada.

There was, however, one man in the English colonies to whom the French threat of domination in North America was very real. He was Colonel Thomas Dongan, appointed in 1682 by James, Duke of York, to be the Governor of New York in the place of Sir Edmund Andros whose tenure of office had been marred by his addiction to wrangling with neighbouring colonies on matters of jurisdiction and boundaries. Dongan saw at once that French control of the Hudson would isolate New England and prevent any future development; it would also provide the French with an ice-free outlet to the Atlantic. Conversely, while the English held New York they were a constant menace to French interests on the St Lawrence. He was a man whose mind rose far above the level of his predecessor's bickering and understood the great strategic issues involved. In his view, sooner or later the current irritations of French attempts at encirclement and interference with the Indian trade would explode into war, and it would be war to decide who was to control the destinies of the North American continent.

As a soldier, Colonel Dongan had begun his career in the French army, as a mercenary, and subsequently transferred to a British regiment, The Queen's (2nd of Foot), with whom he had seen active service against the Moors in Queen Catherine of Braganza's dowry port of Tangier. Thus, when he came to New York he brought with him an understanding of what it was like to fight against 'savages'—the Moors' idea of warfare was painfully uncivilized. He knew what might happen in a war in which a high proportion of the 'troops' taking part would probably be Indians in full war-paint, who had their own views on how to treat women and children in lonely frontier settlements. He lost no time in making a firm alliance with the tribes of the Iroquois who formed a buffer state between the English and French colonies, and he had no difficulty in doing this because, despite the French enthusiasm for meddling with Indian affairs, they had never been able to affect the preference the Iroquois had always shown for the English.

Soon after Dongan's arrival the French became overtly aggressive. They destroyed the factories of the Hudson Bay Company, founded by Prince Rupert of the Rhine and a group of business associates in 1670; with skilful use of treachery they trapped, captured and murdered a number of Iroquois at Fort Frontenac; they plundered English traders and further strengthened the fort at Niagara. All this created a very awkward situation in Europe where France and England were supposed to be on very good terms, with Charles II to a large extent financially dependent on his cousin Louis XIV. The two kings signed a little treaty in 1686 to tidy things up and put matters right, but it had virtually no effect on their respective colonists.

Dongan's protests to his own government were, as Fortescue says, 'vigorous to the point of discourtesy' and his importunate demands to be allowed to retaliate were at last answered. He was authorized to use force to prevent further aggression against the Iroquois. He at once assembled a force of local militia and Indian warriors at Albany, demanded the destruction of the fort at Niagara and then turned the Iroquois loose upon Canada. They spread their own particular type of terror right up to the walls of Montreal.

Dongan was recalled to England in 1688 and Andros was restored to the office in which Dongan had succeeded him six years previously. Affairs in North America had now reached the point of crisis, and just at this moment William of Orange, arch-enemy of Louis XIV, Roman Catholicism and all that France stood for, replaced his uncle and father-in-law James II on the throne of England in what is so inaccurately described by the Whig enemies of James as the 'glorious revolution'. With William, and James's daughter Mary, jointly on the throne, England at once became involved in William's war against France, brought to an uneasy, temporary cessation by the Treaty of Ryswick in 1697. But in North America, New England and New France had entered upon a conflict which, with practically no intermission, was to last for nearly seventy years.

4 The West Indies

On Friday, 3 August 1492, Christopher Columbus set sail from Palos, a little port in the Gulf of Cadiz, with three ships, the *Santa Maria*, the *Pinta* and *Nina*, and headed for the Canary Islands. He was quite convinced in his own mind that the Canaries and Cipangu (Japan) were in the same latitude, and that west of Cipangu lay Cathay. All he had to do was sail due west. Since by his reasoning any land of considerable size lying to the west had to be Cathay he arranged for King Ferdinand of Aragon and Queen Isabella of Castile to provide him with letters of introduction addressed to the Grand Cham, or Khan.

Leaving the Canaries on 6 September, he reached an island of the Bahamas only thirty-six days later (October 12). Very appropriately he named it San Salvador, out of gratitude to the Saviour. Believing he was now in Far Eastern waters Columbus assumed that the kindly and peaceful Arawaks were Indians, always referred to them as such, and persisted in this belief. Acting on the instructions of the people of San Salvador he sailed on to Santa Maria de la Concepción (subsequently named Rum Cay by less devout travellers), Long Island and then the north-eastern shores of Cuba.

Recording this last discovery in his log he wrote, 'I believe that it is the island of Cipangu', but when he had taken a closer look he was disconcerted to find it was quite unlike anything Marco Polo had written of Japan. He came to the conclusion that Cuba must be Cathay, and having sent off a formal embassy to find the Emperor of China he gave the name Alpha and Omega to the eastern tip of the island on the grounds that it was the beginning and the end of the Asian continent. He then went across the neck of water to what he christened *La Isla Española*, Hispaniola—modern Haiti and

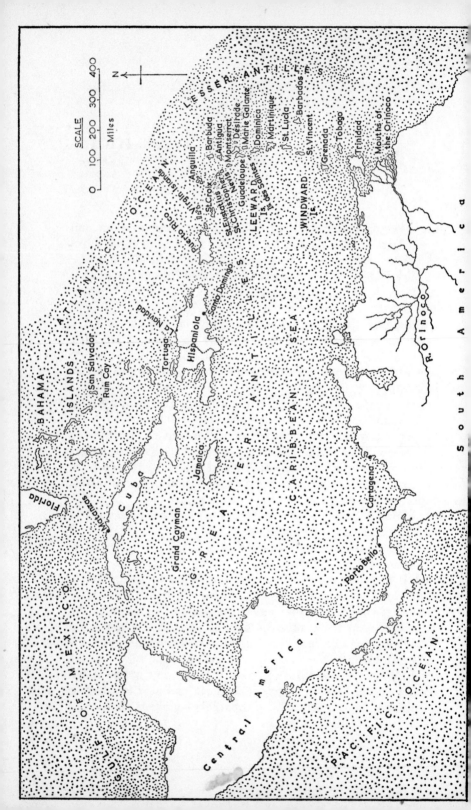

the Dominican Republic*—and here he obtained by barter a number of gold nose-plugs, bracelets and other small ornaments, which at once changed the whole concept of his expedition. Hitherto it had all been very interesting but he had found nothing sufficiently attractive from a commercial point of view to encourage anyone in Spain to finance another voyage. The 'Indians' of Cuba and the small islands to the north—of whom Columbus wrote, 'they remained so much our friends it was a marvel'—eagerly exchanged parrots and woven cotton for red caps and glass beads, but parrots, if they survived the journey, were not likely to excite the merchant adventurers of Spain. Gold, even in such small quantities, was quite a different proposition. It also sealed the fate of the trustful and happy islanders who, under the impact of so-called European civilization, were to be extinguished.

The first colony in the West Indies was planted more or less by accident. On Christmas Eve, 1492, the *Santa Maria* was driven ashore in a storm and wrecked on the north coast of Hispaniola, the crew being saved. The *Nina* was so small she could barely accommodate her own crew of twenty-two, and the *Pinta* was not there because her captain, Martin Pinzón, and crew had deserted. So, on Christmas morning Columbus was faced with the problem of finding transport to carry his men back to Spain. There was no solution. Thirty-nine Spanish mariners became the first colonists in the New World— as discovered by Spain—and they were all volunteers. In fact it was an arrangement satisfactory to them and to the local inhabitants. From the Spanish point of view the country, the climate and the women were delightful. Food was plentiful and above all there was the promise of gold. Once Columbus had gone, taking the rest of the expedition with him, they

* The various names given at various times to this island tend to cause great confusion—San Domingo, Santo Domingo, St Domingue, and so on. Columbus named it Hispaniola, and subsequently a defended port on the south coast of the eastern end of the island was called Santo Domingo. By the terms of the Treaty of Ryswick (1697) the Spaniards recognized the French occupation of the western part of the island (St Domingue) and during the period covered by this book the island changed hands and was attacked on several occasions. To simplify matters, rightly or wrongly the island has been referred to as Hispaniola throughout, and Santo Domingo is the port.

49

Sketch Map of the Caribbean Area

could get on with the serious and exciting business of finding where the gold came from.

The local people were Arawaks, the least warlike of people whose only weapon, according to Columbus, was a sort of wooden dart either pointed at the end or with a fish hook attached to it. Thus they were an easy prey to an active and bellicose race of marauders coming north along the line of the Lesser Antilles and already gaining a foothold in Puerto Rico, easternmost of the big islands. The Spaniards called these raiders 'Caribs', meaning cannibals, since cannibalism for food and ritual purposes was their chief characteristic. The Caribs adopted hit-and-run tactics, swooping suddenly on a village, snatching what they wanted in the form of fresh meat or bedfellows and disappearing. The local Arawak *cacique*, or chieftain, Guacanagari, felt that the Spanish would be a useful protection against the Caribs, but in their own way the Spanish were to prove to be no less a menace—snatching what they wanted and then infecting the islanders with European diseases.

Early in 1493 Columbus left his colony of La Navidad—so named to commemorate its founding on Christmas Day—and set sail for Spain. On the way he was blown off course by a storm in the eastern Atlantic and had to land in Portugal, where he was not at all welcome. King John II thought he had been down to the Guinea coast, trespassing in an area reserved for Portugal under the terms of the Papal Bull 'Aeterni Regis' of 1481 and the Treaty of Alcáçovas, with Spain, which gave Portugal jurisdiction over a region vaguely defined as 'south of the Canaries and west of Guinea'. He claimed all Columbus's discoveries, Spain appealed to the Pope, and the whole thing was more or less sorted out by the Treaty of Tordesillas in the following year.

When Columbus finally got back to Spain in March 1493 he said that he had found the archipelago long known to exist off the south-east coast of Asia, that in other words, he had reached the outskirts of Cathay. Although there was a certain amount of disappointment at his meagre specimens of the fabulous riches, the general feeling was that any gold at all indicated the presence of ore which people as primitive as those Columbus described had probably failed to exploit.

Columbus returned to the Caribbean in that same year, reaching Hispaniola on 3 November, but instead of going to see how his colony was faring he went straight to the island of Marie Galante, raised the crucifix and the royal standard of Spain, and took possession in the name of King Ferdinand. Then he sailed for *Los Islas de Canibales*, the Carib bases for their attacks to the west, naming and claiming Guadeloupe, Désirade, Les Saintes, Montserrat, Antigua, Nevis, the Virgin Islands and Puerto Rico, among others. At length he went to La Navidad and had some difficulty in finding it at all. The place had been razed to the ground and there were no survivors. Apparently the Spaniards he had left there had been raiding local villages in search of gold, murdering, plundering and stealing women, until one day they went too far, into the lands of Chief Caonabo who had Carib blood in his veins. Caonabo descended on the Spanish settlement and took the action he felt was needed. From that time onwards the Caribs were left alone, which was an error of strategy, because by failing to occupy the islands of the Caribs the Spaniards left them available for other European nations, especially the English and the French, who seized them in due course.

Another colony was established, further along the north coast of Hispaniola, and named Isabella, but progress was very slow. The trouble was that Columbus was a sailor and not an administrator, and he was caught between conflicting aims. On the one hand, his men wanted gold, which was found in some quantity at 'Cibao', the native name for what is now called the Cordillera Central; while on the other, his sponsors, Ferdinand and Isabella, wanted full-scale conversion of the natives to the Roman Catholic faith. Columbus soon found himself in a situation he could not control, and finally he so alienated Queen Isabella and the colonists that in August 1500 his governorship was terminated and the Spanish Crown assumed direct control of his discoveries. In effect, governors such as Francisco de Bobadilla, sent to replace him, were no better and sometimes worse than he was, and the early history of this part of the New World is a sombre tale of the exploitation and extermination of a once-happy people whom Columbus had described as 'very well made, of very handsome bodies, and very good faces'.

For many years the Spaniards gained little from the Caribbean or from their discoveries on the nearby coast of Central America. They realized this New World was not Asia but another continent altogether; and King Ferdinand had nothing to show for the money spent and lives lost on the Spanish Main except a handful of pearls and a little gold. At length, twenty-six years after Columbus had first landed on San Salvador, a Spanish expedition sent from Cuba to Mexico heard stories of the Aztec civilization and found traces of large stores of gold. In 1521 Hernán Cortés, a settler in Cuba, gathered together all the soldiers he could find and, helped by local tribes which for generations had been horribly oppressed by the Aztecs, conquered Mexico. Vast stores of treasure were captured and, to the consternation of the rest of Europe, the steady flow of gold and silver into Spain began.

Less than ten years later, Spanish explorers in the isthmus of Panama heard tales of a land to the south even richer than Mexico, and in 1532 Francisco Pizarro with a force rather less than 200 strong invaded Peru. Whereas Cortés, attacking a tough and warlike people, had had to fight with desperate valour to prevent the annihilation of his expedition, Pizarro found the Peruvians to be far milder and, in their dislike of war, much easier to defeat. These *conquistadores*, by their greed, revolting cruelties and initial refusal to accept the authority of the Spanish government, have earned their own place in history, and when their rebellion had been crushed the mines of Peru produced greater wealth for Spain than all her other possessions. Inevitably Spain transferred the focus of her attention from the apparently unproductive islands of the Caribbean to these great stores of treasure on the mainland.

Hispaniola had been the centre from which, directly and indirectly, all the other Spanish colonies in the Caribbean had been founded, particularly those in the Greater Antilles, and virtually all progress in them now ceased. They began to contract rapidly. In Jamaica there were only scattered groups of hunters; all settlements disappeared from the north coast of Hispaniola; in Cuba only Havana and Santiago de Cuba held evidence of Spanish occupation. No attempt was made to expand into the Windward or Leeward Islands or into the Bahamas, but this was because the Spaniards had no liking

for the guerrilla warfare in which the Caribs were disconcertingly adroit, and they had an understandable horror of
being cooked and eaten. Yet although their garrisons and
naval units in the Caribbean soon became little more than a
token force, they still claimed that only they had the right to
navigate in Caribbean waters.

The British and French did not dispute this claim, they
behaved as if it had never been made, and indeed the Spanish
were aware they could not defend it. Philip II of Spain knew
only too well that his country did not possess the resources of
manpower and material to hold and maintain exclusive rights
on these islands, or adequately to protect the shipping lanes of
his treasure fleets. Naturally enough, the Caribbean became
the happy hunting ground of pirates of many nations, perhaps
the most famous being Sir Francis Drake who, considering
himself permanently at war with Catholic Spain, was liable to
attack a Spaniard whenever and wherever he found him. Yet
despite all the careful plans of great captains like Drake and
Hawkins, and their determination to sever the arteries of
Spain, they were never able to catch one of her bullion fleets
in the Caribbean.

The long Elizabethan war of attrition on the high seas,
culminating in the disaster of the Armada, not only reduced
the sea power of Spain to a dim shadow of its former glory but
tolled the knell of the Spanish empire, and with both Spain
and Portugal being forced to drop out of the battle for empire,
the field was left open to France and England.

In the sixteenth century the English and French had made
no attempt to plant any colonies in the Caribbean. To do so
would have been to invite immediate attack by the Spanish,
jealous of their exclusive rights in the area; it remained theirs
for a hundred years and their claims were not disputed. But
the waters where great treasure-galleons assembled before
sailing in protected convoys across the Atlantic were alive
with privateers and pirates who lived by plunder—and died at
the end of a rope if the Spaniards caught them.

At the beginning of the seventeenth century Spain's maritime rivals, the English, French and Dutch, made their first
tentative efforts to gain a footing in the islands, and when they
found how easy it was the early trickle of colonists became a

flood. It was easy because Spain had never been able to occupy or garrison all the territory she claimed and, for fear of the Caribs, had left the Lesser Antilles severely alone. Islands such as Martinique, Guadeloupe and Dominica, the obvious and natural ports of call for any ships coming from the east, were left unguarded. What should have been the outer defences of Spain's colonial empire, protecting the sources of her huge mineral wealth, became instead the convenient and sheltered bases for her enemies. This strange lack of foresight had left the Caribbean exposed to the privateers, and where they found sanctuary the colonists followed.

Sir Walter Raleigh, the first English colonizer, whose efforts in Virginia had failed, was also the first Englishman to penetrate the Spanish Main. He went to Guiana, searching for gold, and some of the ships' boats from his little fleet travelled four hundred miles up the Orinoco. His last attempt, in 1617, was in every way disastrous. James I had imposed on him the impossible condition that he was not to fight the Spaniards, who had built a fort at San Tomé to guard the Orinoco. No gold was found, his son was killed in an assault on San Tomé, one of his captains committed suicide and disease and desertion forced him to return, whereupon he was beheaded by James I to give the Spaniards their revenge.

Away to the north-west, further attempts were made to redeem Raleigh's failure on the Orinoco. In 1604 Charles Leigh and forty-six men and boys tried to establish a town they called Mount Howard on the Wiapoco (Oyapock) river, the boundary, subsequently, between French Guiana and Brazil. In 1606, after two years of work on the making of a tobacco plantation, fever and other diseases wiped out the little colony, and a relief force of sixty-seven potential colonists in the ship *Olive Branch* failed to reach the distressed settlement and were landed on St Lucia in the Lesser Antilles. Attacked at once by Caribs, all these unfortunate people perished, and this first English attempt at colonization in the West Indies was, like so many similar efforts elsewhere, a catastrophe. Three years later Robert Harcourt tried to re-establish Mount Howard, and in 1610 Sir Thomas Roe, who four years after was to be England's first ambassador to the court of the Mogul Emperor, founded another small colony which was also to be a trading port on the Amazon. Lack of capital at home, lack of regular supplies and the devastating effect of tropical diseases soon reduced both enterprises to a handful of survivors living on local resources. Yet despite this the Amazon Company was formed in 1619 by Roger North, who had been one of Raleigh's officers, to develop and exploit the Amazon-Guiana area. It never really had any chance of succeeding. Apart from the appalling casualty rate from fever, dysentery and septic sores caused largely by malnutrition, settlers on the banks of the Orinoco, Oyapock and Amazon were under the constant threat of extermination by Spanish expeditions sent to root them out.

In that area it was much easier to defend an island colony than one on the mainland which could be surprised and overrun by a silent enemy moving along secret game paths in the jungle. In 1623, at the instigation of the Spanish Government, a Portuguese expedition from Brazil made a determined effort to suppress once and for all the activities of the English and Dutch on the Wild Coast. Many of the settlers were killed or captured and only a few escaped—among them was Captain John Warner. On his way home Warner landed at several of the islands in the Caribbean but found none suitable for what he had in mind until he came to St Christopher, better known today as St Kitts. The soil and the climate were ideal for planting tobacco and, much to his surprise in view of all he had heard about the cannibals, he found that the local chief, Tegramond, was extremely friendly. Having explored the island during a stay of several months, Warner continued his journey to England to raise money and recruit men for his new project—the development of tobacco plantations on St Kitts.

With the support of Ralph Merifield, Charles Jeaffreson, navigator and old schoolfriend, and a number of merchants, Warner was able to make detailed plans. The response to his recruiting campaign in his native county of Suffolk was disappointing—it yielded only fourteen men, but it was arranged that he would go first to Virginia, to obtain seeds for his plantation and persuade more men to join him, and then go to St Kitts. While he was doing this, Jeaffreson would acquire a ship, load it with everything the colonists needed, and sail it to St Kitts as soon as he heard that Warner had arrived there. Warner invested everything he possessed in this undertaking and took with him his wife and thirteen-year-old son. The Virginians gave him seeds, but no one wanted to go with him—perhaps because of the cannibals—and on 28 January 1624 he arrived at his island, established himself in what is now called the parish of Old Road Warner, put up huts and planted tobacco and maize. A few months later practically everything was swept away in a hurricane, but Jeaffreson brought badly needed help in the ship aptly named *Hopewell*. The colony survived, its roots deepened, and after a short time Warner returned to England with the first shipment of its produce, nearly four and a half tons of tobacco.

His real object in going home was to obtain royal recognition for the new territory and collect more colonists. He may well have been slightly apprehensive. James I was so unpredictable, and might be going through a phase of appeasement with Spain.

But all was well, and the patent signed by James dealt with the problem of any Spanish claim:

> Thomas Warner hath lately discovered several Islands in the Main Ocean towards the Continent of America, the one called the Isle of St Christopher, alias Merwar's Hope [the first syllables of Merifield and Warner] and other the Isle of Mevis and other the Isle of Barbados* and other the Isle of Monserate which said Islandes are possessed and inhabited only by Savage and Heathen People and are not nor at the Time of Discovery were in the possession or under the Government of any Christian Prince State or Potentate.

Thomas Warner was appointed King's Lieutenant and Governor of St Kitts, Barbuda, Nevis and Montserrat; the first English Governor in the West Indies. He was also successful in obtaining recruits, and from 1625 there was a steady flow of colonists into the northern group of the Lesser Antilles. Many of them came from Suffolk, where Warner's name was well known. Tobacco plantations on St Kitts and Nevis began to yield heavy crops, and this caused great anxiety in Virginia

---

* This is clearly an error for the neighbouring island of Barbuda. Warner had never been anywhere near Barbados.

where such competition was fiercely resented. Many unsuccessful appeals were sent to London asking the mother-country to stop all tobacco-growing in the West Indies, but within fifteen years, before any serious trouble could develop, Virginia's rivals had turned from tobacco to sugar.

Sugar had been introduced into the Canary Islands as early as 1491 and Columbus, on one of his voyages, had taken seeds and expert cultivators from there to Hispaniola. In the first half of the sixteenth century it grew to be a major industry, involving no less than forty sugar mills, and shipments of this expensive luxury* went back to Spain in the treasure galleons. Oddly enough the sugar industry in Hispaniola does not seem to have prospered for long. In 1550 it was regarded by the Spaniards as one of the great sources of wealth in the Spanish Main, by the end of the century it was virtually dead. The centre of it was transferred to Cuba and not until the end of the seventeenth century did the French revive it in Hispaniola.

By 1625 the English, under Warner's governorship, were firmly established in the four islands named in the patent of James I. They had come by the hard road of Guiana and Virginia to the lush green islands in the sun, and then just when the future seemed reasonably secure, the French arrived.

It was all strangely accidental, reminiscent of the forming of the first Spanish colony at La Navidad.

For more than a century the French had been the scourge of the Spanish Main. Pirates and privateers preyed on all shipping, especially the bullion ships of Spain, and went on doing so despite a long series of treaties between France and Spain in which the French King undertook the hopeless task of controlling

---

* Sugar production was an extremely costly business with its own special problems. To set up a mill for crushing the cane cost anything up to 12,000 gold ducats. Another 5,000 ducats were needed to organize a labour force of 100 slaves, to provide the herd of cattle needed to feed them, carts to carry the cane, fuel for the refining vats, and irrigation systems in the cane fields. One of the problems was that sugar cane is highly perishable and must be milled within forty-eight hours of cutting, so the cultivator had to be a manufacturer as well. Add to this the problems of shipping, the provision of casks for transporting molasses, the labour problems endemic to a slave force, shortage of overseers, runaways forming bands in the hills and periodically attacking the settlements, and it can be seen that production even on a small scale and by crude methods kept the price of sugar high.

his subjects. Somewhat half-hearted attempts to plant factories in Guiana had failed because French traders had been quite unable to cope with the hostility of the natives, who probably thought they were Spaniards. Other types of settlement on the mainland of Central America had been equally unsuccessful and would-be colonists had gone back to the sea to make their living.

In the autumn of 1625 two privateers, Pierre Belain, Sieur d'Esnambuc and the Sieur de Rossey, attacked a Spanish galleon off the Caymans, south of Cuba, and were beaten off, losing ten of their crew of forty men. In their badly damaged ship they ran eastwards to find an island where they could make repairs and refit. They reached St Kitts and asked Warner for help.

Warner was glad to see them. The expansion of his original settlement into the three other islands had left him with comparatively few men and he had recently had a lot of trouble with the Carib Chief Tegramond. Becoming bored with cheap English penknives, beads and mirrors which he now felt were inadequate compensation for the land he appeared to be losing, Tegramond had been planning to wipe out the colony. Warner had reacted swiftly, launching a surprise attack on the people who had greeted him with such friendliness, killing some and driving the rest to another island. They now constituted a major threat, and naturally Warner was relieved to see other Europeans, particularly ones as tough as these Frenchmen, who might be able to help him solve his problem. He persuaded Esnambuc to stop being a pirate and become a planter, and the French decided to stay.

It was just as well for Warner that they did, because a few months later the Caribs expelled from St Kitts collected allies from other islands and attacked in strength. The battle was long and fierce. The Caribs were determined to win back what they had lost, but they were repulsed, and though they went on raiding the islands held by the English and French for many years they were never able to drive the white men out. This story of native hospitality leading to the expulsion of the rightful owners of the islands reflects no credit on the early settlers in the West Indies, and the Caribs of these islands, like the charming Arawaks of the Greater Antilles, could not withstand the effects of European invasion. Today, only in Dominica is there a small Carib reservation, and on some islands a few families claim descent from the Caribs.

They were replaced by a society divided into three distinct grades: the landowners and administrators; indentured and transported white labour, and negro slaves. The slaves came mainly from West Africa, brought across the Atlantic by slavers operating ships in which the conditions, for sheer horror, defy description. The indentured white labour were people who made a contract to serve without pay, usually for a period of five years, in return for a passage to the West Indies and food and lodging, in the hope that at the end of their bondage they could make their own fortunes. This was fairly popular while there was plenty of land to be had, because 'freedom dues' at the end of the contract included a grant of land, a few implements to work it and sometimes a sum of money. The transported labour came from the prisons, and the harshness of the penal code in England ensured a constant supply.

About a year after his arrival in St Kitts, Esnambuc went back to France for the same reasons that had prompted Warner to seek an audience of James I, and like Warner he took with him a large quantity of the excellent tobacco grown on the island. The price it fetched in Paris at once aroused the interest of French financiers and came to the notice of Richelieu. The Cardinal, as the chief minister of France, took no chances with the Papal authority and applied to Pope Urban VIII for permission to do what Esnambuc had already done—found a colony in the New World in defiance of the edicts of Pope Alexander VI. On 13 October 1626 Richelieu received Papal recognition of France's right to plant colonies in the West Indies; and this was the first official recognition of Spain's inability to defend her prerogative. Richelieu at once formed the Company of St Christopher, with himself as the largest shareholder, and gave it a mandate to colonize St Kitts, Barbuda and 'other islands at the entrance to Peru, between the 11th and 18th parallels not possessed by any Christian Prince'.

Since in high places there was great enthusiasm and support

for his project, Esnambuc had little difficulty in recruiting from the ports of Normandy and Brittany nearly 500 French seamen and peasants. Conditions were so bad for them in France that they could not very well be worse in St Kitts, even though this island paradise might not be quite as Esnambuc described it. They set sail in three ships which took ten weeks to cross the Atlantic. Of seventy new colonists in one vessel only sixteen survived the voyage. It was not a good beginning to the French colonial empire in the Caribbean.

Although while Esnambuc was in France he must have heard of the rivalry now developing between his country and England over North America, he made a most peculiar arrangement with the English almost as soon as he returned to St Kitts in 1627. He and Warner drew up a treaty that is unique in colonial history. The most important clauses laid down that there were to be no hostilities between the English and the French in the West Indies, even when their countries were at war with one another, unless their home governments issued specific orders that they were to fight. Another clause stipulated the pooling of all resources against external enemies, assumed to be the Caribs and the Spanish. All roads, harbours, salt-ponds, and hunting and fishing rights were common property, and St Kitts was to be divided into three areas. The English, who got there first, were to have the fertile centre of the island while the French had the two ends—Capesterre and Basseterre.

The natural enmity between the two nations, so deeply implanted in the first Hundred Years' War, made any such arrangement hopelessly impractical, and there were other factors. The English settlements, once they had recovered from the disruption of the first hurricane, had never looked back. They had been well supported by their sponsors in England who were better organized and more generous than their French counterparts. The French, interested solely in trade and profits and caring little for the place as a colony, were unpleasantly parsimonious. The English had obtained from their American colonies a great deal of experience, while the French, even taking Canada and Acadia into consideration, had gained comparatively little. In England, manpower for new colonies was no problem, for the unscrupulous enclosure of land by the rich was depriving thousands of their livelihood, and they came overseas to escape starvation. By 1640 the white population of Barbados was in the region of 18,000. The French peasant, though wretchedly poor, was not harried by enclosure and was always reluctant to leave his beloved country. In any case, only Catholics were allowed to emigrate. Their colonies grew slowly. After fifty years in the Caribbean the combined white population of their two largest islands, Martinique and Guadeloupe, amounted to only just over 10,000.

In St Kitts the population and prosperity of the English increased rapidly, while that of the French did not. Inevitably the English began to encroach on French land, neglected because of a shortage of labour. The treaty had to be renewed and the boundaries redrawn six times in the next forty years, but it did nothing to remove the underlying bitterness and jealousy between the rival—and they were rival—colonists on the island; nor did it prevent war between them.

It was the Dutch who brought matters to a head. In 1628 Admiral Piet Hein of the newly formed Dutch West Indies Company, with a fleet of thirty-one sail, attacked and captured a Spanish treasure fleet in Matanzas Bay, off the north coast of Cuba. When this news reached the Spanish government a battle squadron under the command of Don Fadrique de Toledo was at once dispatched to rescue their fleet and escort it back to Mexico, if this were possible, and in any case to drive the English and French out of their settlements in the Lesser Antilles. Richelieu, whose intelligence service rivalled that of Sir Francis Walsingham in the reign of Elizabeth I, heard of this and sent ten ships and 300 colonists, led by the Sieur de Cahuzac, to make sure that no matter what might happen to the English, French interests would be protected.

Ignoring the clause in the treaty about pooling defence resources, Esnambuc used the French reinforcements to try to drive the English off what he said was French land. Cahuzac and his fleet seized English shipping in the harbour, and Thomas Warner's son Edward, acting as Governor while his father was away in England, was forced to give up the disputed border areas. After this, there could be no combined opposition to Don Fadrique when he arrived, and the French made no attempt at all to resist him. In fact, as if to make everything easier for the Spaniard, Cahuzac dispersed his ships and men before the enemy arrived.

The island of Nevis was the first to be attacked. Its fort, warehouses and plantations were destroyed while its inhabitants ran for the hills. The Spanish fleet then anchored off Basseterre and the French fled to Antigua. Edward Warner and the English colonists stayed to fight but achieved little in the face of a well-organized attack. Some of their shipping was taken and 700 men were carried off as prisoners to Cartagena and forced to work in the mines of Mexico and Peru. Of these, 300 eventually escaped and reached Plymouth in Devon.

Don Fadrique's descent upon the English and French settlements had no lasting effect. When it became clear that they could not defend their property on St Kitts many of the English took to the woods, to emerge and start all over again as soon as the Spaniards had gone. Thomas Warner came back from England and his driving energy soon restored the plantations. The French returned too, and at first the English tried to keep them out, on the ground that by running away at the first sign of danger they had forfeited any rights they might have had on the island; but after a while the situation became much as it had been before the Spanish attack.

Once again, the English flourished while the French struggled. High costs and low yields in the French plantations destroyed morale, many settlers died or gave up and went away to America or France, and of the 1,200 who came to the island in the four years after Esnambuc's treaty with Warner, less than 300 remained. The causes for this decline lay with Richelieu's Company of St Christopher and its policy of exploitation rather than development, but total failure, which seemed inevitable, was averted by the dissolution of the company and the founding of the Company of the Isles of America in 1635.

The new company not only developed the French portions of St Kitts but planted colonies in Martinique, Guadeloupe and on the north coast of Hispaniola. Progress on these three islands was slow but steady and laid a firm foundation for the enormous success that came to them in the eighteenth century. None approached the early prosperity of Barbados whose colonial history began at the same time as that of St Kitts.

Lying about eighty miles east of the rest of the Lesser Antilles, in a position where a combination of the trade winds and the Caribbean current made the voyage from other islands slow and difficult, Barbados was uninhabited until Captain John Powell, blown off course while returning from a trading visit to Brazil in the *Olive*, anchored off what became Holetown at the end of 1624. Impressed by the fertility of the island, its forested hills rich in logwood (used for dyeing), its beauty and its freedom from Carib and Spanish interference, Captain Powell nailed to a tree a board with the inscription: 'James, King of England and of This Island'. After this annexation he went first to St Kitts where he told Warner of his discovery, and then returned to England. In London he persuaded his employer, the merchant Sir William Courteen, to finance a colony. The joint-stock company, Courteen and Associates, was formed in 1627 and a large party of settlers, led by Captain John Powell and his brother Henry, went to the island, founded what was first called Jamestown and subsequently Holetown and began to clear the forests. Dyewoods were exported to England, and tobacco, maize and cassava were planted and tended by thirty Arawaks, freemen and volunteers, who had come to teach the colonists how to cultivate the crops.

The immediate success of the colony aroused Warner's envy and jealousy, and in the nasty little situation which developed, the competing groups of private investors in London began an undignified scramble for patents and patronage. Warner acquired the support of the able but spendthrift Earl of Carlisle while Courteen's patron was the Earl of Pembroke, one of the favourites at the court of Charles I. Both noblemen sought and were granted patents which included Barbados, but after extremely complicated and dubious intrigues Carlisle arranged for himself to be appointed 'Lord Proprietor of the Caribbee Islands' which specifically included St Kitts, Nevis and Barbados. He appointed Warner as his 'Lieutenant-General' and confirmed his position as Governor of St Kitts, but he installed his own nominee, the uncouth and unpopular Hawley, as Governor of Barbados. The Earl of Pembroke's patent was set aside, Courteen lost the £10,000 he had invested, and in the disorders which broke out in Barbados many of his colonists lost their lands.

Warner, who had started all the trouble, got nothing out of it. Carlisle died in 1636 and his son became Lord Proprietor, but when the Civil War began, all proprietary power lapsed.

By this time, in 1642, the French and English colonial possessions in the West Indies were becoming firmly established. St Kitts had been the joint source of considerable expansion. Nevis had been settled from there in 1628, and Antigua and Montserrat in 1632—largely as a result of religious dissension in the tradition of the New England colonies. The French in 1635 had spread out into Guadeloupe, Martinique and Hispaniola. In addition to these colonies, St Croix in the Virgin Islands had been settled by the Dutch and English in 1625; in the same year an attempt had been made to move into Tobago; and from 1638 until 1641 there had been a colony in St Lucia—from which the Caribs had been successful in driving away the planters.

French progress in Martinique and Guadeloupe was considerably hampered by the warlike Caribs whose sudden savage raids forced settlers to live in a state of defence, and this inhibited development. The partnership established in St Kitts still existed but was wearing very thin. Apart from constant boundary disputes and the regrettable Cahuzac incident—which had in fact occurred while England and France were at war and the Duke of Buckingham was trying to take La Rochelle—there had been no open warfare. The real reason for this comparatively peaceful state was that for the moment there was not much to fight for. Tobacco crops were still on a small scale and had to compete in the European market with American production. Sugar had not yet risen to the status it was to achieve in the next century.

The large islands of the Greater Antilles—Cuba, Hispaniola, Puerto Rico and Jamaica—were all regarded as Spanish property until the French moved into the western part of Hispaniola. The failure of the Spanish to prevent this intrusion, and their inability to do anything about it once it had happened, showed Oliver Cromwell how vulnerable were their possessions in the Caribbean.

Cromwell had won the Civil War with his New Model Army, thereby giving even more weight to the ancient principle that true political power must, in the end, be secured and maintained by military strength. And, like many dictators before and since, he found that having created military strength and used it to gain supreme power he had to find employment for troops who, for want of active service, were constantly plotting against him.

His attention was first drawn to the West Indies by a renegade priest, Thomas Gage, who had lived for some years in the Antilles and had written a book about the Spanish Main. In reading of the riches of the Caribbean, Cromwell, whose treasury was empty, felt the time had come to exercise his idle troops and benefit financially at the same time. With his Puritan's hatred of Papism it was not difficult to justify an act of aggression: he saw no reason why Spain should have exclusive rights in American waters, and he could avenge the Spanish attack on St Kitts and the massacres of Englishmen at Tortuga in 1638 and Santa Cruz in 1642.

The obvious base for operations was Barbados, which had the great strategic advantage of being to windward of the whole Caribbean archipelago, and a certain Colonel Thomas Modyford of Barbados, glad of an opportunity to ingratiate himself with the all-powerful Cromwell, assured him that the island would give him every support. Gage suggested the Orinoco as the objective of offensive operations, Modyford recommended Cuba or Hispaniola, with special reference to the rich Spanish port of Santo Domingo.

The original idea of a comparatively simple raid on Hispaniola grew into a vast plan to drive the Spaniards out of the whole area of the south Atlantic. Two English fleets were to be employed: one to create havoc on the Spanish Main and the other to cruise off the Spanish coast, capturing treasure fleets coming from the west and reinforcements sailing from Spanish ports. All through the autumn and early winter of 1654 secret preparations, centring on Portsmouth, caused considerable alarm in Holland, Spain and France whose spies sent back to their masters a stream of imprecise but worrying reports. Unfortunately, the plan which involved equipping a total of sixty-five warships and transporting

6,000 men across 3,000 miles of ocean to undertake operations in tropical conditions of which no one had any experience, was simply not feasible. After all the upheaval and expense of the Civil War and the campaign in Ireland it was far beyond the country's capabilities. In charge of all the preparations was Major-General John Desborough who, despite his military rank, was a Commissioner of the Admiralty. He was not mentally equipped to think out the immensely complex problems facing him, nor was he disposed to do so. Apparently he had a childlike faith that everything would be all right in the end. He was deluding himself.

The error which sealed the fate of Cromwell's great plan was entirely his own fault. Instead of detailing complete units under their own officers for the land force element of the expedition he created new corps mainly of drafts from regiments and supplemented by recruits. It is astonishing that Cromwell, who knew a great deal about soldiering, should have done this, for, as every soldier knows, commanding officers tend to look upon the compulsory provision of drafts as a heaven-sent opportunity to get rid of men they do not want. Recruits, of course, were useless, for not only was there no time to train them but they were liable to be restless, worthless undesirables.

The command structure of the expedition was not exactly an advantage. The land forces commander was General Venables, a man whose military reputation rested on the atrocities of Cromwell's terrible campaign in Ireland, but he was probably chosen because he was reckoned to be 'Cromwell's rival in military glory', and therefore a man to be got out of the way. The Admiral was William Penn whose gallantry and ability are overshadowed by the fact that he was the father of the Quaker who founded Pennsylvania. Having divided the command of what should have been a joint force, Cromwell made things worse by appointing three Civil Commissioners, virtually the equivalent of political commissars. One was Gregory Butler, who had been an army officer in the Civil War, another was a government official named Edward Winslow, and the third was Daniel Searle, the Governor of Barbados. Winslow's main function was that of a spy; he was required to report on the conduct of Venables who was under suspicion of treachery, and Penn who was distrusted for much the same reason.

After much administrative difficulty the expedition put to sea on 26 December 1654 and reached Barbados on 29 January 1655. It had had to sail without many of its stores, for example there were no water bottles for the 6,550 troops, but Modyford had told Cromwell not to worry because the people of Barbados would be only too happy to make up any deficiencies. It turned out that Modyford's opinions were his own; they were not shared by anyone on the island. On the ground that they would probably need every man and every piece of equipment for their own defence they refused to give any help of any sort, and in fact did their best to obstruct the expedition in every way. There was some justification for their attitude. If the Spaniards discovered, as they were almost bound to do, that the expedition had been launched from Barbados, they would probably take their revenge and repeat what they had done to Nevis and St Kitts.

Venables wasted a few weeks on Barbados, set off for Hispaniola, picked up a regiment of colonial volunteers collected by Gregory Butler in St Kitts, and arrived off the enemy coast on 13 April. His immediate objective was the town and harbour of Santo Domingo. The naval officers, Admiral Penn, Vice Admiral Goodson and Rear Admiral Blagge, wanted to attack at once and take the place by surprise. The civilian, Winslow, refused to allow this because, he said, the soldiers would plunder the town and he wanted all the plunder for the Treasury at home. Since plunder was the main reason why the undisciplined, disordered force had remained together for so long, the order forbidding it very nearly started a mutiny before any operational plan was made. Finally it was decided to follow the precedent set by Sir Francis Drake when he raided the port in 1586. The force was divided. Venables was to land thirty miles west of the town while Colonel Buller with the other half was to go ashore on the east of it. Both would then converge and attack from the landward side.

Nothing went right. Half-mad with thirst because they had no water bottles the troops ate whatever fruit they could find and drank from any pond or ditch. Hundreds fell out, sick and dying of dysentery, and when an attack was at last made against an outlying fort the troops would not stand against the fire of its defenders. Led by their officers they turned and ran, only to be caught in an ambush. The advanced guard and main body became wedged in a defile where they served as admirable targets for the guns of the fort and the lances of a body of Spanish cavalry. Leaving behind 300 dead the demoralized force withdrew to the ships, to face the contempt of the whole fleet. Admiral Penn asked to be allowed to take the town with his sailors but Venables and Winslow forbade it. This turned the contempt of the seamen into abuse, and in shame, leaving Santo Domingo intact, the fleet sailed for Jamaica.

Columbus had been the first European explorer to see Jamaica, on 3 May 1494, when he was off the coast of Cuba, and a local fisherman told him the island was called Xaymaca, 'land of many rivers'. He christened it St Jago, but the name did not survive, and he took possession in the name of King Ferdinand when he landed at Discovery Bay on 4 May. There was no Spanish settlement there until 1503 and, like the founding of La Navidad, it came about through misfortune when Columbus, returning from his disastrous expedition to Veragua, had to seek refuge by running his sinking ships ashore at St Anne's Bay. It was here that he had to deal with a mutiny, and Bridges points out that 'the first European blood which was shed in the New World by European hands stained the virgin soil of Jamaica'.

Columbus left the island on 28 June 1504 for the last time, and in 1509 the Court of Spain authorized Alfonzo d'Ojeda and Diego Nicuessa 'to make what use they pleased out of the unoccupied island of Jamaica'. It was not by any means unoccupied and the unhappy Arawaks soon found themselves under what Bridges calls 'the iron yoke of merciless captivity'. By 1528 French pirates had established bases in secluded, swamp-protected areas such as Bloody Bay on the extreme west of the island, but Jamaica belonged to Spain. This ownership was never challenged until Admiral Penn's fleet, piloted by local pirates, sailed along the south coast towards where Kingston is today. His attack was in fact the first government-sponsored attempt made by the English to take the colony of another European power by armed force.

As soon as he was within striking distance Penn announced

that since he could not and would not trust the army he would lead the assault landing himself, which he did, in one of his flagship's boats. Only one defence work, Passage Fort, protected the approach to the island's capital at Spanish Town, and after a feeble show of opposition the garrison surrendered and the English flag was hoisted.

The soldiers then came ashore under the threat of a General Order which laid down that the first man to turn his back was to be shot by his neighbour. 'Some,' says Bridges, 'suffered this ignominious fate.'

There is a story that this order was the result of the behaviour of the troops at what was called Drake's Landing at the mouth of the Rio Hayna near Santo Domingo. As the landing craft, rowed by sailors, approached the shore there was a tremendous rustling in the dry reeds and undergrowth just above the tide line, and convinced that a strong force of the enemy was waiting, concealed, to fire a murderous volley, the men would not land. The rustling was nothing more than the alarmed movement of hundreds of land crabs which live in sand holes at the edge of the sea, but no doubt the noise was frightening enough to men whom Penn described as 'a mixture of all that was base, ignorant and cowardly'. (Anyone who walks today beside the shore of the north coast of Jamaica, for example between Salt Marsh and Flamingo Beach, can hear what they heard, but on a reduced scale.)

The capital, and with it the island, of Jamaica capitulated to Penn and Venables on 11 May, and the looting and demolition of Papist churches began at once. It was not reported to Cromwell, or to his Secretary of State Thurloe, that French pirates had joined the English fleet for the attack on Hispaniola and helped in the conquest of Jamaica. However, they were invaluable with their experience of the inshore waters, their knowledge of the position of Passage Fort, the route to Spanish Town and of local conditions and language generally.

As soon as they had settled themselves in on the island the sailors and the soldiers began to fight one another in earnest, and after the various commanders had spent six weeks quarrelling continuously, Penn and Venables gave up and went home, leaving the troops and a large proportion of the fleet behind them. Cromwell was extremely displeased by their failure to win an empire and sent both of them to the Tower. They were set free in due course but both remained in disgrace until the Restoration.

Yet Jamaica had been won. The English flag now waved over one of the most beautiful islands in the world, and this new possession had to be defended. The first garrison was formed from the troops left behind by Venables. It was commanded by Colonel Richard Fortescue of the New Model Army who, encouraged by a letter from Cromwell thanking him for filling the breach created by the desertion of his commander, set out with great enthusiasm to tackle the multitude of problems facing him. He soon discovered there was one problem to which there was no solution, the scourge of yellow fever, known then as 'the black vomit', an enemy far more deadly to the English and French in the Caribbean than their rival forces.

Cromwell in his letter had promised reinforcements, and they arrived in October 1655 under the command of Major Sedgwicke. He found Fortescue on his deathbed, the garrison greatly reduced in numbers and hardly a man fit for duty. Within a week or two of his arrival the men he had brought with him began to die at the rate of twenty a day. Sedgwicke himself was dead within nine months, having long given himself up for lost. Colonel Brayne arrived in December 1656, and in lasting ten months he managed to outlive two-thirds of the draft that had come with him. At length a certain Colonel D'Oyley who had been in Penn's original expedition took over the command. He must have been a very fit, resolute man with far more will to live than his predecessors, and he was so successful in restoring order and morale that a determined attempt by the Spaniards to recapture the island in May 1658 was beaten off with heavy enemy losses.

This confirmed England's possession of Jamaica, and so, despite administrative chaos, incompetent and in many cases cowardly officers, mismanagement, divided command and in general a positive nightmare of a combined operation, England's first great military expedition to the tropics had achieved a concrete result. It was also the first of many attempts to take Spain's empire in the west away from her,

and nearly all were disastrous. Furthermore, it put ideas into
the heads of the French, who could see that the secret of
success in the acquisition of other people's colonies was sea
power. They could also see that sea power was not so much
the domination of the oceans of the world by an invincible
navy as a proper application of the principle of war summed up
in the words 'concentration of force'. A small fleet,
carrying troops, could achieve notable results if it concentrated
all its efforts in the right place at the right time.

The conquest of Jamaica put a different complexion on
the always strained relationship begun by Captain Warner
and the Sieur d'Esnambuc in St Kitts. There could be no
more 'local arrangements' over a matter now raised to the
level of international politics. Moreover, other governments in
Europe were beginning to realize the potential of these islands
for the production of tobacco and sugar. Holland's chances of
becoming a great maritime power were seen to be slender at
the end of Cromwell's First Dutch War; they had gone for
ever by the end of the Third Dutch War fought by Charles II
and his brother James. Portugal, unable to sustain the bright
promise of the fifteenth and sixteenth centuries, was declining
rapidly. Spain's failure to recover Jamaica underlined her
inability to prevent further depredations, and thus, of the
five Atlantic European nations, only two remained strong.
Inevitably, to the French and the English, what had been
regarded as a limited area of parochial settlements in the
West Indies suddenly became a new area of conflict in the
battle for empire.

There was nothing sudden about the change from partnership to rivalry because the whole history of the uneasy col-
laboration is one of quarrelling. The seeds of enmity were
always there; not much was needed to make them flower into
a state of war, particularly as Louis XIV's attitude to warfare
echoed that of medieval chivalry. He thoroughly enjoyed it.

The reaction of Philip IV of Spain to Cromwell's attack on
Jamaica was to make an alliance with Cromwell's greatest—
though at that time somewhat ineffective—enemy, the exiled
Charles II. Charles was then living in Cologne, while his
brother James was serving as a Lieutenant-General in the

French army under Marshal Turenne, and fighting a war against Spain in the Spanish Netherlands. Cromwell at once allied himself with Cardinal Mazarin, the virtual dictator of France during the minority of Louis XIV, and all the diplomatic moves that these alliances entailed created much awkwardness for the exiled House of Stuart. James had to leave the French army and join that of Spain. Thus he was on the losing side in the Battle of the Dunes outside Dunkirk, when Turenne and a force of British infantry, sent over by Cromwell, defeated the Spanish army commanded by Philip IV's bastard son, Don Juan of Austria. It had been many years since a British force had fought on the Continent for the French.

The Anglo-French alliance was continued throughout the reigns of Charles II and James II, not just because they were cousins of Louis XIV but because the Stuarts relied heavily on his financial support. It was never a very happy arrangement. Charles and his brother had been dependent on the French court for too long during the years of exile to forget their unfortunate position as poor relations, and the autocratic Louis was obsessed by the problem Louis XI had created all those years ago. Louis XIV was determined to push the vulnerable north-eastern frontier of France up to what he regarded as the natural boundary, the Rhine. This would absorb the Spanish Netherlands and most of Holland. The Dutch fear of annihilation and England's fear of subsequent invasion brought about the marriage of William of Orange with James's daughter Mary in 1677, and in 1686 William took a further step in his own defence and formed the alliance known as the League of Augsburg against Louis. It was William of Orange, when he had made himself William III, who brought England into his war with France, and it was a strange reversal of the course of history. Anglo-Dutch rivalry in the third quarter of the seventeenth century had left the French virtually free to increase their influence in North America and the West Indies; now an Anglo-Dutch alliance meant a sudden upsurge of resistance to the colonial ambitions of France. Beginning in 1689, King William's War started the second Hundred Years' War which did not come to an end until that June evening in 1815 when the British cavalry and infantry, sweeping down the slope of Mont St Jean in the last overwhelming charge, destroyed the *Grande Armée* and the political career of the Emperor Napoleon.

From the English point of view the war began badly. Local French troops, better equipped, better disciplined and more numerous, rapidly overcame all British resistance in St Kitts, but in the following year (1690) a small naval squadron arrived from England on temporary duty. St Kitts was recaptured and the island of St Eustatius, held by the French since the end of the Third Dutch War, was taken. The Governor-General of the Leeward Islands, Sir Christopher Codrington, petitioned for a permanent naval force to be stationed in the Caribbean for, as he said himself, 'all turns upon the mastery of the sea', but there was too much trouble at home.

Somewhat misguidedly Louis XIV was supporting the efforts of James II to win back his kingdom through Ireland, and Admiral Château-Renault brought 3,000 reinforcements for James's army into Bantry Bay. Admiral Herbert, later Viscount Torrington, stood in to engage the squadron covering the landing and was driven off by the heavy accurate fire of the French gunners. This so-called Battle of Bantry Bay, on 9 May 1689, was reported to James as a great victory over the British Navy, but James, who had done so much to make the navy what it was, received the news with the cold remark, '*C'est donc le premier fois*'.

Nevertheless, it showed the French what they could do, and in the following year they felt they had a good chance of seizing control of the Channel from the Anglo-Dutch fleet— the essential preliminary to invasion. On 22 June 1690 the French Admiral Anne Hilarion de Costentin Tourville put to sea from Brest and sailed up the Channel with a fleet of seventy-five ships of the line, six frigates and twenty fireships, the largest naval striking force since the Armada. His objective is said to have been London, following the same tactics as those used in June 1667 when the Dutch admiral de Ruyter had captured Sheerness, broken through the chain at Upnor, sailed up the Medway and bombarded Chatham without any difficulty.

From an intercepted dispatch Tourville had learned that the combined fleet of the enemy, consisting of fifty-eight

73

ships and under the command of Admiral Herbert, was lying at anchor off St Helens in the Isle of Wight, and he hoped to make contact within forty-eight hours of leaving Brest. It took much longer than he had planned for the last of his ships to clear Brest roads, and then the wind dropped. For three more days he was becalmed, and when he finally reached the Isle of Wight on 5 July the enemy had gone. He asked for a volunteer to reconnoitre the English coast farther up the Channel, and Jean Bart, a pirate well known in the Caribbean but at that time serving in the French navy, came forward. He knew something of the area because he had been a sailor in the Dutch flagship on the Medway raid, and setting off in a small craft disguised as a fishing boat, he found the Anglo-Dutch fleet anchored off Eastbourne, between Beachy Head and Pevensey—called Béveziers by the French, the name they gave to the subsequent battle.

Jean Bart returned to the French fleet on 8 July and reported the enemy strength as eighty-four ships when in fact the figure was now sixty. Beating slowly north-east, Tourville at length brought his fleet into action on 10 July, and the battle lasted all day. The French account of it implies that Admiral Herbert was a coward who set the example for the rest of his fleet, but in fact the damage and casualties were much the same on either side. By evening the wind had swung round to the west, to Tourville's advantage, and it seemed that he might yet win a decisive victory. Herbert gave orders for the towing away of disabled ships and this was interpreted by the French as a prelude to withdrawal. Then the wind died away and the tide turned. Instead of being able to bear down on the enemy, Tourville found himself being carried away westwards on the ebb. Herbert, very sensibly, anchored and stayed where he was. Helpless to do anything but drift slowly out of range, Tourville sat down to compose his dispatch. 'The enemy,' he wrote, 'has fled.'

He did, however, during the next two days inflict tremendous damage on the unfortunate Dutch who had not been able to follow Herbert into the shelter of the Nore, taking or destroying seventeen ships of their fleet without loss to his own, whereupon William III sent Herbert to the Tower. Although the Admiral was tried by court martial at Sheerness on 10 November 1690 and acquitted, the King refused to believe he had not deliberately sacrificed the Dutch while he made good his escape, and dismissed him from the Navy. With good reason, William never really trusted the senior officers who had served under his father-in-law.

Tourville had won a victory. His fleet was apparently still operational, and in a very real fear of imminent invasion England called out the Trained Bands. But battle casualties, damage to his ships, bad weather and a sick list of 6,000 men suffering from scurvy and other diseases compelled Tourville to lay up the French fleet for the winter.

Ex-King James, his Irish plans ruined by the Battle of the Boyne—fought nine days before the battle off Beachy Head—returned to France. His cousin began to collect a force for the invasion of England and final defeat of the Protestant Champion. The invasion army camped near St Vaast-la-Hogue, and it was Tourville's responsibility to convey it safely to the shores of England. Unfortunately the Marquis de Seignelay, the Minister for War who had provided Tourville with the means to win the battle off Beachy Head, had died in November 1690 and his successor, Pontchartrain, had made a mess of everything. So much so that when he gave peremptory orders for Tourville to put to sea on 12 May 1692, only thirty-nine ships of the Brest fleet were in commission and more than twenty had to be left behind because they had no crews, ammunition or supplies. Tourville was joined by five ships from Rochefort but twelve more, coming up from Toulon under the command of Admiral Victor Marie d'Estrées, were held up by contrary winds and failed to reach him.

Within sight of the cliffs where James and Marshal de Bellefonde stood watching, Tourville once more engaged an Anglo-Dutch fleet, this time under Russell and van Almonde. The French were greatly out-numbered and after a battle lasting nearly forty-eight hours only ten of their warships remained afloat. The English and the Dutch controlled the Channel and England was secure. The Battle of Cap la Hogue, which the French call the Battle of Barfleur, put an end to any hopes James may have had of returning to the Palace of Whitehall.

The effect of these great battles in the English Channel was to reduce the naval assistance that either the French or the English could provide in the Caribbean, and to emphasize to the colonists in the West Indies that both nations were now properly at war. The English naval squadron which had come to support Sir Christopher Codrington went on from the capture of St Eustatius to take Marie Galante. An assault was then made on Guadeloupe but this failed because of disease, the difficulties of the mountainous country and lack of supplies. The ships went back to England at the end of 1690 without having achieved the tasks set them by the authorities in London. By any standards they were slightly ambitious: the conquest of Martinique, Hispaniola and Canada, all within twelve months.

In the following year Jean-Baptiste du Casse, who already had a considerable local reputation, first as a slaver and then as a privateer, was appointed Governor of the French territory in Hispaniola, and he played a notable part in the war against England. In 1694 he invaded Jamaica, in 1695 he successfully defended his area of Hispaniola against a joint Anglo-Spanish attack, and in 1696, at the head of a force consisting of a French naval squadron considerably augmented by buccaneers, he captured Cartagena, and with it an immense booty.

His attack on Jamaica stemmed indirectly from two vastly different events: one was the earthquake of 1692 which destroyed a large part of Port Royal, at the entrance to Kingston harbour, and the other was Cromwell's campaign in Ireland, which spread so great a hatred of England that there were many Irishmen who would seize upon any opportunity to gain a little revenge. Two Irishmen, Stapleton and Lynch, informed du Casse of the wretched state of the fortifications of Port Royal, telling him that 'two hundred could capture the place and another two hundred could march in any part of the country, the people were so thin and so little used to arms'. They also told him that at least 500 men, 'some Catholics and others affected to King James II', would join him if he attacked.

On this information du Casse planned his campaign, and three French men-of-war were sent to help him. By chance, his intentions became known. A certain Captain Stephen Elliott

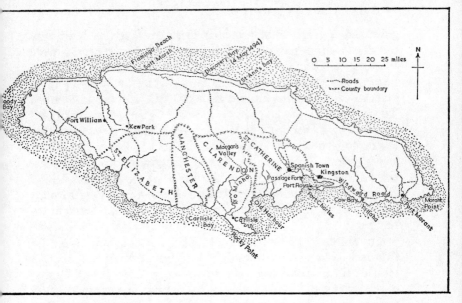

Sketch Map of Jamaica

of Jamaica, in his sloop *Pembroke*, was attacked by the French and he was taken, as a prisoner, into Petit Goave on the west coast of Hispaniola. On the way he overheard some valuable information, and he managed to escape from Hispaniola in a small canoe with two companions. On 31 May 1694 he reached Jamaica and at once warned the Lieutenant-Governor, Sir William Beeston, that du Casse with a fleet of twenty sail and 3,000 men was on his way to invade the island. His hazardous escape and timely warning were later rewarded by William III who sent him a gold chain, a medal worth £100 and the sum of £500 in cash.

Beeston went straight to the House of Assembly and thereafter things began to move swiftly. The House adjourned its normal proceedings for a month, called a Council of War, proclaimed martial law and ordered every officer to his post. Colonel Beckford, who was in command at Port Royal, at once put Fort Charles into excellent order and fortified the town. Fort Charles had grown from one small tower, built originally to protect Port Royal, to a large fortress of thirty-six guns and a garrison of 700 men. Another fort was built very rapidly on the parade at Kingston and breast-works were erected at Old Harbour and Carlisle Bay. According to Elliott, the French intended to land at one or other of these places before moving inland to attack the capital at Spanish Town.

In his own account Beeston says he realized it was hopeless to try to protect the whole coastline, so he concentrated his forces, regular and militia, in the Kingston–Port Royal area but left 'some few' to defend the breast-work at Carlisle Bay. He gave orders for the guns at Fort William and Port Morant to be spiked, the shot buried and the powder brought to Kingston.

On Sunday, 17 June, the French fleet, commanded by Admiral Rollon in his flagship the 54-gun *Téméraire*, making a total of three naval warships and twenty-three armed 'transports', many of them belonging to buccaneers, appeared off the eastern end of the island. Eight ships remained off Port Morant while the remainder went to Cow Bay, near Yallaha, some six miles to the west, where the troops and pirates disembarked. They laid waste the country, burned plantations, plundered houses, slaughtered every white man they could find and 'generally behaved with barbarity'. According to contemporary records, Charles Barber was tortured and James Newcastle 'murdered in cold blood', among many others. Having done as much damage as it could in the neighbourhood of Port Morant, the fleet set sail again on 15 July, moved west, reconnoitred Port Royal and then put back into Cow Bay. Fearing a land attack on Kingston, Beeston reinforced the troops guarding the approaches on the 'Windward Road' to the east, but on the morning of 18 July he counted seventeen ships making for what he rightly judged to be Carlisle Bay, thirty-six miles to the west of Spanish Town.

He at once sent off two troops of Horse and elements of the militia regiments of the counties of St Catherine, Clarendon and St Elizabeth, having given orders that the infantry were to mount themselves on any horses or mules they could find. (The island's garrison at this time consisted of one regiment of cavalry, 500 strong, and seven regiments of Foot, totalling 5,000 men. They were planters, merchants and white servants.)

The cavalry and mounted infantry reached Carlisle Bay that night, and those on foot 'marched so hard' that they came up to the defensive position at ten o'clock next morning, 19 July. Meanwhile the enemy had anchored in Carlisle Bay on the previous afternoon.

Into the breast-work, commanded by Colonel Sutton of Clarendon County, were crowded 250 men; Beeston says 'in addition to negroes' so it is not clear what the strength was. No doubt the Negroes were the 'some few' he refers to earlier in his story, but the figure of 250 refers to 'those of the several regiments who had come in during the night'. Beeston was highly critical of the whole position: 'the fort was ill-made and worse contrived . . . on the south was the sea, on the west a large river [the Rio Minho] and on the east they had left a wood standing which provided a natural covert for the enemy'. The garrison had no provisions either for man or horse.

At first light on 19 July the enemy landed between 1,400 and 1,500 men about one and a half miles east of the breast-work. A small outpost or piquet, which Colonel Sutton had had the good sense to send out during the night, fired on the invaders and then withdrew into the main defensive position. Following up, the French attacked the breast-work fiercely. Colonel Claybourn of St Elizabeth's was killed, so were his Captain, Lieutenant Vassell, Lieutenant-Colonel Smart of Clarendon, Lieutenant Dawkins and others. Under this assault the defenders were compelled to withdraw westwards across the Rio Minho, but just as the enemy were closing in to occupy the breast-work they were suddenly taken in the right flank by the infantry who had marched all night from Spanish Town. Four companies of the St Catherine Regiment, one of the St Elizabeth Regiment and a troop of Horse, 'although weary, footsore and hungry, fell on bravely, charging the enemy so warmly' that they not only prevented the French from pursuing the troops who had withdrawn across the river but threw them back and forced them to retreat. 'Captain Rakestead and some others were wounded, and some killed.'

This was a splendid little action by the local militia, and an unpleasant surprise for the French and their buccaneer allies who had been assured by the renegade Irishmen that nothing like this would happen.

For the next two days there were only minor skirmishes, when French reconnaissance parties were beaten off by the Jamaicans, and then on Sunday, 22 July, the French launched a planned attack on the house of a Mr Hubbard, which had a garrison of twenty men and a good store of provisions. The attack was repulsed, and Major Richard Lloyd, learning from a prisoner of war that a more determined effort would be made next day, put another fifty men into the house and laid an ambush on the approach to it. But the French had lost a lot of officers and men during this attack and had begun to realize they were not going to get any deeper into the island without losing a great many more. The defenders were far too alert and determined. As nearly always happened, the irregular force of buccaneers proved to be hopelessly unreliable, and feeling they had been badly let down by their Irish informants, the French gave up.

Du Casse set fire to the little town of Carlisle, named after the Earl of Carlisle, Governor of the island from 1678 to 1680 and son of Captain Thomas Warner's patron, and after spiking guns and doing what mischief they could, they withdrew to their ships. On Tuesday, 24 July, the enemy fleet sailed away. Admiral Rollon, du Casse and the three warships went straight back to Hispaniola and the rest put in to Port Morant to take on water and land the prisoners they had taken in the fighting. The French had lost about 700 men, of whom 550 had been killed or died of wounds at Carlisle Bay, whereas the Jamaican casualties were about 100 killed and wounded. A great deal of damage had been done. Fifty sugar works had been destroyed, a large number of plantations burnt and 1,300 valuable negro slaves carried off. This was a serious loss.

Louis XIV rewarded du Casse with a pension of 100 pistoles a year (about £60), and William III paid out the very large sum of £4,000 as compensation for those who had suffered from the French invasion. Sir William Beeston pocketed most of it.

According to Beeston, although the French invasion force disappeared over the horizon on Saturday, 28 July, 'their numerous cruisers still harassed the northern shores of the island, and once, M. Ponti [Admiral de Pointis] feigned an attack but our Admiral Neville pursued him and captured one of the richest ships of his squadron, with about £200,000 sterling; after which they never made any serious attempt upon Jamaica'.

There was another invasion threat in 1709. Some well-intentioned friend of Jamaica sent a letter from Paris, 'giving warning of the intention of M. du Guy Trouin to make a descent upon Jamaica with the force that was then preparing', but nothing came of it although the piracy and what Beeston calls 'depredations upon the coasts' continued.

The English attempt, in 1695, at a reprisal for the damage done in Jamaica failed not so much because of du Casse's defence of Hispaniola but through their own fault. The attack was to be a joint effort by the English and Spanish, assisted by five naval vessels sent from England, but the dilatoriness of the Spaniards and their jealousy over who was to command what, bogged everything down. There was a complete lack of co-ordination between naval and military units; the invasion took place during the rainy season, at the worst possible time of year and, as always, the black vomit played havoc with the troops. In effect the venture was no more than a repetition, on a much larger scale, of the English failure against Guadeloupe in 1690.

Du Casse's naval operation in 1696 against Cartagena, carried out by a French naval squadron commanded by Admiral de Pointis and a force of buccaneers, was not part of the struggle between England and France. Its object was to weaken Spain by making it as difficult as possible for her to find the money for keeping forces in the field. The expedition was financed by public subscription, with the incentive of huge dividends from loot, but it probably could not have been undertaken at all without the buccaneers. Du Casse was well aware of their lack of discipline and spirit, and he must have been desperate for manpower if he had to call again upon men whose reputation was founded upon greed, cowardice and brutality. Admiral Penn and General Venables had employed them, to no particular advantage except in local knowledge as pilots, guides and interpreters, though the English in Jamaica had thereafter given them considerable encouragement to raid and sack Spanish possessions, provided they brought their loot back to Jamaica; but it was soon realized that their value was limited.

In the context of the Anglo-French conflict the real significance of the French attack on Cartagena is that it was the last occasion on which French policy was influenced by the buccaneers. After the spoils had been divided the buccaneer element of du Casse's force was disbanded and paid off. Some became planters, some became straightforward pirates, but because du Casse and his successors maintained a firm rule in Hispaniola, supported by a naval force in the West Indies station, they were never again a serious menace.*

From the governorship of French Hispaniola, du Casse went on to greater things. Promoted to the rank of admiral—his service rank while he had been governor was that of a captain in the French navy—he served with great distinction in the War of the Spanish Succession and became a Knight of the Order of Saint Louis. His real achievement was the acquisition by France of the territories, known to the French as St Domingue, in Hispaniola that were formally ceded to her by the

---

* The difference between a buccaneer and a pirate became, by common usage, difficult to define, although initially the definitions were clear enough. The buccaneer was a 'boucanier', 'one who hunts wild oxen', the name first given to French hunters of Hispaniola who lived by selling hides and smoked and dried meat to the crews of passing ships.

The pirate, from Latin and Greek derivations, is simply one who robs and plunders on the sea.

In all the islands of the Greater Antilles there were huge herds of pigs and cattle running wild, the descendants of animals imported by the early Spanish settlers, from whose farms they had escaped. These herds provided a livelihood for runaway servants and slaves, escaped criminals, deserters from naval or military forces, marooned or shipwrecked sailors and the social misfits to whom organized society was anathema. Many of them were wont to raid settlements or attack passing vessels as a change from hunting.

By the middle of the seventeenth century the buccaneers had developed into bands of seaborne outlaws, well organized and armed and, when they chose to follow, well led. From outlawry they moved into power politics and were sometimes employed by ambitious and aggressive colonial governors as mercenaries. Bloodthirsty and almost invariably unreliable, most of them were savage scoundrels who lived by the sword and died by it. Although the buccaneers contained desperadoes of many nationalities, the majority of them were French or English. They were not of great significance in the contest between England and France.

Treaty of Ryswick in 1697 which brought King William's War to an end.

The Treaty of Ryswick also marked the end of the age of the buccaneers who, particularly under men like Henry Morgan in the period from 1655 to 1661, had instituted a reign of terror in the Caribbean. Morgan was subsequently knighted and made Governor of Jamaica from 1675 until 1682, strictly on the principle of joining those you cannot beat. His name lives on in 'Morgan's Valley' in the parish of Clarendon.

While the buccaneers flourished it was impossible for any government or governor or colonist to develop the Greater Antilles, and it became essential, for political, strategic and commercial reasons that they should be suppressed. Once this had been done, Hispaniola, hitherto the focus of their depredations, became a land of large sugar plantations and, in the eighteenth century, was generally regarded as the most valuable, in relation to its size, of all tropical possessions in the world.

Their extinction did not end the fighting, nor did the Treaty of Ryswick bring a lasting peace to Europe. The pattern of warfare now changed. The spasmodic fighting between largely local gangs of thugs and ruffians, mainly for private profit at the expense of the industrious individual, was translated to a far higher, international level where the two ancient enemies, France and England, fought to win an empire.

5 India

In 1023 the Sultan Mahmoud of the dynasty of Ghuznee established the first Mohammedan garrison two hundred miles south of the great river Indus, at Lahore. This was the first major Mohammedan penetration of Hindu territory. Not until the end of the twelfth century did his descendant Shahab-ud-Din push as far south as Benares on the Ganges and then come back to the north-west and make his capital at Delhi. He died in 1193, while Richard Cœur de Lion was on his way back from the Third Crusade, and by this time, only a few years before the Mongols, or Moguls, under Genghis Khan began to sweep like a tidal wave across Asia and Eastern Europe, India had become a separate kingdom, distinct from the countries to the north and west of the Indus.

The Mogul invasion of India culminated in the Battle of Delhi in 1526 and Babar became the first of the Mogul Emperors. His grandson, Akbar, the Great Mogul to whom Queen Elizabeth I sent a letter, was by far the most able of the Mogul dynasty. He conquered the whole of Hindustan and a large part of the Deccan, and he divided his empire into eight administrative districts, each governed by a subahdar. But he had defeated the Hindus and not the Mohammedan chieftains who claimed allegiance to the previous dynasty. Incessantly quarrelling amongst themselves they were unable to co-ordinate resistance to the Moguls and so, during the next hundred years, were gradually subdued until Shah Jehan—Akbar's grandson and builder of the Taj Mahal—felt confident he had completed the task begun by his grandfather. His confidence was misplaced, for in the reign of his son Aurungzebe the Mahrattas, tough Hindu hillmen from the Western Ghats, began to infiltrate the Mogul Empire, coming down from their mountains and hiring themselves as mercenaries to the dissident Mohammedan chiefs. The field

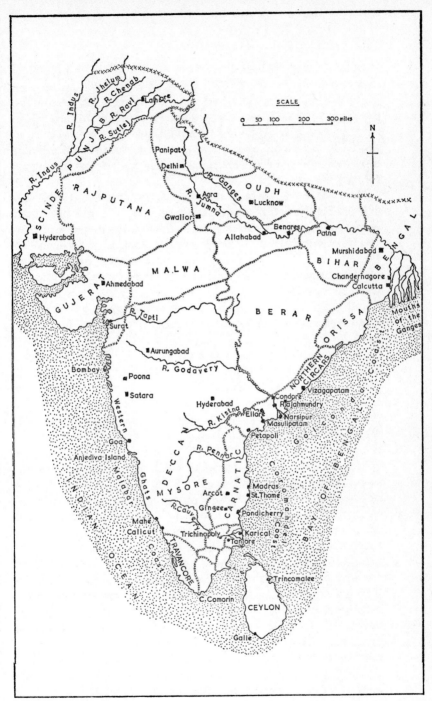

Sketch Map of India

strength of these Mahrattas grew steadily until in 1672 they met and defeated the Mogul army in a pitched battle. The Mahratta chief, Sevaji, died in 1680—five years before the death of Charles II—and Aurungzebe took up the sword in earnest. He chased the Mahrattas back to their hills, then turned southwards, overthrowing all who dared oppose him until he had crossed the river Kistna and added part of Mysore to his conquests.

Now at last it seemed that India, so long a battleground of emperors, chieftains and invading hordes, could be united in peace under one strong man, but when Aurungzebe died in 1707 the whole structure of his empire, shaken and cracked by the Mahrattas, fell apart. A shadow of the great Mogul Empire lingered on for another fifty years, seemingly making way for the Mahrattas, but the new Indian Empire was founded not by them but by a race of foreigners whose representatives, ridiculously small in numbers, came from Europe.

No doubt the difficulties encountered by Sir James Lancaster in the reign of Elizabeth I made the English reluctant to seek their fortunes in India, for the first two voyages the Merchant-Adventurers—the association which became the East India Company—followed in the wake of Dutch merchantmen to Java and Sumatra. On the third voyage, in 1607, after being forced by storms to shelter on the coast of Sierra Leone, Captain William Hawkins sailed his ship, the 300-ton *Hector*, direct to Surat, about 150 miles north of Bombay. Here he found encouraging openings for business, but permission to open a factory had to be obtained from the Mogul court at Agra. On 1 February 1609 he set off on the long walk of nearly 600 miles, taking with him a hired escort of fifty Pathans. It was just as well he did, for he was ambushed on the way, not by bandits who were a recognized hazard but by Portuguese merchants determined to preserve their trade monopoly. The Pathans dealt very capably with the ambush and in due course Hawkins was received by the Emperor Jehangir, Akbar's eldest son, and was granted valuable trading concessions. They did not amount to very much in the end because the Portuguese were already well established at the imperial court and the Jesuits wasted no time in undermining any English influence in what they regarded as their territory.

Two years later one of the East India Company's ships put in to Galle on the southern tip of Ceylon and then sailed up the east, or Coromandel Coast of India as far as Masulipatam. A factory was set up at Petapoli. By now the anger of the Portuguese and Dutch at the intrusion of English merchants in their rich markets was being actively expressed. The Dutch company trading in the Eastern Archipelago had four times the resources of the East India Company in manpower, shipping and general commercial influence, and during the next ten years they drove the English out of the islands altogether. In India the Portuguese had much the same advantages as the Dutch had in the islands but they had never recovered from the annexation of their country by Philip II of Spain. They seemed to have little or no will to resist the new threat to their commercial life-lines. In 1612 the English Captain Best, with only two small ships, drove a large Portuguese squadron from the mouth of the Tapti river in the Bay of Surat. His victory so impressed Jehangir that the Emperor not only threw out the Portuguese claim to a monopoly of the Indian trade but signed a treaty with the English. Under the terms of it the English received extremely worthwhile privileges and Jehangir agreed to accept an English ambassador at his court. After a six months' voyage round the Cape of Good Hope Sir Thomas Roe reached Agra in September 1614. He found himself in a world very different from the fever-plagued banks of the Amazon,* and during a visit which lasted a year he concluded a proper commercial treaty and arranged for all the existing concessions to continue.

The Portuguese never regained their influence, but the Dutch could not be disposed of so easily. During the troubled reign of Charles I, who succeeded his father James I in 1625, the English were too distracted by the domestic problems which led to the Civil War to spare much thought, let alone armed forces, for mercantile projects on the other side of the world. The affairs of the English company began to decline although the men on the spot established one factory at Masulipatam, another further along the coast and, in 1640, two years before

* See p. 54.

the Civil War began in England, a third at Madras, called Fort St George.

The Dutch took full advantage of England's preoccupation, but after the Civil War the East India Company petitioned Oliver Cromwell's Parliament for redress of injuries and depredations inflicted by them. This led to the First Dutch War and a series of sea battles which did much harm to Dutch naval strength. In 1651, by a very lucky chance—in the current state of medical knowledge it must have been a combination of chance and luck—the daughter of Shah Jehan, Jehangir's son, recovered from what was generally accepted as a fatal illness while under the care of an English surgeon at Surat. In gratitude, Shah Jehan gave the company full rights for free trade with Bengal—though the factory at Calcutta was not founded until 1690.

By the time of Cromwell's death in 1658 the East India Company was in a very sound position. Its main headquarters at Surat was responsible for the trade with Persia. A subordinate headquarters at Madras handled the business of all the factories on the Coromandel Coast and in Bengal, and a third, at Bantam in Java, dealt with the Eastern Islands. Its affairs prospered even more after the Restoration in 1660, for Charles II granted a new charter which authorized the sending out of warships, soldiers and war material for the defence of the factories, and furthermore gave permission for the island of St Helena in the south Atlantic, which for the last ten years had been a port of call on the voyage to India, to be fortified. The company's trade route was to be protected, if necessary by force.

In the following year Charles II married Catherine of Braganza, the Infanta of Portugal, and she brought to the English Crown as part of her dowry the ill-defined area of Bombay. Despite the arrangement made by their sovereign, the Portuguese were extremely reluctant to hand over so valuable a possession, and when Sir Abraham Shipman and 400 troops arrived there in 1662 there was a dispute over whether the word 'Bombay' in the marriage treaty meant only the island on which the port was built or the island and its dependencies on the mainland.

The unfortunate soldiers, ill-equipped and in no way

prepared for the sticky heat of the Malabar Coast, had to remain on the island of Anjediva, not far from Goa, while the controversy was being sorted out. Many of them died. After two years on the island the few survivors were transferred to Madras, now threatened by Dutch attacks in the long-foreseen Second Dutch War which actually began on 4 March 1665. When at last the Portuguese moved out and allowed the English to occupy Bombay in March 1665, the new garrison had been reduced to one officer and 113 men.

In 1668 Charles II relieved some of the constant pressure on his slender financial resources by leasing Bombay and all its military stores to the East India Company for a rent of £10 a year. He also gave the company power to raise its own private army, enlist officers and men for its own service on three-year contracts, and to transfer his own regular troops to this company force to fill vacancies. The company drew up its own military code and articles of war, and thus introduced the first military establishment in India.

The French East India Company, which the duc de Sully had resuscitated in 1664, celebrated its revival by another attempt to plant a colony in Madagascar. It failed because of the strenuous hostility of the local inhabitants, and so the company transferred its attentions further east and occupied two far smaller islands which were named Bourbon (after the Royal House of Louis XIV) and l'Île de France (later La Réunion and Mauritius). These became the naval bases which France felt she needed if she was ever to gain a firm footing in India.

In 1668 François Carron founded the first French factory in India, at Surat, alongside the English, a reminder of the uneasy partnership in St Kitts begun some forty years before. French influence was increased in the following year by the grant of another factory concession at Masulipatam, again beside the British, and vastly encouraged by this progress the French company then made a determined attempt to set up a post at Trincomalee in Ceylon. The Dutch, regarding Ceylon as part of their Eastern Archipelago, threw the French out. Then in 1674 they pursued the French traders to St Thomé, just south of Madras, where they had built another factory after their flight from Trincomalee. The garrison, under its commander François Martin, defended their factory with great gallantry but were forced to surrender, albeit with the honours of war. Martin had felt this might happen and had already made alternative plans. With sixty men, all that were left of his original force, he went south along the coast and settled at Pondicherry. In 1693 the Dutch attacked him again, with overwhelming strength, during King William's War. Louis XIV's wars had ruined his country and made it impossible for the French East India Company to send effective aid to its outposts in India, and once again Martin had to surrender a settlement which showed every sign of becoming a success. Pondicherry was restored to France by the Treaty of Ryswick four years later.

The French company's financial position deteriorated to such an extent during King William's War that the original factory at Surat had to be abandoned, but there was some compensation for this in the growth of the factory at Chandernagore in Bengal, for which formal permission had been granted in 1688. French commercial interests were now grouped on the east coast of the sub-continent, and when Pondicherry was handed back to France it became the company's principal factory, the headquarters of their *Directeur-général* in the East. François Martin was the first to hold this new appointment, and he died in office in 1706.

The Mogul Emperor Aurungzebe died in the following year, having divided his empire among his three sons who at once began fighting one another to gain the whole inheritance. This went on for a year, but when the oldest of them, Shah Bahadur, emerged as the winner he found that his troubles were just beginning. He made an appreciation of the somewhat confused situation and came to the conclusion that the Mahrattas in the south were the real threat to his security. He therefore made a rather precarious peace with them, only to find himself faced by a rebellion of Rajputs in Rajputana to the west and a serious insurgency among the Sikhs of the Punjab in the north.

Shah Bahadur died in 1712, after only five years on the now tottering throne which his forbears had invested with unparalleled splendour and power. Without a man like Jehangir or Shah Jehan to impose his will on the multitude of turbulent races in the empire all the smaller chiefs and provincial governors began to have their own dreams of sovereignty.

It was against this unstable background of disputed succession, shifting loyalties and personal ambitions that the French and English sought to establish their factories, negotiate further concessions, and keep on the right side of local rulers on whom the success and the future of their trading ventures seemed to depend. Neither nation was represented in any real strength. The headquarters of the British East India Company, established at Bombay in 1684, had an alarmingly small garrison of only 600 men (Europeans), an auxiliary force of two companies of Rajputs amounting to about 200 men, and about 100 cannon, mounted for the defence of Bombay's fortifications. The French had far less. Neither company was well enough organized or settled in to risk really active, and if necessary armed, competition with one another in areas where the local powers might become irritated with their antics and drive them out altogether. Thus in the period between 1688 and 1714, during King William's War and the War of the Spanish Succession, there was no outbreak of hostilities between the English and French in India, and both made local arrangements on virtually the same lines as Esnambuc's agreement with Warner in the West Indies.

The death of Shah Bahadur at a time when Indian politics were becoming extremely complicated merely made everything worse. After the traditional and inevitable quarrel over who was to succeed him, his grandson Farokshah became Emperor and inherited Shah Bahadur's unsolved problems. The Sikhs were brought under control but the Mahrattas increased the scale and scope of their raids into Mogul territory and at the same time expanded and developed their military strength. Meanwhile Persian and Afghan raiders came across the north-west frontier, at first in small bands seeking women, cattle and loot, and then in far greater force to carve out their own kingdoms in the fertile lands watered by the Five Rivers: the Punjab.

The descendants of Akbar's subahdars had by now come to look upon themselves as monarchs with powers of life and death over the smaller states within their provinces, and these states each had its own rajah or nawab who considered himself independent. When Farokshah died in 1719 any semblance of centralized control and settled order vanished entirely. The people of India became like a rudderless ship, unable to do anything but drift in whatever direction the political winds might blow, while all the time on the southern horizon the black storm cloud of the Mahratta confederacy grew larger. The rulers of the fragments of the Mogul monolith became too absorbed in local affairs to realize the threat. Their new freedom was so much more enjoyable than the rigid autocracy which Babar had imposed, and they used it to indulge in the delights of anarchy.

The dissolution of the whole political system which had safeguarded their interests made the European trading companies realize they were now in a very awkward situation. If they were to remain in India at all they would have to defend the concessions they had been granted, certainly by every political means and probably by armed force. The Dutch withdrew. They devoted all their energies to the area they knew and where they had very little competition, the Eastern Archipelago. They left their representatives in Bengal and the Carnatic, ready to start again if things got better, but for the moment they were prepared to cut their losses and wait and see what happened. The French and English remained, unaware initially that the Mahratta policy of destroying piecemeal the remnants of the Mogul Empire would create a political vacuum which, whether they liked it or not, only they could fill. Their contest in the East was to decide which of them would fill it.

Just before Farokshah died the English East India Company acquired from him a large extension of their territory on the Hooghli, an area some ten miles long on both sides of the river, and with this possession at Calcutta and the two very prosperous settlements at Bombay and Madras, the company's future seemed secure. Being so widely separated it was most unlikely that these large commercial installations could be attacked simultaneously, so no matter what happened there was bound to be at least one still in business at any one time. Bombay, well fortified on its island, was a great asset. It was never captured, and when the great storms of the monsoon made the Coromandel Coast unsafe for all shipping, British fleets were able to shelter in its harbour.

While the English prospered, the French declined, largely because of Louis XIV's ruinous wars which reduced their company almost to insolvency. They had only one major settlement, at Pondicherry, which was their headquarters, and their other reasonably large factory, at Chandernagore on the Hooghli, could not be reached by ocean-going ships and was easy to blockade. The little factory at St Thomé was not a success; it had no harbour and was difficult to defend. The nearest refuge for their shipping during the monsoon was Mauritius, more than 3,000 miles away.

Thus, at the beginning of the contest, England had all the advantages, and about the only asset the French possessed was their excellent relationship with the local native rulers, carefully maintained by all the governors at Pondicherry.

Then there appeared upon the eastern scene a young Frenchman, Joseph François Dupleix, who was to put all the assets and advantages of the rival company at risk. He arrived in Pondicherry in 1720. Five years later a second great Frenchman, Bertrand de la Bourdonnais, a captain in the French navy, came out to India. He was a man of formidable talents and energy. Between them they were to make life very difficult for the English company.

Dupleix was the son of a director of the French East India Company and he had a driving enthusiasm for commerce. He was twenty-three when he joined the company and he at once began to put into effect a plan he had devised for making Pondicherry the commercial centre of southern India; proving its viability by investing his private fortune in the scheme and making a large profit. In doing this he was helped considerably by the action of the French Government in completely reconstructing and rehabilitating the company in 1723.

La Bourdonnais first made his name in 1725 by capturing the little town of Mahé on the Malabar Coast, just north of Calicut. Having abandoned Surat the French needed this western point of access to the trade of southern India. From Mahé, la Bourdonnais went to Mauritius where he showed almost incredible energy and ability. Within two years he converted this thickly forested island into a naval and military base, well fortified and provided with dockyards, barracks, arsenals and everything needed for future operations in

India. When he had finished, his harbour of Port Louis could accommodate the largest fleet likely to be used in the Indian Ocean.

In 1731 Dumas, the governor of Pondicherry, sent Dupleix up to Chandernagore which had been moribund for years and showing no profit against its overheads. Dupleix rapidly revived it and turned it into the most important centre of trade in Bengal, and it was while he was doing this that the French really began to get involved in the complex web of opportunism, treachery and general skulduggery euphemistically described as Indian politics.

The first subahdar formally to establish his independence of the Imperial Court was Nizam-ul-Mulk of Malwa who reached an understanding with the Mahrattas and made himself master of the Deccan. In 1732 one of his subordinates, the Nawab of the Carnatic, died and was succeeded by his nephew, Dost Ali, of whom Nizam-ul-Mulk so disapproved that he refused, as Nawab of the Deccan, to authorize his succession. Dost Ali went to Pondicherry, in his province of the Carnatic, and asked Dumas for French support in his claim, offering trading concessions and a large bribe in return. He and Dumas got on very well together, and the happy relationship was extended to Dost Ali's, son, Sufder Ali, and his sons-in-law, Mortiz Ali and Chunda Sahib—who were all Mohammedans. Chunda Sahib appears to have had the greatest respect for everything French and did his best to further the growth of French influence in the Carnatic.

Three years later the Rajah of Trichinopoly, a much smaller state on the southern boundary of the Carnatic, died leaving the usual quarrel and muddle over his successor. He had been a Hindu. His widow, who strangely enough was one of the claimants to the vacant throne, took the unwise course of asking the Mohammedan Dost Ali to help her. He sent Chunda Sahib, at the head of an imposing army, and as soon as Chunda Sahib entered the city of Trichinopoly he sat down on the throne himself and announced that the whole state now belonged to Dost Ali—the close friend of the French.

Another three years later, in 1738, another Hindu rajah died, this time the ruler of Tanjore, even smaller than Trichinopoly and lying between the eastern boundary of that state and the sea. Again the succession was disputed and an aspirant named Sauhoji offered Dumas the little coastal town of Karical, some seventy miles south of Pondicherry, in return for active support. With the money, arms and ammunition supplied by Dumas, Sauhoji took possession of the throne of Tanjore and then declined to keep his side of the bargain. This so upset Chunda Sahib that he intervened without being asked, forced Sauhoji to keep his word, and Karical became French. It was not of much value from the trading point of view and had no proper harbour, but at a time when the French were trying to expand, it was better than nothing.

The activities of Chunda Sahib began to cause considerable concern to the Mahrattas. They, as Hindus, were determined to check all this Mohammedan empire-building by the Nawab of the Carnatic, and so they attacked Dost Ali, defeated and killed him, and created the utmost confusion from one end of the province to the other. Sufder Ali took his father's place and he and Chunda Sahib appealed to Dumas for asylum in Pondicherry for their families and belongings, now apparently in great danger. Bearing in mind that Dumas had no troops under his immediate command and that to give help to his Mohammedan friends would put him in danger from the powerful Mahrattas, the action he took was extremely courageous. Ignoring the most alarming threats from the Mahrattas he gave sanctuary to the wives and children of Sufder Ali and Chunda Sahib and set to work to put Pondicherry in a state of defence. He strengthened the fortifications, raised a body of infantry from the European population and recruited as sepoys between four and five thousand of the local Mohammedans.

While he was busily doing all this, his 'friend' Sufder Ali entered into a secret arrangement with the Mahrattas whereby they undertook to leave him alone on condition that he betrayed his brother-in-law Chunda Sahib into their hands. Under the terms of this agreement the Mahrattas then laid siege to Chunda Sahib in Trichinopoly, and with no fear of the place being relieved by Sufder Ali, took it after three months, and in March 1741 carried Chunda Sahib off as their prisoner. It is surprising that they did not merely kill him out of hand for they regarded him as a danger to them, a dangerous influence for unity among the Mohammedans of the Deccan, and a dangerously competent soldier.

Having acquired Chunda Sahib's person they then wanted his property. An envoy with a suitably impressive entourage of Mahratta cavalrymen came to Pondicherry and was hospitably received by Governor Dumas. In the cool of the evening Dumas took him for a gentle ride round the city, pointing out the impregnable strength of the reconstructed fortifications, the resolute men prepared to defend them to the end and the extraordinary smartness and enthusiasm of the new sepoy army. He then sent the envoy away with a large case of good French brandy and liqueurs, and the assurance that he would not yield the city so long as there was one man left alive with him. He must have stage-managed the demonstration extremely well because the Mahrattas gave up all thought of an attack and marched away. Dumas found himself the hero of southern India. He had done what no man had ever dared to do: he had defied the invincible Mahrattas. Nizam-ul-Mulk and Sufder Ali extolled his bravery and sent him lavish presents. The effete descendant of the great Akbar invited him to Delhi to receive the honoured title of Nawab, and Dumas, always with a sharp eye to the future, was happy to accept it—with the proviso that the rank would be passed on from governor to governor.

In October of this year of progress (1741) Dumas resigned and went back to France. He was replaced by Dupleix who, after administering Chandernagore for the last ten years and raising it to its paramount position in Bengal, had made himself a vast fortune.

La Bourdonnais, having done all that could be done to turn the island of Mauritius into a springboard for offensive operations, returned to France in 1739, at the time when England and Spain were engaged in the War of Jenkins' Ear. He was told by government ministers that France was likely to enter the Anglo-Spanish war on the side of Spain, and he suggested to Cardinal Fleury, Louis XV's elderly chief minister (he was eighty-six), that it would be a good idea to station a naval squadron at Port Louis now, so that as soon as the war began he could launch a devastating attack on the Coromandel Coast long before the English could augment their meagre forces. There was much argument about this, but at last, in 1741, la Bourdonnais, now promoted to the rank of admiral, was allowed to sail with an armament of five ships and a small force of 1,700 sailors and soldiers. As soon as he had gone, the directors of the East India Company decided there was nothing to be gained by fighting the English in India, and every advantage in renewing the arrangement made for neutrality in the previous war. They persuaded the old Cardinal to order the return of the ships and troops, and when la Bourdonnais reached Mauritius, having first made a reconnaissance of the Coromandel Coast, he found the order waiting for him. He complied with it. The ships put out to sea and a few days later, when they were beyond recall, he received another message, cancelling the order. He must have been a very patient man to do so well under this sort of administration.

France entered the War of the Austrian Succession in the spring of 1741, having pledged her aid to the Bourbon king of Spain in a Family Compact, but it was a long time before hostilities began in the East.

Dupleix, a great lover of pomp and ceremony, especially when he was the central figure, had arranged for himself to be ceremoniously installed as a Nawab before he left Chandernagore, leaving no doubt in the minds of neighbouring princes invited to the function that his rank came from the same authority as theirs, and that henceforth he was their equal if not their superior. He took up his post as Governor of Pondicherry, and when la Bourdonnais arrived on his reconnaissance early in 1742 they discussed the Admiral's plans for an attack on Madras. These were approved and Dupleix undertook to besiege the city on the landward side at the same time. The Admiral then went back to Mauritius to await the signal for action, only to find the message depriving him of the means for putting the plan into effect.

In the meantime the lid had again blown off the political cauldron of the Carnatic and much began to happen, although at a speed related to the climate and the standard of communications—seldom more rapid than a man on foot who frequently found it necessary to rest in the shade.

Sufder Ali had at last been officially accepted as Nawab

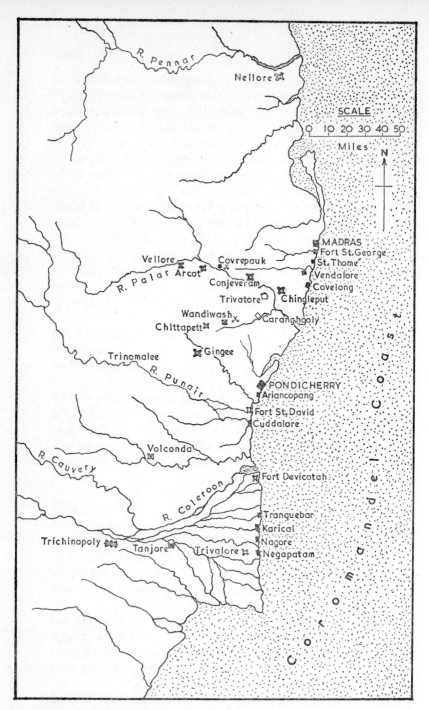

Sketch Map of the Carnatic Area of Operations

of the Carnatic, but as soon as his appointment had been confirmed he refused to pay the accepted percentage of his income to his superior, Nizam-ul-Mulk. Sufder Ali was intelligent enough to realize that this act of open defiance would not be supported by the French. Their policy was at all costs to avoid offending the local Mohammedan rulers who owned the land all round their factories and had large native armies to enforce any eviction orders they might choose to serve. He therefore removed the treasures he had placed in the safe custody of Governor Dumas in Pondicherry and transferred them to the English in Madras.

His brother-in-law, Mortiz Ali, seems to have regarded this switch of allegiance with extreme disfavour for in September 1742 he arranged for Sufder Ali to be assassinated and then announced that he was now the Nawab of the Carnatic. (The other brother-in-law, Chunda Sahib, was still in a Mahratta prison.) Mortiz Ali's subordinates, loyal to the memory of the departed Sufder Ali, took exception to this headstrong action and appealed to the Mahratta chief, Morari Rao, to help them expel the new self-appointed Nawab. Without waiting to hear what the Mahrattas proposed to do, but having a shrewd idea what was likely to happen, Mortiz Ali fled, leaving the infant son of Sufder Ali as the nominal Nawab.

The whole province at once dissolved into anarchy, and the Mahrattas, naturally enough, felt this was the ideal moment for them to annex Trichinopoly, Tanjore and the Carnatic, and put an end to any Mohammedan aspirations in the south of India. Their army, ostensibly in response to the appeal of Mortiz Ali's courtiers, began to march into Trichinopoly in December 1742. At the beginning of the new year, much to their surprise, Nizam-ul-Mulk suddenly appeared, coming from the north, and behind him was an army much larger than theirs, with which he proposed to restore order. The Mahrattas withdrew. Sufder Ali's poor little son disappeared with an abruptness that was probably fatal and one of Nizam-ul-Mulk's officers, a man named Anwar-u-din, was appointed Nawab.

Dupleix, sitting in Pondicherry and watching these events with an interest considerably sharpened by the unexpected involvement of the English in Madras, heard that war between

England and France was likely to be declared at any minute and that a large squadron of English warships was now on its way to attack and destroy Pondicherry. (News of the actual declaration did not in fact reach him until the middle of 1744.) To any man less resourceful this information might have been disturbing. The French fleet intended for exactly similar action against Madras had long since returned to France and there was no naval protection either off the Coromandel Coast or in Mauritius. The fortifications of Pondicherry were all on the landward side and the city lay open to bombardment from the sea; Dupleix had even been forbidden by the company directors to 'waste' money on repairing them. There were less than 500 Europeans to hold off a combined operation by land and sea, and Dumas's sepoy army, too expensive to maintain except on a short-term basis, had dwindled away to nothing. In these circumstances an attack by the English was likely to raise all sorts of problems, but Dupleix was quick to see a solution.

Laying great emphasis on the help given by the French to the Nawabs of the Carnatic in the past, he persuaded Anwar-u-din to declare his neutrality and forbid hostilities on his territory. The British in Madras had to conform to this because there was nothing else they could do, but they made the condition that the same prohibition must apply if the French ever showed signs of attacking them. Their naïveté must have amused Dupleix.

Thus, towards the end of 1745, when the British squadron at length appeared off the coast, Commodore Peyton who commanded it found he was limited to seaborne operations.

Away in Mauritius, la Bourdonnais did not hear of the outbreak of war until the autumn of 1744, and because he was a man in the tradition of great commanders, it was all he needed to know. An admiral without any ships to command, virtually isolated on his little island and knowing that any dispatches or instructions received from France were likely to be anything up to a year out of date, he went ahead as rapidly as he could to make war on his own. He requisitioned every French merchantman that came into Port Louis, told their commanders exactly what he was going to do, and why, armed them with any guns he could lay his hands on, trained their crews for war and supplemented them with auxiliaries recruited from the mixed population of planters, labourers and slaves on the island. Despite his arbitrary behaviour and the driving energy which his subordinates, in that enervating climate, must have found exhausting, he seems to have inspired considerable loyalty and affection.

In January 1746 a 70-gun warship arrived from France, escorting four merchant vessels, and they raised the strength of his naval force to ten ships, of which some were only partly armed. This, he felt, was enough for the task he had in mind. The squadron put to sea early in April and almost at once found itself in the path of a hurricane. All the ships were damaged, some badly; the only warship was completely dismasted, and with difficulty they made their way back to Port Louis. Yet, after only six weeks of immense labour the little fleet was again at sea and it arrived off the south coast of Ceylon at the end of June. On 6 July la Bourdonnais met and engaged the British squadron under Commodore Peyton, but the action was indecisive. At the end of it, for some reason never explained, Peyton took his ships into Trincomalee to repair the slight damage suffered in what could hardly be described as a battle. In doing so he left the way open for la Bourdonnais to sail first to Pondicherry to contact Dupleix and then, if he wished, attack Madras. Thus from the French point of view the sea action off Ceylon had been a success which, provided Dupleix was able to find a way round Anwar-u-din's ban on hostilities in his province, could be the prelude to conquest.

The defences of the town of Madras were almost as inadequate as those of Pondicherry. For the past half-century the directors of the East India Company had economized on the fortifications, largely because they put all their trust in sea power to protect England's interests overseas. There were 300 English—200 of them being garrison troops—in the cantonment area called the White Town which was only about a quarter of a mile long by 100 yards wide, surrounded by a flimsy wall defended by four small batteries set in bastions. Nicholas Morse, the Governor, was a merchant who knew virtually nothing about local politics and even less about soldiering. He had in his office a young clerk who had joined

THE BATTLE FOR EMPIRE

the company two years before, quiet, moody and lonely, apparently unhappy, out of tune with his surroundings and always glad of a chance to try to escape from them in the library of Government House. His name was Robert Clive.

In July, at the end of the month, Morse heard of the warlike preparations being made in Pondicherry and at once appealed to Anwar-u-din to enforce neutrality in the Carnatic, but, being ignorant of local customs, he failed to provide his messenger with a suitable present for the Nawab. In these circumstances the envoy had the greatest difficulty in interesting anyone in his mission. On 29 August la Bourdonnais and his squadron arrived off Madras, bombarded the town for a short while without doing much damage and then sailed away. He returned two weeks later, landed a force of 1,100 Europeans and 400 native troops and began a formal siege. Under his personal supervision approach trenches were dug, batteries were erected; when the guns opened fire Governor Morse abandoned hope.

Unknown to him, Anwar-u-din heard from a source other than the messenger from Madras that the French were ignoring his edict of neutrality, and this apparently contemptuous disregard for his orders enraged him. He was in the act of gathering together a force to go to the aid of the English when he was told that after a siege lasting one week, in which the English had five casualties and the French none, Morse had surrendered. This did not prevent him from sending a message to Dupleix making it very clear that unless operations against Madras ceased immediately he would come himself at the head of an army to put a stop to them.

Dupleix, who had foreseen all this, sent a smooth reply explaining that it had never entered his head to try to capture Madras so that the French could take possession of it. The Nawab was the ruler of the province and it was to the Nawab and to no one else that Madras belonged. Naturally it would be handed over to him as soon as the formalities of the English surrender had been completed.

It is strange that Dupleix, who was usually able to see ahead so clearly, did not foresee the danger lurking in this undertaking, and the complications which could arise as the result of the mutual antipathy between him and la Bourdonnais. The Admiral was a practical, clear-thinking man who seldom had any difficulty over his priorities. He knew exactly what he wanted, and how to get it. Dupleix was an opportunist with a sinuous, supple and subtle mind. Secretive and devious, he delighted in intrigue and was fascinated by all the permutations of Indian politics. The outwitting of a wily Oriental opponent was, to him, more rewarding than any direct advantage gained by it. He greatly enjoyed being a Nawab, dressing himself in flowing robes to act the part, and his success, his great wealth and his place in Oriental society had led him to believe he was perhaps more intelligent and more important than he really was.

Both men were venal and, where making money was concerned, entirely amoral, but public life in the eighteenth century was generally regarded as a lucrative opportunity. The attitude was that anyone who had a chance to enrich himself was simply a fool if he did not take it. Dupleix had already made a great fortune for himself in India, la Bourdonnais had not yet been so successful. Both had agreed on the plan for driving the English out of Madras, but what they had not decided—perhaps not even discussed—was who was going to make the most money out of it.

As the conqueror of the place and the man on the spot, la Bourdonnais reckoned that he, and only he, should decide how to dispose of Madras. Dupleix, with some justification, contended that as Governor-General such a decision could only be made by him. La Bourdonnais was not interested in the opinions of a civilian, and he was well aware there was very little time in which to argue and sort things out. It was now nearly the end of September, the monsoon was nearly due and if he and his ships were caught by it on that exposed coast he might find himself in serious trouble. However, determined to have his own way, he lingered on, drawing up an agreement with Nicholas Morse that all the English captured in Madras would be treated as prisoners of war on parole and that the town would be handed back on payment of a ransom.

There seems to be little doubt that a substantial bribe formed the basis for this amicable arrangement, but while the details were being settled, the monsoon broke—on 14 October —and in the hurricane that heralded it four of the French ships were wrecked and the rest badly damaged. A week later, on 21 October, la Bourdonnais and Morse signed the treaty for the ransom of Madras, all the ships that could be made seaworthy sailed south to Pondicherry and in a confrontation soon after their arrival Dupleix and la Bourdonnais exchanged frank but abrasive remarks on each other's diplomacy. La Bourdonnais then returned to Mauritius, arriving in December, and sailed from there to Europe. On his way back to France his ship was captured by a British man-of-war and he personally was treated with such courtesy and consideration that his countrymen, when he returned to France, were convinced the arrangement he had made over Madras had been very much to his own advantage. He was arrested and confined in the Bastille where he remained for three years. At his trial he was acquitted, no doubt because after that lapse of time it was difficult to produce convincing evidence of peculation, treachery or anything else, but it was generally felt that by the long imprisonment and trial, honour, such as it was, had been satisfied.

In fact la Bourdonnais had sound arguments to support his action. The French Government had expressly forbidden him to make permanent conquests—it was already difficult enough for them to maintain the possessions they had—and though he had reached agreement with Dupleix over the actual attack on Madras, he did not and had never pretended to favour all Dupleix's elaborate political plans. Moreover he was certain in his own mind that, as usual, when the war was over any conquests or acquisitions would be restored to their former owners. It was for these reasons that he had taken what he felt was the commonsense course of granting parole and accepting bills of ransom. The fact that he put the ransom money in his own pocket was not at that time looked upon in any way as a breach of honour.

La Bourdonnais sailed away, never to return, leaving Dupleix furious and embarrassed. Furious because his authority had been flouted and he had gained no financial advantage from the capture of Madras, and embarrassed because he now had to find some way round the undertaking he had made to Anwar-u-din. Meanwhile the Nawab had become highly suspicious that something had gone wrong because there was

so long a delay in handing Madras over to him, and he had
sent his son Maffuz Khan with an army of 10,000 men to
besiege it.

Dupleix's first step after the departure of la Bourdonnais
was to secure Madras. The French now had the preponderance
of European troops in the area, for la Bourdonnais, after the
hurricane, had been compelled to leave more than 2,000 men
behind, and Dupleix, when he heard of the move of Maffuz
Khan and his army, was only too glad to have them. Even so,
his manpower resources appeared terrifyingly small in relation
to the huge native forces opposing him.

He sent a message to the French officer commanding in
Madras, M. d'Espréménil, telling him to offer all possible
resistance to Maffuz Khan and to hold the town at all costs.

D'Espréménil began to suffer from a sort of claustrophobia
with this large native army sitting all round him, and on
2 November he made up a small force of artillery and infantry,
sallied boldly forth from his fortifications and formed up
facing the dense mass of enemy cavalry. He then opened a
tremendous fire from his light field guns with all the speed
and accuracy for which French artillery, even from the days of
Charles VII, had become notable. In the native army a gun
crew capable of getting four rounds off in one hour was
reckoned to be at the peak of efficiency, so it is not surprising
that the ability of French gunners to achieve, for short periods,
a rate of nearly one round a minute, threw Maffuz Khan's
troops into the utmost dismay and confusion. They turned and
ran. M. d'Espréménil marched his men forward and occupied
the enemy camp. It is difficult to say which side was the more
taken aback by the behaviour of the other, but the effect
on the morale of the French was considerable.

Maffuz Khan collected his army and after hanging about
near Madras for another day, marched it to St Thomé, four
miles to the south, to intercept a French detachment which his
spies told him was on its way to relieve d'Espréménil.

Early in the morning of 4 November this force was seen to
be coming up the road, on the last lap of the long march
from Pondicherry, and it consisted only of 230 Europeans and
700 sepoys, under the command of a young Swiss officer,
M. Paradis. He suddenly found himself faced with a tactical

situation of the utmost danger. Ahead of him the road sloped down to a river running across his front. The monsoon floods had subsided and he knew there was a ford, but drawn up on the far bank, completely barring his advance, was an army of 10,000 men with artillery support. Being in full view of the enemy he could not attempt to outflank them, and if he retreated he and his force would be cut to pieces by the enemy cavalry.

Whether he made his plan out of inspiration or sheer despair will never be known, but, with his men closed well up behind him, he dashed through the ford, scrambled up the bank, paused to discharge one volley of musketry and then went straight in with the sword and bayonet. The effect, like that of the French artillery at Madras, was magical. From a reasonably well-ordered force Maffuz Khan's army became a terrified rabble, running for their lives into the streets of St Thomé where they became wedged in appalling confusion. Paradis, following up at once, fired volley after volley into the seething mass, and just at this moment a small party sent down from Madras to make contact with him came up on the rear of the enemy. This caused a panic and the battle became a rout, led by Maffuz Khan himself, mounted on his war elephant which was goaded by its mahout into a lumbering run. At length, with his broken army streaming across the countryside behind him, Maffuz Khan found safety inside the walls of Arcot.

These two actions changed the whole course of Indian history. Hitherto the Europeans in the country, conscious of their weakness in numerical strength, had assumed they could not engage large native armies except with superior numbers, or perhaps equal strength if the ground was to their advantage. They had therefore conducted their affairs, and their relationships with native rulers, with caution. They had been humble, accommodating and sometimes afraid. Even the self-confident Dupleix had been careful to play the courtier when he approached the throne of any native prince. Suddenly, by charging headlong against apparently impossible odds, a single, practically unknown Swiss officer found the key to the conquest of India, and at the same time solved Dupleix's most pressing problem.

Paradis was at once appointed military commander of Madras and instructed by Dupleix to declare as null and void the treaty made between la Bourdonnais and Morse. Henceforth Madras belonged to France by right of conquest. Morse protested strongly but to no avail and he and several officials of the English East India Company were escorted to Pondicherry. The officers of the company's army, rightly feeling that this deliberate breach of faith released them from their parole, escaped to the English stronghold of Fort St David, adjoining the native town of Cuddalore just to the south of Pondicherry. They at once made preparations to defend it, for since the fall of Madras the English officials there had taken over the administration of the company's affairs on the Coromandel Coast. One of the officers who escaped was Robert Clive, recently granted an ensign's commission in the company's army.

Up to now, in all affairs, naval, military and diplomatic, the French had taken and held the initiative and the English had done nothing but accept each reverse as it occurred, with a resignation or an apathy that one likes to think was uncharacteristic. Now, Dupleix's wanton disregard for the customs and usages of war aroused all their latent dislike and contempt for the French, and particularly for a Frenchman who aped the natives and seemed to have no idea how a gentleman should behave.

The English in Fort St David asked Anwar-u-din for help, and he, hoping to have an opportunity to wipe out the disgrace of Madras and St Thomé, sent a force under the joint command of his two sons, Maffuz Khan and Mohammed Ali. Maffuz Khan went so far as to attack Paradis who, having put French affairs in Madras in order, was on his way back to Pondicherry. Although the French detachment was only 300 strong and heavily burdened with plunder from Madras, Paradis repeated his disconcertingly offensive tactics, drove his enemies off with the loss of a few of his men wounded, and reached his destination of Ariancopang, just over a mile from Pondicherry. It was here that Dupleix was collecting a force for an attack on Fort St David, and by the middle of December it amounted to a total of 1,600 men of whom 900 were Europeans. The artillery consisted of six field guns and the same number of mortars. The strength of the English in the Fort was only 300, one-third being native troops.

It was unfortunate for the French that in their army assembling at Ariancopang there were several officers senior to Paradis, and the command was given to General de Bury. He marched on Fort St David, crossed the river Pennar on 19 December and set up his camp in a walled garden about a mile and a half from his objective. So great was his new-found contempt for native armies that he ignored the existence of Maffuz Khan, Mohammed Ali and their army barely five miles away, put out no piquets and posted no sentries. The alarm was sounded while all his men were scattered about the garden, cooking their evening meal, and in a panic they rushed out with the one object of putting the river between them and the enemy. Only the artillery stood firm and thus prevented the annihilation of the force. Leaving twelve Europeans dead and carrying 120 wounded, de Bury hastened back to Ariancopang and did nothing for the next three weeks.

In January 1747 a French naval squadron arrived off Pondicherry, tipping the balance of military force even further in Dupleix's favour and he again got in touch with Anwar-u-din. He pointed out that the English were in a hopeless position; nothing could now prevent him from destroying Fort St David and then, within a few months, removing all trace of the English presence in India. To emphasize the strength of his own position the letter was accompanied by gifts worth £15,000. Anwar-u-din accepted the bribe, abandoned the English, made a separate peace with Dupleix and withdrew his army from the field.

All this was very depressing for the English, driven out of their comfortable headquarters at Madras and now about to be attacked by a European force far larger than anything they could muster. It looked like the beginning of the end, and Dupleix was confident it was.

One or two East Indiamen dispatched by the company in London had reached the Coromandel Coast but had been either captured or chased away by the French. In March 1747 one of them landed a party of twenty men and £60,000 in silver at Fort St David—a welcome reinforcement—and ten days later, on 13 March, the French made another attempt to besiege the fort. They were driven off by the sudden arrival of a naval force commanded by Admiral Griffin who landed 100 soldiers, loaned the garrison a number of sailors and marines, and went off to blockade Pondicherry. More reinforcements arrived in May and June, and by July the total strength of the garrison in Fort St David had increased to 1,200 Europeans and 800 sepoys.

The British now had command of the sea, and a secure base at Bombay to operate from, while Dupleix's superiority in European troops was shrinking fast, and there was no one to replace la Bourdonnais. Dupleix wrote to Mauritius; his letter did not reach Port Louis until December, and it was not until May 1748 that any ships could set out. Even then they were greatly outnumbered by Griffin's squadron, now actively blockading the coast. However, the French admiral was skilful. He lured Griffin into the open sea, slipped past him at night, landed 300 men, all regular French troops, and a large sum of money at Madras and was off to sea again before Griffin could catch him. While Griffin's attention was thus distracted, Dupleix made a third attempt on Fort St David and Cuddalore which was just under two miles from the fort.

He had gathered together 800 Europeans and 1,000 sepoys, and though aware that the English had been reinforced he was reasonably sure of success. What he did not know was that Major Stringer Lawrence, an extremely competent officer, had come out in January 1748 and was now in command at Fort St David.

The French plan was to attack Cuddalore, not the fort, and to attack at night. Dupleix sent his force—a large one judged by the usual size of the tiny 'armies' contending for the empire in India—by a very roundabout route to some broken, hilly ground three miles from the walled town. His orders were that it was to stay under cover until the pre-arranged time to attack. Lawrence, kept well informed by his spies of all that was going on, and knowing that all his movements were overlooked, gave orders for the garrison and guns of Cuddalore to move back into Fort St David as ostentatiously as possible during daylight. As soon as it was dark he sent them back again.

On the night of 28 June, without bothering to take even

the normal precautions, the French marched happily up to the walls of the native town, laid their scaling ladders against them, began to climb and were met by a shattering fire of musketry and grapeshot. Those on the ladders who were not killed or wounded leapt off, most of the troops still on the ground threw away their weapons without firing a shot, and the whole lot, except for the unfortunate casualties, began running wildly in the direction of Pondicherry.

This was the first action fought between English and French troops in India.

It was a great disappointment to Dupleix who, to make matters worse, had just been told that the British Government had resolved to give strong support to the English company. Admiral Boscawen with eight ships of the line and 1,400 regular troops had sailed from England in November of the previous year.

Boscawen had been instructed to take Mauritius and Réunion on his way out to India; being only one month's voyage from the Coromandel Coast they were of vital importance to the French. He reached Mauritius on 4 July but la Bourdonnais had laid out its defences so well that after wasting three weeks in trying to find a vulnerable spot, Boscawen gave up and went on to Fort St David. On 11 August he made contact with Admiral Griffin, and the combined fleet of thirty ships gave the English the greatest advantage over Dupleix they had ever possessed.

Although it was late in the fighting season and the monsoon might break at any moment during the next few weeks, Boscawen laid siege to Ariancopang. Despite his great advantage in men and material nothing seemed to go right. He was badly let down by incompetent engineers who had little or no idea of normal siege procedure. The attack on the fort of Ariancopang was a complete failure, someone forgot the scaling ladders and a quarter of the assaulting force became casualties in trying to do what could not be done. A few days later in a skirmish under the walls Major Stringer Lawrence was taken prisoner and Boscawen lost his best army officer. Ariancopang was finally abandoned by the French when a magazine caught fire and exploded, causing 100 casualties, and Boscawen moved on to the siege of Pondicherry.

Dupleix conducted the defence with admirable skill and tenacity, and the burden of it fell heavily upon him when Paradis died of wounds after leading a sortie against the British lines. At length, on 11 October, with the monsoon overdue, Boscawen had to raise the siege. One thousand Europeans had died, Madras and Pondicherry were still in French hands and Governor-General Dupleix remained triumphantly where he was. Then, in December, came the news that France and England had ended the war in the previous April. The terms of the Treaty of Aix-la-Chapelle were not known in India until the following year, and then it was proved la Bourdonnais had been right. Madras was restored to England in exchange for the fortress of Louisbourg in Acadia—to the fury of the North American colonists, as we shall see.

(Admiral Boscawen formally accepted the restitution of Madras in August 1749, just before he returned to England.)

In Europe, England and France were officially at peace, but while Dupleix remained in India there could be no lasting peace between the British and the French in the East.

The British made the mistake of thinking that if Dupleix could make so much trouble for them with his policy of interfering with the internal affairs of neighbouring Indian states, they ought to be able to do the same to him. Regrettably, they lacked his experience, his extraordinary understanding of the Oriental mind and his inherent diplomatic skill. They lacked, too, his ability to absorb the most crushing disappointments and reverses without any apparent effect on his determination to do what he had set out to do. Yet perhaps his greatest advantage over any British governor on the Coromandel Coast was his almost uncanny talent in forecasting the long-term effect of his plans. Lacking his skill, the British were liable to make mistakes in local politics. Their first was in Tanjore.

Ten years before, Governor Dumas had given French support to the Rajah Sauhoji in return for the town of Karical, and he now came to the British with a long, sad story of injustice. He had been the victim of a *coup* in his state and his enemies had deposed him. He offered to pay the costs of any war undertaken to put him back on his throne and to make over to the British the fort and territory of Devicotah as their reward. He pointed out that he was offering much for very little, because he was so popular in Tanjore that the mere suggestion of British support for his cause would bring the local people flocking to his standard. Impressed by his assurances the company provided a force of 500 Europeans and 1,500 sepoys, which left Madras at the end of March 1749 and marched towards the capital of Tanjore.

Far from causing a rising throughout the state there was a depressing lack of interest at the reappearance of Sauhoji, whose reign had been notable for extortionate misrule, and the force marched back without achieving anything. Instead of drawing the obvious inference and dropping the whole project the company equipped a second force, stronger by 300 Europeans than the first one, put Major Stringer Lawrence in command of it and told him to go and take the fort of Devicotah, the promised reward; from any point of view a risky operation.

Lawrence embarked his troops, landed on the south bank of the Coleroon river, near its mouth, and within a few days had knocked a breach in the wall of the fort with his guns. One of the ships' carpenters built a raft to carry troops across the river and Clive was put in charge of the storming party of 34 Europeans and 700 sepoys. The attack was met by Tanjore cavalry. The sepoys turned tail, the European troops suffered a great many casualties and Clive was lucky to escape with his life. Lawrence attacked again, this time with all his Europeans. Their musketry drove the cavalry off, the fort was entered and found to be deserted. Lawrence took formal possession of it, and the territory promised by Sauhoji, in the name of the company. Having got what it wanted, the company then refused to do anything more for Sauhoji except offer him a pension if he undertook to make no more trouble in Tanjore. No one emerged from the affair with much credit, and the British, without appreciating the implications, had created a dangerous precedent by taking up arms in the cause of local politics and seizing territory by force. The attack on Devicotah opened the way for Dupleix to continue the war, brought to a pause by the Treaty of Aix-la-Chapelle, by allowing his troops to be employed as auxiliaries in support of native factions which, with his peculiar skill, he could manipulate for his own ends. He did not have to look very far for an excuse to play the same game as the English.

Nizam-ul-Mulk, the independent ruler of the Deccan, had died in 1748 having nominated his grandson, Murzaffar Jang, to be his successor. This was at once disputed by the old man's second son, Nazir Jang, and both claimants set out to collect supporters. Murzaffar Jang went off to the Mahrattas and on his travels he came across Chunda Sahib, imprisoned at Satara ever since 1739, when Sufder Ali had allowed the Mahrattas to capture him at Trichinopoly. Because he was an able soldier and a man of Western education as well as Oriental culture the Mahrattas had always refused to release him except for a ransom far beyond his means. He was a long-standing, trusted friend of the French and Dupleix had looked after his wife and family in Pondicherry all the time he had been in captivity. Murzaffar was quick to realize the value of such a man and he went back to talk to Dupleix. To the Frenchman this was an opportunity which might never come again. If French arms established Murzaffar as Nawab of the Deccan the whole vast province would be under French influence, and French influence was only a euphemism for Dupleix himself. It was a delightful prospect, and it all fitted in so tidily. The first and obvious step was to gain control of the Carnatic, and for a long time, ever since the French capture of Madras, relations with the ageing Anwar-u-din had been deteriorating. The time had come to take advantage of this.

Chunda Sahib's ransom was paid, he was released and then provided with 2,000 trained sepoys from the Pondicherry garrison—to whom he added 4,000 men he had collected himself. He joined Murzaffar's army of 30,000 men and the combined force marched on Arcot, Anwar-u-din's capital. On 3 August 1749 the old man came out to fight, but he had nothing to match the well-trained sepoys under their French officers. At the battle of Amore he was defeated and killed. Next day Murzaffar and Chunda Sahib entered Arcot and the Carnatic was theirs.

Murzaffar proclaimed himself ruler of the Deccan and with Chunda Sahib he rode to Pondicherry where Dupleix had arranged a magnificent ceremonial welcome. They made him a large grant of neighbouring territory, and the British, barred from any protest by their ill-judged activities at Devicotah, could do nothing.

Mohammed Ali, Anwar-u-din's son who had escaped from the battlefield of Amore, came to Madras to ask for the company's help and received only 120 men to help him defend his city of Trichinopoly. After this meagre gesture the company officials then acted with incredible folly. Keeping 300 of Boscawen's men for the garrison of Madras they allowed him to return to England, taking with him British naval superiority, the only restraint on Dupleix's designs. There was now only one minor obstacle in the path of French dominance in India and that was Mohammed Ali and his little force in Trichinopoly. All that Murzaffar and Chunda Sahib had to do was take their great army there, crush Mohammed Ali and so open the way to the Deccan. Chunda Sahib would become the Nawab of the Carnatic and Murzaffar, with French aid to remove Nazir Jang, would rule the Deccan.

Everything depended on striking fast, before time could divert the ever-fluid stream of Indian politics into a different channel. Dupleix impressed this upon his Indian allies, but they had spent so much money on celebrating their victory at Amore that they now had none left to pay for the final campaign on which all depended. Between them they decided that the best way of raising money was to demand it with menaces from the Rajah of Tanjore, and so they led their armies up to the walls of his city and called upon him to surrender. The Rajah, Partab Singh, was an expert at procrastination, and while he and his enemies were engaged in polite and prolonged negotiations he sent urgent appeals for help to the British and to Murzaffar's rival for the Deccan, Nazir Jang. The East India Company sent an evasive reply but Nazir Jang came himself, leading a very large army, showing great eagerness to meet Murzaffar in the field, and summoning Mohammed Ali and the British to join him. The company changed its mind and sent him Stringer Lawrence and 600 European troops.

At the end of March 1750 both candidates for the Deccan and their allies were encamped within reach of one another near the fortress of Gingee, midway between Arcot and Pondicherry, but there was no battle. Quite unexpectedly, there was a sudden acceleration in the leisurely tempo of events. The French troops in Murzaffar's army mutinied and in so doing virtually broke up his force. He himself surrendered to his rival Nazir Jang and the whole pattern of Dupleix's careful plans appeared to be torn to shreds. In no way daunted, Dupleix switched his attention and his persuasive diplomacy to Nazir Jang. When rebuffed, which was no surprise, Dupleix attacked his camp at night with a handful of men and caused so much distress and confusion that Nazir Jang withdrew at a brisk trot to Arcot. The British, finding themselves abandoned, retired to Fort St David and once again the field was left clear for Dupleix's next move.

It followed swiftly. Mohammed Ali and the force he had brought from Trichinopoly, now isolated near Pondicherry, were the next to be attacked, and Dupleix, with a far smaller force, compelled him to flee to the north. Dupleix then sent the marquis de Bussy to deal with the remnants of Mohammed Ali's army which had rallied under the massive walls of Gingee and showed signs of linking up with Nazir Jang in Arcot.

Bussy was by far the best French military commander in the whole story of India, and his tactical genius has been equated with that of Clive. He had come out from France as an impoverished aristocrat, seeking fame and fortune in the East as a last resort. He found both. After twenty years he returned to a happy retirement in France with the reputation of being one of her ablest leaders and one of the richest men in the country. He now marched with only a small party of men against Gingee, routed the force in front of it and then, to the amazement of everyone, carried by escalade the fort which for generations had been considered absolutely impregnable. This was one of several sensational feats of arms by Europeans in India, and it provoked Nazir Jang into trying to show that anything Europeans could do, his troops could do better.

In September he moved against Gingee with 100,000 men, an army far too large to control. He arrived just as the monsoon broke. Military operations became impossible and he sat doing nothing for three months while Dupleix's agents were busy in his camp. Dupleix's programme of subversion and psychological operations was most successful, for when the French attacked in December the huge host was easily defeated and a small party of conspirators murdered Nazir Jang.

With no loss of time Murzaffar was hailed as Nawab of the Deccan and duly installed as such at Pondicherry with Dupleix, splendidly robed, sitting beside him to receive the homage of lesser beings. Everything was turning out just as Dupleix had planned. He himself was appointed Nawab of the whole area south of the Kistna river to Cape Cormorin; Chunda Sahib was made Nawab of the Carnatic; Mohammed Ali, glad to be still alive, renounced all claims to anything and the French East India Company received a great number of new concessions and privileges. The fleur-de-lis was now supreme and the end of the year 1750 marks the zenith of French affairs in India.

All that remained was for Murzaffar Jang to move into his official residence in his new capital at Aurungabad, and Bussy was detailed to escort him. On 15 January 1751, while they were on the road, a party of malcontents—possibly supporters of the late Nazir Jang—attacked the caravan. Though they were easily dispersed by the French artillery, Murzaffar, a choleric, vindictive man, rode forward with a drawn sword to dispatch his enemies personally and was shot and killed—on the very threshold of all his worldly ambitions.

The marquis de Bussy being, like la Bourdonnais, a very practical man to whom one political puppet was as good as another, attached little importance to the incident because he was well aware that Dupleix was the real ruler of the Deccan. He chose Salabad Jang, a younger brother of Murzaffar, to be Nawab in his place and rode beside him when they entered Aurungabad in state on 29 June. Bussy and his troops also took up their quarters in the city, with every sign of making a prolonged stay. Thus the whole area from the Tapti river, which flows into the Indian Ocean at Surat, to Cape Cormorin was either under Bussy's military control or the direct rule of Dupleix.

In Madras the British appeared to be incapable of offering any opposition to the rapid and startling growth of the French empire. Dupleix had outwitted and outmanœuvred them at every turn, and Mohammed Ali, the only local personality with a cause likely to attract sympathy and supporters, had withdrawn from power politics and, keeping out of the lime-light, was quietly governing Trichinopoly. The extinction of the British East India Company seemed to be almost inevitable.

Early in January 1751 Thomas Saunders was promoted from managing a small factory to be Governor of Madras. He had heard that Stringer Lawrence, the veteran of Culloden Moor and the company's only answer to Bussy, had returned to England in October 1750, and he had come to the conclusion that the company had to act quickly. The French had to be resisted, every move they made would have to be countered, and this could not be done without an Indian ally who could provide an excuse for active intervention in the sort of politics which Dupleix exploited with such success.

Mohammed Ali, unexpectedly, provided the necessary excuse. Dupleix, now the all-powerful Nawab of the province, ordered him to surrender his city of Trichinopoly, largely because he had supported the British cause. Saunders could see that if Mohammed Ali were stripped of all authority and Trichinopoly became French, there would be no opening for any further intervention and the British might easily be driven from the Coromandel Coast. So when Mohammed Ali, desperate under the pressure being applied by Dupleix to enforce obedience, appealed somewhat hopelessly to the British in February 1751, Saunders at once sent him a force of 600 men, half of whom were British.

This was an overt act of war at a time when France and England were at peace, but since it did not break the local rule that the troops of either company should fight only as the auxiliaries of Indian rulers and rivals, and not as principals, Dupleix could make no complaint. Saunders, a very astute and capable man, knew that sooner or later the question of who was to control India would have to be answered. Dupleix had recognized this and acted accordingly ever since he had been made governor of Pondicherry, and it had always been a matter of some surprise to him that the British, a race which every Frenchman knew to be crafty and devious, had done so little to stand in his way. He saw that the great issue now

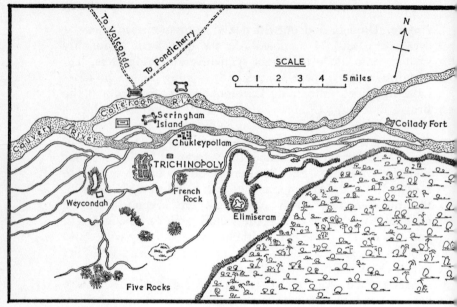

Trichinopoly

turned on the possession of Trichinopoly and so he arranged that Chunda Sahib, with his own army of 8,000 men, stiffened by a force of 400 French under their own officer, Jacques François Law, should march on the city.

Law was the nephew of the Scottish banker John Law who in 1716, at the time of the Regency before Louis XV was old enough to rule, tried to solve France's fiscal problems by devising the system of creating apparent resources by the printing of money. Though in fact basic to the modern concept of credit, his idea led to a full-scale financial crash and his hurried departure from France. His nephew inherited very little of his boldness or acumen.

Saunders reacted to the news of Chunda Sahib's move by dispatching a further force of 500 Europeans and 1,000 sepoys led by Captain Gingen and accompanied by Clive, who had resigned his commission in the autumn of 1749, as his commissary. Gingen was reluctant to march straight to Trichinopoly at the head of his own force because there had been no declaration of war, and so he waited at Fort St David until the middle of May. Then he was joined by 1,600 of Mohammed Ali's troops, and since this converted his status into that of a legitimate auxiliary he was able to set off for Volconda, on the road between Arcot and Trichinopoly, to intercept Chunda Sahib's army.

The engagement began with an exchange of cannon shots, and for some unexplained reason the British troops took fright and threw away their arms. Even Clive, remarkable for his coolness in action, was unable to rally them. Gingen had no option but to fall back on Trichinopoly, closely followed up by Chunda Sahib. Three days later, after a certain amount of desultory skirmishing, the British force crossed the Coleroon river and took refuge in the city. Dupleix was very gratified by the way things were going. Practically all the British military resources were now locked up in Trichinopoly without any prospect of rescue, and all the French had to do was starve them out. It was now simply a matter of time before Chunda Sahib and his French allies put an end to all British interests and activities in the Carnatic.

It was in this month, July 1751, that Clive again applied for and was granted a commission in the Company's army. This time it was that of Captain, and on his past record he also became the leading British officer in southern India. A few British reinforcements arrived from England and in two expeditions Clive succeeded in getting them all into Trichinopoly and thus raising the European military strength in the city to 600 men. The French had nearly 1,000, a superiority which seemed to seal the fate of Trichinopoly, and of British influence in India.

Clive's passage through the lines of the besiegers of Trichinopoly was not quite as easy as it sounds, for on the first occasion he was lucky in being able to fight his way out and avoid capture, but it must be assumed that he penetrated at the weakest spots and that Chunda Sahib's men were not very alert sentinels. After his second adventure he returned to Madras with a depressing report and a plan so bold that only a man as intelligent and far-sighted as Saunders would have accepted it.

Clive pointed out that although most of the British force was inside the city, most of Chunda Sahib's army was needed to keep them there. This meant that Arcot, Chunda Sahib's capital, could not be adequately defended. The only way to relieve Trichinopoly was to attack Arcot. Chunda Sahib must either raise the siege of Trichinopoly and go to the relief of Arcot, or accept the loss of his capital, for which Trichinopoly was a very poor exchange.

With great difficulty Saunders scraped together a force of eight officers, 200 Europeans, 300 sepoys and three field guns. Four of the eight officers had, like Clive, been clerks in the company. This left less than 150 men to guard Madras and Fort St David. The risk was enormous. Clive must have been quite exceptional in his ability to inspire confidence, but Saunders must have realized the game had reached the stage where he had to stake all to win, or lose.

Clive and his little army marched the sixty-four miles from Madras to Arcot in five days. Ten miles from the city he halted for a while and then marched on through the full fury of a tropical thunderstorm. Spies from the city rushed back and said the British were coming, through thunder, lightning, howling wind and lashing rain. The garrison of the half-ruined fort felt it would be tempting Providence to oppose an enemy who defied even the elements and wisely slipped away before they arrived. Clive occupied the deserted fort, repaired the defences and mounted the guns that were lying about. When he had made all the necessary preparations to withstand a siege he sallied out to attack the native garrison which had camped about six miles away. He struck them twice, on 15 and 17 September, reduced them to a gratifying state of unsteadiness and then, a week later, learning that they had been reinforced to a total of 3,000 men, stormed into their camp in the deceptive darkness of a starlit night, killed some, filled the remainder with abject terror, watched them flee and then returned to the fort at Arcot without losing a man.

This forced Chunda Sahib to act, and he detached 4,000 men from the siege of Trichinopoly to recover the fort. Dupleix, though unwilling to dance to Clive's tune because he saw all the dangers in the situation, nevertheless sent 100 Frenchmen and they, with other levies, brought the strength of the army sent to relieve Arcot up to 10,000 men. Commanded by

Rajah Sahib, Chunda Sahib's son, it entered Arcot city on 4 October and laid siege to the fort.

On the next day Clive did what Paradis would probably have done. He went out and attacked the besiegers before they had had time to sort themselves out and settle down to the routine of a siege, but he was driven back with what, in his weak state, were very serious losses. Two officers and thirty-one European soldiers were either killed or wounded. More reinforcements for Rajah Sahib's army arrived on the following day, increasing his force to 150 Europeans and 11,000 natives, and a fortnight later the siege artillery arrived. On 10 November, having blown a breach in the wall, Rajah Sahib observed the formalities and invited Clive to surrender. He got the reply he probably expected, but he knew the garrison was running out of supplies and so he hesitated to storm a fort which in a few days would have to yield.

During the fifty days of the siege Governor Saunders had not been idle. He had collected reinforcements and had also persuaded the great Mahratta leader, Morari Rao, already very sympathetic towards men who could hold out for so long against odds of nearly twenty to one, to come in on the British side. As soon as Rajah Sahib heard that the Mahrattas were coming he decided to storm the breach. One of Clive's agents discovered the date and time of the assault, and when it came all was ready. Cannon were trained on the breach and every serviceable musket in the fort, including all those found in the armoury, lay ready loaded, to be used in relays to keep up a continuous fire. The attack was made at dawn on 25 November. For a loss of six men killed or wounded and the expenditure of 12,000 cartridges, Clive and his few men inflicted 400 casualties and threw back the enemy from the breach. Next day Rajah Sahib raised the siege and marched away in disorder, leaving behind him several guns and a great deal of ammunition. With less than half his original force still able to fight, Clive was left in victorious possession of the capital of the Carnatic.

Clive's defence of Arcot established him as a soldier of fearless genius, respected and admired by his allies and feared by his foes. Suddenly, from a position regarded by French and

Indians alike as one of contemptible inferiority, the British had risen up to show they were active and dangerous opponents. With Bussy far away in Aurungabad, Dupleix had no military commander able to compete with Clive who, not content with driving Rajah Sahib out of Arcot, was now following up with a most inconvenient energy.

On the evening of the day Rajah Sahib abandoned Arcot, reinforcements of men and four guns reached Clive in the fort. They enabled him to leave a small garrison behind and go after the retreating enemy with a force of 200 British and 700 sepoys. But the enemy virtually melted away during the pursuit, for most of Rajah Sahib's men decided that soldiering was not a profession in which they were really interested and, disbanding themselves on the line of march, went home to their villages. In a short time their commander was left with only a few of the men he had brought with him from Trichinopoly, and his French allies. With these he made for Vellore, due west of Arcot, where he was joined by 300 more French troops sent by Dupleix and some native levies provided by his father. He then set off south-eastwards towards Pondicherry. On the way he was attacked, somewhat rashly, by Mahratta cavalry, and the repulse of them improved the morale of his men. He pushed on, feeling more confident, but unaware that Clive, recently joined by 600 Mahratta horsemen, was hot on his heels and moving by forced marches.

Clive caught up just as Rajah Sahib was about to cross the river Arni. With odds of three to one against him Clive completely outmanœuvred the enemy force, inflicting casualties of fifty Europeans and 150 native troops and capturing all their artillery for the loss, in killed and wounded, of eight sepoys and fifty Mahrattas. Immediately after this battle Clive marched north-east to Conjeveram, on the road between Arcot and Madras, captured it after a siege of three days and dismantled the fort. He then strengthened the garrison of Arcot and at the end of December returned to Fort St David to make arrangements for the relief of Trichinopoly.

Dupleix, realizing that from the way things were going Clive would undoubtedly achieve his object, moved quickly. At his instigation Rajah Sahib repaired the fort at Conjeveram and garrisoned it, thereby cutting off communications between

Madras and Arcot, and began a series of nuisance raids almost up to the walls of Madras. This forced Clive to postpone his plans for Trichinopoly in order to deal with the latest threat, and on 13 February 1752 he marched out of Madras with a force of 380 Europeans, 1,300 sepoys and six guns. His intention was to find and destroy the enemy army. Hearing of his approach Rajah Sahib did not wait for him but withdrew to a fortified camp at Vendalore, twenty-five miles to the south-west. Arriving there at three o'clock in the afternoon, Clive found the camp deserted, but after a few hours learned that the enemy had gone to Conjeveram, thirty miles to the west. At four o'clock next morning he came up to the fort he had recently dismantled and the garrison surrendered to him without firing a shot. He was then told that Rajah Sahib had gone to attack Arcot. Having marched fifty-five miles in less than twenty-four hours Clive's men were too tired to move without some rest, but at noon they marched on and just as the sun was setting they came to Covrepauk, sixteen miles on their way.

Here, without warning, the advanced guard was suddenly fired on by a battery of nine field guns out on their right flank. The enemy had been to Arcot, and finding the garrison too alert and strong had come back down the road and laid an ambush. Clive and his troops, their alertness no doubt dimmed by fatigue, had marched right into it.

The battle of Covrepauk, which lasted for four hours and was fought by the light of a full moon, is chiefly remarkable as an illustration of Clive's astonishing ability not only to sum up an extremely dangerous situation with immediate accuracy but to see almost at once the only possible course of action which would be successful. Rapidly disposing his exhausted men to hold the enemy they could see he launched a right flanking movement which came up behind the French artillery and put the gunners to flight. Although out-numbered as usual—in addition to 400 Frenchmen the enemy had 2,000 infantry and 2,000 cavalry—Clive inflicted a crushing defeat. At first light next morning the bodies of fifty Frenchmen and 300 sepoys were found in the ambush position. Sixty Frenchmen had been taken prisoner and once again all the artillery had been captured. Of the rest of the enemy there was no sign. The cost to Clive in killed was forty Europeans and thirty native troops.

This defeat put an end to Rajah Sahib's career as a military commander and ally of Dupleix. His army, having lost all confidence in him, dispersed, and with only a small bodyguard he rode to Pondicherry to explain what had happened. For once, Dupleix's mask of smooth diplomacy slipped badly and he made no attempt to hide his feelings.

During this time the French Commander, Law, with 900 French troops, 2,000 trained sepoys and Chunda Sahib's 30,000 levies had been idly sitting in front of Trichinopoly. Mohammed Ali was still inside the city, waiting with traditional Oriental patience for his British friends to rescue him. In March 1752 an army of 400 Europeans, 1,100 sepoys, eight guns and a large convoy of supplies left Fort St David to deal with the problem of Trichinopoly. It was commanded by Stringer Lawrence who had just returned from England, and Clive was his second-in-command. Between the two was a strong bond of mutual liking and respect.

The orders which Law had received from Dupleix were that as soon as he heard of the approach of Lawrence's army he was to leave the absolute minimum of troops to keep the besieged garrison inside the walls, march out with the rest and give battle. This he did, and being an ineffective and incompetent commander, was defeated. He took refuge on the island of Seringham, formed by two channels of the river Cauvery. Dupleix then instructed an elderly officer, M. d'Auteuil, to extricate the force on the island, and a relieving 'army', 500 strong, marched out of Pondicherry on 10 April. By 13 June it was all over. D'Auteuil was a prisoner of war, outwitted and captured by Clive; Law had surrendered, Chunda Sahib was in the hands of his enemies, Trichinopoly had been relieved and once again all Dupleix's plans lay in ruins.

Chunda Sahib had been quick to make his own surrender arrangements but he was assassinated a few days after his capture. His head was sent in a basket to Mohammed Ali who then proclaimed himself Nawab of the Carnatic, and the British spent the rest of the year in establishing his authority. Lawrence, Clive and other British officers, commanding small columns, captured all the French garrisons in southern India.

Dupleix refused to be discouraged. In July the annual reinforcement of troops reached him from France, and by taking sailors from the ships he raised a force of 500 Europeans. He then resolved to recapture Trichinopoly on behalf of Chunda Sahib's son Rajah Sahib. While he was making his preparations, Bussy, away to the north, who had been guarding Dupleix's interests by protecting the puppet ruler of the Deccan, once more became an operational soldier. He moved across to Masulipatam and used it as a base from which to conquer the Northern Circars, the province on the Golconda Coast to the north of the Carnatic.

Dupleix, when he was ready, continued his war against Colonel Stringer Lawrence although Britain and France were at peace. He gained some local successes but the tide of events had turned against him. Bussy advised him to cut his losses, make peace with the British and give his attention to the promising situation in central India. But Dupleix would never accept defeat. By the spring of 1754 his treasury was empty. Princes such as the Rajah of Tanjore, who at one time had been flattered by any invitation to the 'court' at Pondicherry, were now steadfast in their allegiance to the British. Yet he held on, believing that with the next reinforcement from France he could retrieve all that had been lost.

Unknown to Dupleix the directors of the French East India Company in Paris had been growing more and more disturbed by the activities of their Governor-General who never bothered to keep them informed of his intentions and plans. Having lost touch they also lost confidence. In August 1754 a certain M. Godeheu arrived in Pondicherry, introduced himself to Dupleix as his successor and, in accordance with his instructions, sent Dupleix home on the next ship. By any standards, this was a disgraceful way to treat him after he had served the company for thirty-four years.

Opinions on this sudden development differ widely. Dupleix himself, naturally, was shattered, claiming he was on the point of complete victory. Local feeling at the time was that France stood only to benefit from his dismissal. He lived for another nine years, persecuted and poor, a sad example of how the mighty can fall. Much has been written to denigrate him, no doubt because in the end he did not win, yet there is much truth in Fortescue's comment, written in 1899: 'Excepting Napoleon, England has known no such dangerous and uncompromising enemy, nor can it be said that he was beaten, even at the last.' Although no doubt a paranoic he was a man of great vision, ambition, adroitness, resilience and resource, possessing unlimited tenacity of purpose. Yet in the end, had he been allowed to run his course, he could not have won because he could not counter the sea power of his enemy, the factor that must prove decisive in any colonial war.

When he had gone, Godeheu at once drew up a treaty with the Madras government. Under the terms of it Mohammed Ali was officially recognized as the Nawab of the Carnatic and both sides agreed to meddle no more in Indian politics. The French were allowed to keep their factories, and Bussy remained in control of the Deccan.

No decision had been reached. The problem of who was to control the great colonial empire of India remained unresolved. The Treaty of Aix-la-Chapelle had merely shelved and not answered the questions—the last round had still to be fought.

6 Louisbourg

The conflict in North America between New England and New France did not reach the state of declared and open warfare until the beginning of King William's War in 1689, and bearing in mind the great disparity in numbers between the populations (Canada 12,000, New England over 90,000) it should have been brief and decisive; but the French had advantages to make up for their lack of manpower. The greatest of these was their social structure. They were close-knit, united and loyal to one commander who was also a soldier of skill and experience. Furthermore, the majority of the male population had a great deal of military training, for Louis XIV had made a point of giving generous bounties of land and money to officers and men of his armies to encourage them to settle in North America. Thirdly, those who did settle were not agriculturalists. They tilled the soil with reluctance in order to provide themselves with essentials, and their real interests lay in fishing and hunting and living the pleasantly free life of the Indians in the great forests. Thus, naturally enough, a very large proportion of the men likely to be called upon to fight were marksmen—within the limited capabilities of the smooth-bore musket—canoeists and trackers, able to live off the country for long periods. They felt thoroughly at home in the woods which were to be the battlefields in the war against England.

On the other side the English settlers were either farmers or, if they lived near the coast, fishermen. To them the forest was something to be cleared so that more land could be brought under cultivation. Far from being united, they lived in separate colonies which, because of a long history of religious and political dissension, were regarded by their inhabitants as individual and autonomous. It was the legacy of past quarrels, and the innate difference between the early colonists pursuing commercial ventures and the Puritans in search of 'freedom', that delayed for so many generations any suggestion of 'united states' of America. Each colony had its own militia in which, by law, the whole male population between the ages of sixteen and sixty was required to serve, and this was a straightforward defence precaution against attack by the Indians. In the early days the colonists had been very aware of the dangers of moving into Indian territory and had gone to some trouble to obtain competent army officers who could teach them something about war. Indeed, such men as Miles Standish and Captain John Underhill had enabled them to take the offensive. In 1637 a band of some seventy colonists had attacked and annihilated a force of 400 Indians, showing a mastery of the principles of this type of unconventional war. But with the passage of time and the gradual extension of boundaries inland from the coastal settlements, the dangers seemed to recede, taking with them the sense of urgency. Military efficiency declined rapidly, as did any enthusiasm for military matters. The war in 1671 against the Indian chief Philip was a series of horrible catastrophes simply because militia officers knew nothing of soldiering. The men, brave enough and tenacious enough by nature to satisfy any commander capable of leading them, had no discipline whatever, and in common with all militia anywhere, were reluctant to go far from their homes.

These failings were magnified by the jealousy and selfishness of the separate colonies which sometimes flared up into something worse. For instance, during the very real perils of 1671 the Quakers of Rhode Island refused to help anyone, for their own good reasons, with the result that a few years later Connecticut took up arms with every intention of dealing once and for all with what Fortescue describes as the 'cantankerous little community'.

Thus the French of New France were capable of swift, concerted action on the outbreak of war, and the English of New England were not. King James II, a soldier and a sailor of international repute and a commander with a sound grasp of strategy, saw the danger clearly enough and did his best to put matters right by trying to unite New England, New York and New Jersey under one Governor, the Guards officer

Sir Edmund Andros—not a very successful choice. The idea
was excellent, and could have solved many problems, but in
effect it entailed amalgamating the representative assemblies
of the different colonies and so had no chance of success.

During their early struggles for existence the American
colonies received very little military aid from England, and
it is characteristic of the Puritan New Englanders that at no
time, no matter how great their need, did they ever ask for
any. James II, when he was Duke of York, had formed an
independent company of regular troops for the defence of
New York, and for a short time there was a similar company in
Virginia, but they were locally recruited men, engaged on a
regular basis. The first troops of the English regular army
to be stationed in America were in a battalion made up from
the Grenadier and Coldstream Guards, brought over to deal
with the rebellion in Virginia in 1677. When Sir Edmund
Andros took up his appointment in New York he brought a
company of infantry with him, and though on paper the
colonies under his administration could muster a total of
nearly 12,000 men, the only trained soldiers under his hand
and immediately available to him were the two infantry
companies in New York. In Canada, apart from the large
percentage of the population trained by past experience and
their mode of life for guerrilla warfare in the forests, there was a
regular force of thirty-two companies, located at Montreal
and Quebec.

In the years just preceding the outbreak of King William's
War in 1689 the tension in North America had been mounting.
In Newfoundland the privilege granted to the French in 1635
of being allowed to dry fish on the shore, on payment of five
per cent of the produce, had become their first fingerhold.
Twenty-five years later they had planted a colony at Placentia,
well fortified. Fifteen years later they persuaded Charles II
to abolish the five per cent levy, and gradually they took over
a large part of the island. Their encroachments in Newfoundland were one of the reasons William III gave for making
war on Louis XIV.

Louis felt the war was more than justified. In Western
Europe he was rapidly becoming omnipotent and only in

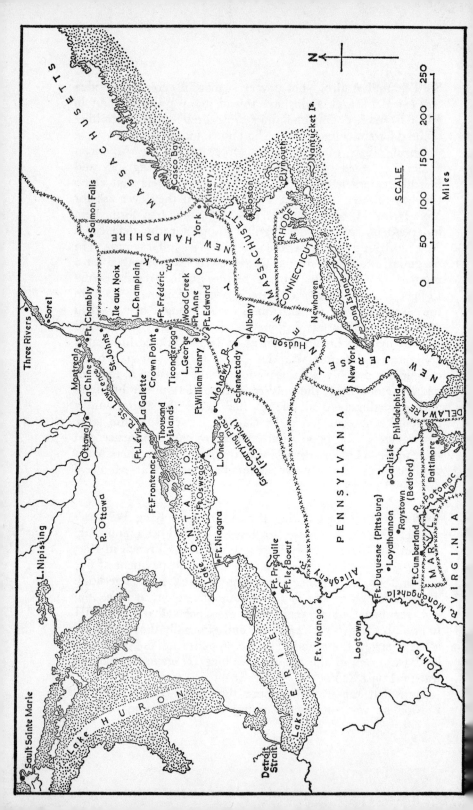

North America were the growth and glory of the French empire being inhibited, by what he regarded as crude colonial peasants. Worse than that, his people in Canada were being slaughtered by savages, the Iroquois, incited by the English.

The scope of his plan was prodigious, and the means to execute it were proportionately inadequate. The whole population of the colony of New York, some 18,000 English and Dutch settlers, was to be uprooted and there was to be no further argument about who controlled the great waterways of the St Lawrence and the Hudson. Two ships and 1,600 troops were allotted for the task. The comte de Frontenac, who had already served one term as Governor of Canada, from 1672 until 1682, was to be reappointed, and he was to return at once and be responsible for the whole operation. The two ships, carrying the soldiers, were ordered to sail to Chebucto harbour in Acadia and there await instructions. As soon as he reached Quebec, Frontenac was to mobilize his land forces, invade the province of New York along the Richelieu river, and so co-ordinate the movement of his troops and the force at Chebucto that the main attack on the town of New York became a combined operation.

Delays in fitting out the ships, and storms in the Altantic, made it impossible for Frontenac to co-ordinate anything, and in the winter of 1689 he assembled three separate columns, or war-parties, of Canadian bushrangers and so-called 'Christian' Indians from the Jesuit missions. One column, starting from Quebec, had the New York village of Schenectady as its objective; another, from Three Rivers, was to go to the village of Salmon Falls in New Hampshire; and the third, from Montreal, to Casco Bay. The approach marches, in the depths of winter, must have been uncomfortable but the first two columns attacked at night, achieving complete surprise against undefended settlements, and murdered men, women and children in their beds. Those villagers who escaped the hatchets and knives died of exposure and starvation in the woods. At Casco Bay the New Englanders defended the small fort with great gallantry, holding out against great odds for several days. When at last compelled to surrender they did so upon honourable terms with solemn pledges of protection from the 'Christian' Indians. The Frenchman in command, a man

131

Sketch Map of the Hudson and Ohio Areas of Operations

named Pontneuf, broke the pledge as soon as the settlers laid down their arms. The people in the fort were scalped and then provided entertainment for the Indians until they died. The fort and village were completely destroyed.

It was a shortsighted policy. The butchery and other atrocities at Casco, Salmon Falls and Schenectady could not really be related to the Iroquois raids into Canada three years before. The operation was conceived, mounted and led by Frenchmen, working under the orders of Frontenac. His object had been the same as that of Oliver Cromwell in Ireland: in Cromwell's own words, 'to spread a helpful terror'. Undoubtedly this appalling form of warfare must have frightened a great many people, but in far more people it aroused a most dangerous determination to be revenged. The comte de Frontenac may well have been one of New France's greatest governors, but he was also the man who changed the whole aspect of the struggle for Canada from a contest of policy and persuasion to what Roberts describes, perhaps a little luridly, as 'a death-grapple of mutual hate'.

After these massacres the settlers of New York appealed for help to New England, and it was then learned that Massachusetts had risen in revolt against the Crown at the news of King James being driven from his throne. The Colonial Assembly had ordered the arrest of Sir Edmund Andros and, lest there should be any doubt about who was master now, had cancelled all the arrangements he had made for the defence of Maine and New Hampshire, leaving nothing to oppose Frontenac's war-parties. Something had to be done, and early in 1690 the representatives of New York and New England met in council and decided to counter-attack. Their resolve was quite as sweeping as that of Louis XIV. They were going to conquer Canada.

The first move was to send Sir William Phipps, commanding a fleet of seven small vessels, to strike at Acadia. His attack on Port Royal was completely successful, largely because the French governor, Menneval, had no troops to defend his ruined fortifications. The fort and the church were looted; any private citizens prepared to sign an oath of allegiance to the King of England were not molested; the rest lost everything of value that was portable. But there were no atrocities.

Phipps went back to Boston with his booty and found that

plans for a far larger campaign were well advanced. He was to command a fleet provided by Massachusetts and go and take Quebec, while Colonel Winthrop was to lead an army raised by New York to destroy Montreal. It was the first of several similar designs. In the land force, things began badly and got worse. Supplies and transport, in the form of canoes, were inadequate, sickness gradually reduced the fighting strength, the Iroquois failed to give the help promised, and the expedition got no further than Lake Champlain. A number of men volunteered to go on but all they achieved was a raid on the border village of La Prairie. Again, there were no atrocities.

Frontenac heard of this abortive attempt against Montreal while he was actually in the town, dancing the war dance with the Indians of Michillimackinac, decked in feathers and paint on the French principle of getting close to the natives. This seemed the right moment to divert the energies of the dancers from leaping round a fire to advancing down the warpath, and he was planning an attack on Colonel Winthrop's weakened and discouraged force when news from another direction sent him back to Quebec in a hurry. The New England fleet was already at Tadusac.

Sir William Phipps had been given a fleet of thirty-two ships of various sizes and a force of 2,200 men. The ramparts and batteries of Quebec, towering above the river on the apparently impregnable heights, contained 2,700 regular troops and militia. From the beginning, Phipps had a hopeless task yet he sent a messenger to Frontenac, curtly demanding immediate surrender. In his reply Frontenac said that Phipps would hear his answer from his guns. The New Englanders, untrained and undisciplined yet resolved to kill Frenchmen in revenge for what had happened in the previous winter, fought for three days with great gallantry to get across the Charles river, but the Canadians and their Indian allies were too much for them. In the end, leaving five of their cannon stuck in the Beauport mud, they were forced to withdraw to their ships and sail back to Boston. *Te Deums* were sung in all Canadian churches, a chapel was dedicated to *Notre Dame de la Victoire*, and Louis XIV, when he heard about it, ordered a medal to be struck bearing the inscription *Francia in Nova Orbe Victrix— Kebeca Liberata A.D. MDCXC.*

The war went on, but neither side seemed capable of making any further major effort and so the fighting deteriorated into a series of raids and counter-raids in which the people who really suffered were the wretched women and children in the border settlements. One of the worst of the massacres was perpetrated by the Iroquois who killed or captured every single inhabitant of the Canadian village of La Chesnaye. Of the stories of courage and endurance, the best concerns a child of fourteen. She was Madeleine de la Verchères, daughter of the Seigneur de la Verchères, who lived in a settlement so exposed to Iroquois attack that it was known as *Château Dangereuse* [*sic*]. One morning, when her father was away in Quebec and nearly everyone was out at work in the fields, she was left in the little fort with two militiamen, her two younger brothers and an old man of eighty to act as garrison. Suddenly a war party of Iroquois appeared, and it seems that the men in the fort at once became the victims of acute depression. According to Roberts, the girl 'shamed and threatened them back to manhood'. 'By a show of confidence,' he says, she held the savages at bay until a few women from the fields got back into the fort, and she then settled down to defend it. Her two brothers, aged twelve and ten, 'handled their guns with wondrous skill and hardihood', and a week later, when help arrived from Montreal, instead of the usual smoking ruins and mutilated corpses the relieving force found the garrison safe and sound, and young Madeleine tired but triumphant.*

In 1696 Frontenac led a strong fighting column into the heart of the Iroquois country, burned the great meeting-house of the whole tribal confederation, destroyed the towns of the Onondagas and the lands of the Oneidas, and brought the leaders of the Iroquois to Quebec, suing for peace. While the talks were dragging on, news came of the Treaty of Ryswick. In November 1698 Frontenac, the strong man of Canada, died in Quebec, and the news must have brought great relief to the English of the northern colonies.

* The questions to which this sort of story gives rise are legion and no doubt a careful historian would reject such a tale as mere legend. On the other hand, as Edward Gibbon wrote, 'History is little more than a register of the crimes, follies and misfortunes of mankind', and therefore any lightening of the shadows on a sombre page is perhaps worth recording.

Most of the raiding and fighting took place in the area of the great waterways but in King William's War Canada was only one of several theatres of operations in North America; the others were Acadia, Newfoundland and Hudson Bay.

In Acadia, although Phipps had captured Port Royal in 1690 he was unable to keep it, and the French came back. The new governor, Villebon, realizing how vulnerable the place was to what he called 'visitors from Massachusetts', built a fort at the mouth of the Nashwaak, opposite modern Fredericton, and moved his headquarters there. He then began a systematic campaign of terror against defenceless New England villages, particularly those of York, Oyster Bay and Wells, where Baron St Castin, at Frontenac's instigation, proved himself adept in directing the slaughter of women and children. Frontenac always excused this barbarity on the ground that it was the only effective means of heartening his Indian allies and preventing them from changing sides. It is easy to condemn, but the Iroquois had been every bit as savage and barbaric as the French Canadians, in fact one might say they started it, and once the elements of a blood-feud have been introduced there is no limit to man's inhumanity. Rightly or wrongly, the French took revenge for all they had suffered from the Iroquois, but when they took prisoners, except in the case of the attack on Casco Bay, they treated them reasonably well.

In 1692 the New Englanders rebuilt Fort William Henry at Permaquid which had been burned by the Abenakis Indians. They made a strong stone structure, jutting out into the sea, and it virtually put an end to Indian raids along the coast. Two years later the French commander d'Iberville, with two warships, set out to destroy it once again. In the Bay of Fundy, where he was to pick up Villebon and a contingent of Indians, he was attacked by two light frigates and a Boston sloop. In the fierce battle which followed, the English vessels were hopelessly out-gunned; one frigate was captured when on the point of sinking but the other two ships escaped in fog. With Baron St Castin's Abenakis accompanying him in their canoes, d'Iberville then sailed to Fort William Henry and took it without much difficulty because its governor, Chubb, was terrified of falling into Indian hands. The fort was levelled to the ground and d'Iberville went on to Newfoundland where

135

he destroyed the English settlements at St John's, Bonavista and Carbonear. From there he sailed into Hudson Bay, captured three English merchantmen after a hard battle, and took Fort Nelson, thus bringing the whole of the Hudson Bay area under French control. After this unbroken chain of successes d'Iberville turned his attention southwards and devoted his boundless energy to founding for France the great colony of Louisiana.

By the Treaty of Ryswick England and France restored to one another all the places they had taken during the war, and eight years of bloodshed and barbarity had decided nothing. There were two results. Frontenac had broken the power of the Iroquois who never again gave any serious trouble to the French. Callières, his successor as Governor of Canada, continued the policy of subjugation and alliances, and the tribes of the north and the south turned towards France. The other result was that the war crystallized in the minds of all the colonists in North America the true nature of the contest. It was now clear that there could be no lasting peace until one side or the other became the undisputed master of the continent. In 1697 it looked as though the flag of the Bourbons would triumph.

The reason for French superiority lay not so much in the skill, organization and unity of the French as in the disarray of the English colonies, who seemed incapable of appreciating the issues at stake. Undisciplined and unco-operative, many of them refused to take any part in the war. New England and New York, the 'front line' colonies whose border settlers had been massacred, had certainly taken offensive action, although their efforts to take Quebec and Montreal had failed. The trouble was they had aimed too high. The French went for targets on a lower scale, concentrated all their available force against them, and were successful. It is ironical that their success stemmed directly from the attitude of the English settlers to the English Crown. Out of animosity tempered by jealousy the colonists refused to supply the contingents of militia requested by the English commanders for the defence of strategic points. The numbers asked for were not large. According to Parkman the total was only 1,008, divided on a pro rata basis between Massachusetts, Virginia, Maryland,

Connecticut, Rhode Island and Pennsylvania. Virginia and Maryland did make some gesture by sending money instead of men, but money cannot defend a settlement.

After only five years of fidgety peace, war broke out again in 1702, ostensibly over the question of who should sit upon the throne of Spain. England and her allies Austria and Holland supported the claims of the Archduke Charles of Austria; Louis XIV and Spain upheld those of Philip of Anjou, grandson of the French king. Yet although the war bears the name of the Spanish Succession it was in fact a conflict for the empire of the New World. Louis XIV's main object in placing his own candidate, and relation, on the Spanish throne was to gain a large share in the enormously profitable Spanish trade monopoly in Spanish America, so that France and Spain together could extinguish not only the vital commerce of the English colonies but the whole of England's ocean trade. For four centuries after the Norman Conquest England had tried to conquer France, now at last France felt she had a chance of bringing about the economic collapse of her hated rival. It can thus be said that the Duke of Marlborough's great battles, on which so much has been written, Blenheim, Ramillies, Oudenarde and Malplaquet, were fought to decide the great issue of who would have an empire and who would not.

In North America the war took the form of what the French call *la petite guerre* and the Spanish the *Guerrilla*, the little, deadly war of sudden raids and surprise attacks. Indians, incited and often led by the French, massacred and tortured the border settlers for no military objective or gain, repeating the horrors of five years before. Once again the colonies showed little interest in the danger threatening them all. The apathy of New York was equalled only by the aloofness of Connecticut; after much sordid haggling Rhode Island reluctantly supplied a few men and a little money. Massachusetts was alone in showing vigour, particularly against the French privateers which were making life intolerable for her coastal settlements. In 1707 Port Royal was attacked again, but the attempt failed because of the ignorance of commanders and the indiscipline of the troops. Almost at the same time the marquis de Vaudreuil, who had succeeded Callières as Governor in Quebec, sent a war-party of Indians and French to attack the village of Haverhill on the Merrimac river. Once again women and children were hacked to death, some prisoners were taken and anything of value carried back to Quebec. Again the New England colonies were roused to fury, and they realized that the only solution to their problems was the conquest of Canada, once described in the Massachusetts Assembly as 'the unhappy fountain from which issue all our miseries'.

An address was sent to Queen Anne, praying for ships and men to help in the reduction of Canada and Nova Scotia, and for the first time a plan was made for joint action by imperial and colonial troops against the French. England was to supply a fleet and five regular battalions, and these, with 1,200 men from Massachusetts and Rhode Island, were to sail against Quebec. Simultaneously a column of 1,500 men from the other colonies—except New Jersey and Pennsylvania who wanted no part of such perilous exercises—was to march on Montreal by way of Lake Champlain. Training cadres of British officers came across the Atlantic to muster and drill the colonial militia, and in due course, in 1709, the land force set out up the Hudson valley, building Fort Edward at the carrying-place from the Hudson river, on the way. At Wood Creek, where the journey by water to Lake George was to begin again, Fort Anne was built, and there the little force halted until news should come of the arrival of the fleet from England. It never came. The whole plan had been disrupted by a battle fought long before, in Spain.

In the summer of 1706 the Earl of Galway, Britain's commander of her expeditionary force operating in Spain, had succeeded in placing the Archduke Charles on the Spanish throne and had arranged for him to be proclaimed King Charles III. Unfortunately the political chicanery of rival factions soon destroyed all he had achieved, and within a few months he had to withdraw from Madrid, followed up by a large force under the Duke of Berwick, a Marshal of France. (The Duke of Berwick was the illegitimate son of James II by his mistress Arabella Churchill, sister of the first Duke of Marlborough. Berwick had accompanied his father into exile at St Germain-en-Laye and joined the French army.)

In the following year, Berwick, whose army of French and

Spanish troops considerably outnumbered Galway's force, took up a position in two lines on what Smollett describes as 'the fatal plain' in front of the town of Almanza, and was attacked by a mixed force of British and Portuguese. The Guards and The Queen's (2nd Foot) attacked Berwick's centre 'with the greatest impetuosity' and in pushing the enemy back they exposed their right flank, which should have been protected by the Portuguese advancing with them. But the Portuguese did not care for the intense artillery fire and were stampeded by the French cavalry. The British lost 4,000 killed and wounded, 3,000 taken prisoner and 5,000 'dispersed during the fight'. In effect, thirteen battalions became either prisoners of war or otherwise ineffective, and this defeat, on 25 April 1707, put an end, for some time, to any transatlantic expeditions.

Hearing of the British plans against him, Vaudreuil proposed to attack the land force waiting at Fort Anne, but he was not a great leader and the force he collected melted away before it reached the borders of New England. The Iroquois deserted too, leaving their English allies weakened by epidemics and totally disheartened. The whole project was called off.

In June 1710 offensive operations that were rather more successful began when a combined fleet of ships of the Royal Navy and the colonies, carrying four New England militia regiments and one of Marines, left Boston for Port Royal in Acadia. The French governor, M. Subercase, short of supplies and almost out of ammunition, nevertheless put up a stout though brief resistance, for the glory of France, and when he capitulated he was allowed to march out with drums beating and Colours flying. This time Port Royal passed finally into English hands. The commander of the land force, Colonel Nicholson, changed its name to Annapolis Royal, in honour of Queen Anne, and repaired its defences. This was a wise precaution, for as soon as the warships had sailed away that savage old woodsman Baron St Castin and a horde of his Indians emerged from the forest and besieged the strong garrison. They could make no impression on Annapolis Royal and after a time, like Vaudreuil's forces, by twos and threes they slipped away.

For the first time a British force from England had played a major part in the long struggle between the French and English in Canada, and the capture of Annapolis Royal marked the beginning of the end. And it marked the beginning of the end of something else too. Francis Parkman quotes an extraordinarily prophetic remark made by a Frenchman at this time. 'If the French colonies should fall,' he said, 'Old England will not imagine that these various provinces will then unite, shake off the yoke of the English monarchy, and erect themselves into a democracy.' Sixty-five years had to pass before he was proved right.

This success in Acadia made very welcome news in England where Robert Harley, first Earl of Oxford, and Henry St John had just succeeded in bringing about the removal from office of the Duke of Marlborough. They felt that the capture of Canada under their leadership would more than offset the victories of the great soldier—the victories which had made it possible to spare troops for America. With the enthusiastic support of Massachusetts another expedition was mounted, and in July 1711 a fleet of fifteen men-of-war and transports, commanded by Admiral Sir Hoveden Walker, sailed into Boston harbour. In the transports were seven of Marlborough's best regiments, veterans of the Continental campaigns, led by General Sir John Hill.

A militia force of New Englanders set off again up the Hudson valley. Vaudreuil called his people to arms, strengthened the defences of Quebec and posted his regular troops at Chambly to cover the approach to Montreal. He knew that this time the attack on Quebec would be no amateurish effort on the lines of Phipps's failure. Against so large and seasoned a force New France might well succumb. Yet, as Fortescue points out, the expedition 'was in fact simply a political move, conceived by factious politicians for factious ends instead of by military men for the benefit of the country, and accordingly it fared as such expeditions must inevitably fare'.

Admiral Walker refused to heed the warnings of his pilot when he reached the mouth of the St Lawrence and took the fleet too near the northern shore. In a high wind, among the reefs and shoals of the Egg Islands, he lost eight ships and 700 soldiers were drowned. Neither the Admiral nor the General felt able to persist after such a disaster. They dropped the whole plan immediately and went home.

From every steeple in Canada the bells pealed a thanksgiving.

The land force which Colonel Nicholson was taking up the Hudson heard the news while on the waters of Lake Champlain. There was nothing Nicholson could do except march back along the way he had come. Three years later the war was ended by the Treaty of Utrecht, and the old tradition of handing back all gains to the previous owners was broken. Acadia, Newfoundland, Hudson Bay Territory and the island of St Kitts were all ceded by France to England, although the long-standing and vexed problems of the boundaries of Acadia were not resolved. In Acadia, France retained the island of Cape Breton, known then as l'Île Royale, the islands in the Gulf of the St Lawrence, including what is now Prince Edward Island, and she was also granted certain fishery rights along the Newfoundland coast.

New France was shrinking, and some might say that the tide of conflict was turning in favour of England. Yet despite the inroads made upon her territory the future for France was very bright indeed. She still held Cape Breton, gateway to the St Lawrence. The St Lawrence, the Mississippi and the Great Lakes were all hers. There had been no attempt to take either by force or by treaty the fort built early in the war by the legendary Canadian fighter and fur-trader la Motte Cadillac. He had built it at Detroit, and dominating the waterway connecting Lakes Erie and Huron, it secured the link between the St Lawrence and the Mississippi and kept open the highway between Canada and Louisiana. To the east of this highway lay the English colonies of North America. To the west lay boundless, unexplored possibilities, now inaccessible to the English colonists.

In these circumstances the Treaty of Utrecht, like the Treaty of Ryswick, was only a pause in the undecided conflict. The French, with what they regarded as the trifling exceptions made at Utrecht in 1713, still claimed the whole of the North American continent and took steps to regain what they had lost.

On Cape Breton Island they chose a harbour, somewhat ironically named Port à l'Anglais, on the east coast, and there they began to build the great fortress of Louisbourg. This would command the gateway to Canada and be the base for future operations against New England and Nova Scotia. The fortification was designed on principles laid down by the great military engineer Vauban, and the men who worked on it called it, with pride, the Dunkirk of America—the fortified English Channel port being then regarded as impregnable.

Unfortunately for the French, the building of Louisbourg revealed one or two snags. Constant sea mists and rain in the short spring and summer prevented cement from drying out, and in the piercing cold of late autumn and winter the damp cement froze, split stones and demolished the walls. Maintenance had to be continuous, the expense was enormous—in the region of one million sterling—yet the fortress was never in good repair. Another point that the French did not apparently consider was that the value, and indeed the very existence, of such a stronghold depended on sea power, an asset they did not possess.

The building of Louisbourg was not simply a long-term project in preparation for the next war. It was the home of the French privateers who preyed on all shipping in the coastal waters of the English colonies, and as such was a perpetual threat to their trade. It was also intended to be a symbol to the people of Acadia, reminding them that one day the country would come back under the French flag and therefore there was no need for them to accept English rule. The psychological warfare aimed at keeping the Acadians in a state bordering on rebellion and the Indians in a state of war against the English was carefully developed and fostered by a chain of mission stations along the line of the Kennebec river and Lake Chaudière. The English colonists, goaded beyond endurance, finally retaliated by using armed force to root out the pernicious 'Christian' missions, and in a state of outward peace there was always covert war.

Furthering their policy of making secure their claim to the northern continent, the French built a new fort at Niagara, another at Chambly to protect Montreal from any English attack coming up from Lake Champlain, and in 1731 a large stone fort was built at Crown Point, on the west side of Lake Champlain. This, named Fort Frédéric, was actually inside the Colony of New York, whose Assembly was too busy quarrelling with New Jersey to do anything about it, except express fury and resentment within the walls of their own council chamber.

Thus the French, tirelessly active, constantly alive to the problems of the future, were making their preparations. The only English response was to set up a fortified trading station at Oswego on Lake Ontario as a counter to the French post at Niagara. Strangely enough, this was done by Governor Burnet of New York out of his own pocket because his Assembly refused to vote any funds. He never received any recompense.

During this time the French had also been opening up the far north-west. The Sieur de la Verendrye began to explore in 1731. At the junction of Red River and the Assinaboine he built Fort Rouge, site of the city of Winnipeg, and eleven years later one of his sons crossed over to the Missouri river, paddled far up it, and on New Year's Day 1743 saw the dim, bluish snows of the distant Rockies. Then the age of discovery in western Canada was interrupted by the War of the Austrian Succession.

The long peace of twenty-seven years after the Treaty of Utrecht had been a period first of exhaustion and then of preparation for the next encounter. As Roberts says, 'England and France only awaited an excuse for flying again at each other's throats'. The excuse was provided by the death of the Emperor Charles VI, who had nominated his daughter Maria Theresa as his heir, setting aside the provisions of the Salic Law in a declaration known as the Pragmatic Sanction which had been agreed by most of the European powers. Nevertheless, as soon as he was dead, France, Spain and Bavaria leapt into the arena, denied the right of Maria Theresa to succeed and put forward their own candidate, Charles Albert of Bavaria, for the Imperial Crown.

England at once came forward as the champion of the young Empress, an action which seemed bold, self-sacrificing and chivalrous, whereas the practical reason was that once more France and Spain had formed a partnership to destroy her colonies and her commerce. War had broken out between England and Spain in November 1739, much against the will of Sir Robert Walpole, England's Prime Minister, who was finally compelled by the pressure against him in the House of Commons to yield over a matter which he felt could easily be settled by negotiation. The story really belongs to the West

Indies for it was there that the ear of the notorious Captain Jenkins was allegedly cut off by the Spaniards. This War of Jenkins' Ear merged into the War of the Austrian Succession. When the Emperor died, in 1740, and Europe took sides over who was to reign in his stead, it was only natural that France and England should oppose one another, but at first they were only auxiliaries and not principals in the dispute. In 1743 the Bourbon kings of France and Spain formally renewed the Family Compact and not until 1744 was war declared with equal formality between Louis XV and George II.

French aggression in the oft-disputed area of the Netherlands brought the Dutch into the war. England could not ignore the threat to Antwerp. George II crossed the Channel with his army and, with Dutch and Hanoverian assistance, won the battle of Dettingen—the last occasion on which an English monarch led his troops in the field. The French responded with a plan to invade England in support of a Jacobite rebellion—from the point of view of the House of Hanover, James II's grandson, the Young Pretender, was being particularly tiresome at this time. Ten thousand French troops assembled at Dunkirk and a large fleet was fitted out at Brest. The invasion force put to sea in February 1744 but was broken up by a tremendous storm off the Sussex coast before an English fleet under Admiral Sir John Norris could engage it. While this was happening an English squadron led by Admiral Mathews fought twelve Spanish warships and the French Mediterranean squadron off Toulon in a battle which was neither a victory nor a defeat. The only officer to come out of the affair with any credit was Captain Edward Hawke who captured an enemy ship. Fifteen years later Admiral Sir Edward Hawke was to win the great Battle of Quiberon Bay.

In North America the French at Louisbourg heard of the outbreak of war some weeks before the news reached Boston, and the French military governor of Louisbourg, du Quesnel, felt he had an opportunity to strike a swift blow for the glory of France, and himself. Du Quesnel has been described by one of his compatriots in Louisbourg as 'capricious, of an uncertain temper, inclined to drink, and when in his cups neither reasonable nor civil'. He was extremely unpopular, having offended everyone of any consequence in the garrison, and was subsequently described as 'the cause of all our disasters'. This accusation was perfectly fair, for *l'habitant de Louisbourg* who is the principal source of information on the campaign added, 'Perhaps the English would have let us alone if we had not first insulted them. It was in the interest of the people of New England to live at peace with us, and they would no doubt have done so if we had not taken it into our heads to waken them from their security. They expected that both parties would merely stand on the defensive, without taking part in this cruel war that has set Europe in a blaze.'

Du Quesnel's idea was to hit the English hard before they knew there was a war on, and the easiest and obvious target was the little fishing station of Canseau, at the southern end of the strait of Canseau which separates the Acadian peninsula from Cape Breton Island. The only defence was a wooden stockade held by about eighty New Englanders who were primarily fishermen.

Early in May 1744 du Quesnel dispatched a force of seven or eight hundred men under Capitaine du Vivier, escorted by two small armed vessels, and the English surrendered on condition that they were sent to Boston. This was agreed, and Canseau was burned to the ground. Emboldened by this victory du Quesnel raised his sights somewhat and aimed at Annapolis Royal. On all the available evidence, the capital of Acadia was even less of a problem than Canseau. During the long peace the British Government had so neglected its upkeep that 'its sandy ramparts were crumbling into the ditches, and the cows of the garrison walked over them at their pleasure'. The garrison consisted of about 100 men, commanded by a Frenchman named Major Mascarene, a Huguenot whose family had been driven into exile and the British service by Louis XIV's revocation of Henry IV's Edict of Nantes.

Du Vivier and a mixed force of French and Indians arrived in front of the fort in August, established a camp behind a ridge overlooking it and advanced with confidence towards the 'crumbling ramparts'. They were greeted by such rapid and accurate cannon fire that they changed their minds about making an open assault and decided to harass the defenders into surrender by keeping them on the alert all night. Under a flag of truce du Vivier informed Mascarene that at any moment two French warships, *Ardent* and *Caribou*, would arrive from Louisbourg carrying 250 regular troops and a siege train of artillery. It might therefore be wise to arrange surrender terms which need not be put into effect until the ships actually appeared. Mascarene said he would make up his mind when he saw the ships, meanwhile he would accept the fortunes of war. The ships never did arrive, for the good reason that when the unlovable du Quesnel gave orders to their captains they refused to comply with them because they had not come from the King. Du Vivier failed altogether to persuade the neighbouring French Acadians to join with him in an attack; they very naturally declined his invitation because he was unable to answer their question about what would happen to them if the attack failed. For three weeks the besiegers made a nuisance of themselves, showing extreme reluctance to use the scaling ladders the French Acadians had made for them as a gesture of compromise, and at the end of September Mascarene received a reinforcement of fifty Indian rangers from Boston. Du Vivier and his men disappeared during the following night.

'The expedition was a failure,' wrote *l'habitant de Louisbourg*, 'though one might have bet everything on its success, so small was the force the enemy had to resist us.' And it caused a lot of trouble. It had first alarmed and then annoyed the New Englanders, and by way of retaliation they decided to mount their own expedition and capture Louisbourg.

There is a lot of argument about who first suggested the idea, not that it matters; with a different outcome the question might not have arisen. Yet as a serious strategical and tactical project the whole thing was nonsense. It had taken the French twenty-five years to build the huge fortress; a French officer had said it could now be held by an army of women against any assault, and there was some justification for his remark. It lay at the extreme end of a low ridge of rock jutting out into the Atlantic between the harbour on one side and Gabarus Bay on the other. The ground behind it was largely a morass which made any movement of troops or artillery extremely difficult. Strong batteries of 42-pounder guns were mounted in bastions covering all approaches by land or sea. In the mouth of the harbour was a separate fortification known as the Island

Battery and at the back of the inner basin, immediately opposite the harbour mouth, stood the Grand Battery which could pound to pieces any ship that managed to survive the combined fire of the Island Battery and the fortress itself. Thirteen hundred regular troops formed the garrison.

It was ridiculous to imagine that the raw militia of Massachusetts would get even within musket shot of such a place. It had been designed by a professional military engineer to be defended by professional soldiers; the odds against success by the military talent available in New England were so great that the idea should have been discounted as totally impracticable as soon as it was put forward—as indeed it was.

However, it appealed greatly to Governor William Shirley, an English barrister who had come to Massachusetts in 1731 to practise and prosper in his profession. Advised by a man named William Vaughan, who said he knew something of Louisbourg, Shirley made a plan, but it could not be put into effect without the approval of the Assembly of Massachusetts. On 9 January 1745 the General Court of Massachusetts was slightly surprised when Governor Shirley announced to what Parkman calls 'this convention of grave city merchants and solemn rustics from country villages' that he had a communication to make; a communication so critical that he wished the whole body to take an oath of secrecy. Shirley was a popular, persuasive man, and the members agreed. He then made his proposition. They listened, appointed a committee of the two Houses to consider it, and after several days of deliberations the committee turned it down flat. Meanwhile the secret had come out. Naturally enough, in this deeply religious community the members of the committee when faced with a difficult decision were wont to seek guidance from the Almighty; a right and proper thing to do. One member, whose piety exceeded his discretion, prayed with such power and fervour that he was overheard. Within a few days Shirley's plan was all over the province.

Shirley was not the man to take no for an answer. He arranged for a petition to be presented by the merchants who suffered most from the French privateers based on Louisbourg. This, supported by testimony from militiamen captured at Canseau who spoke of mutiny and grievous lack of supplies in the fortress, reversed the decision. Apparently Louisbourg could not possibly hold out against a siege without replenishment of all necessities from France. To attack now was to ensure success. To invoke the aid of England would be to let slip a golden opportunity. The plan was put to the vote and carried, by a majority of one, because one member of the opposition fell and broke his leg while hastening to the House.

Once the decision had been taken, the work of assembling a force went ahead briskly. Governor Shirley wrote to all the colonies as far south as Pennsylvania asking for their help, and with the exception of Connecticut, New Hampshire and Rhode Island, they all found some excuse or other to explain why, just at that moment, they found themselves unable to co-operate. So it became a New England affair and a Puritan crusade. Those who on reflection might have been daunted by the magnitude of the project were made resolute by the thought that, after all, this was a war against the Papists and therefore, by their own peculiar logic, must have the approval of the Almighty. In all families and churches there was much insistence on this point, and God was constantly reminded which side He was on.

The Reverend Samuel Moody, known as Parson Moody, the minister of York, was appointed Senior Chaplain to the Forces. Parkman says that his irritable temper and thick-skinned insensibility made him as invulnerable as a rhinoceros. The old man possessed lungs of brass which enabled him to keep his flock standing for two hours while he communicated with Heaven in a voice of thunder, and then followed up with a sermon expounding his own brand of sulphurous theology for another two hours. When he sailed with the force he took with him an axe, to be used, he said, 'to hew down the altars of Antichrist and demolish his idols'.

In a remarkably short space of time the energy and resource of Governor Shirley had brought together a force of 4,000 men —each man bringing his own clothing and gun and receiving pay of sixpence a day. The officers had no experience of war or training except for the occasional drill on muster day, when it was the custom for militia officers to supply their soldiers with rum to make them better inclined to obey such words of command as could be remembered. The commander appointed to lead the army was William Pepperrell, a merchant of Kittery, whose selection appears to have rested on his popularity—there was a reasonable chance the men might obey someone they liked—and the fact that he possessed 'as little military incompetency as anyone else who could be had'.

The naval commander was Captain Edward Tyng who had distinguished himself in the previous summer by capturing a French privateer far larger and better armed than his own ship. He fitted out a brig named *Massachusetts* as his flagship, converting her into a 24-gun frigate, and the invasion fleet assembled in Nantasket Roads. It consisted of *Caesar* and *Shirley*, both of 20 guns; a 16-ton 'snow', similar to a brig, and probably with 16 guns; one sloop of 12 guns and two of 8 guns each; the *Boston Packet* of 16 guns; two sloops from Connecticut each with 16 guns; a privateer of 20 guns hired in Rhode Island; the Connecticut government sloop *Tartar* carrying 14 carriage and 14 swivel guns; and the entire navy of New Hampshire, a sloop of 14 guns. This total strength of 218 guns of all sorts of different calibres and ranges would be hopelessly out-gunned by as small a force as three French 74s.

Artillery was a problem. Ten 18-pounder cannon were borrowed from New York and there were a few 22-pounders available locally but these were far too light to make any impression against the walls and bastions of Louisbourg. So Shirley put his faith in being able to capture and use the heavy French cannon in the isolated batteries protecting the harbour, and the fleet carried a large store of 42-pounder cannon-balls for this purpose. As one chronicler remarks, this was 'like selling the skin of the bear before catching him'.

While the other colonies looked on with amusement tinged with contempt the final preparations were made, and Shirley, miles from the scene of operations and knowing very little about the ground, sat down and wrote out the force commander's orders in immense detail. Yet he did have the good sense to add a last paragraph which in effect cancelled out most of his labours: 'Notwithstanding the instructions you have received from me, I must leave you to act, upon unforeseen emergencies, according to your best discretion.'

Without a single professional officer or even an engineer, with men who were farmers, fishermen and shopkeepers, without adequate artillery but with boundless optimism the army embarked in ninety 'transports', mostly fishing boats and coastal traders, and the fleet set sail on 24 March 1745.

It seems that no one had any real idea of what they were taking on. The swiftly promoted General Pepperrell had received a great deal of serious advice. For instance it was suggested to him that before storming the walls of Louisbourg 'two trustworthy persons should cautiously walk together along the front of the French ramparts under cover of night, one of them carrying a mallet with which he was to hammer the ground at short intervals. The French sentinels, on hearing this mysterious thumping, would be so bewildered as to give no alarm. While one of the two partners was thus employed, the other was to lay his ear to the ground which would return a hollow sound if the artful foe had dug a mine under it. Whenever such secret danger was detected, a mark was to be set on the spot, to warn off the soldiers.' (A remarkable forecast of modern minefield clearance.)

On Friday, 5 April, Captain Tyng led his fleet into the harbour of Canseau which, despite du Vivier's efforts to destroy the settlement, had been quietly rebuilt and reoccupied by the English. Here Pepperrell learned that Louisbourg, further to the north, was still blocked by winter ice and there was nothing he could do until it had melted. On Thursday, 18 April, there was a sea battle, ending in a running fight, between Tyng and his warships and the French frigate *Renommée* of 36 guns, but the French vessel got away and sailed back to France to report what she had seen. On Tuesday, 23 April, the expedition was joined by a small British naval squadron under the command of Commodore Warren. He was in the *Superbe* of 60 guns and was accompanied by *Launceston* and *Mermaid*, both of 40 guns. This was a most welcome addition for it would now be possible to blockade Louisbourg and offer reasonable opposition to any French ships attempting to relieve the fortress.

During the three weeks while the troop transports lay at Canseau much of the time was spent in drilling the men and organizing them into units and columns for the assault. Parson Moody preached some powerful sermons on such texts as 'Thy people shall be willing in the day of Thy power', and heightened the crusading zeal. Then at last on the morning of Sunday, 29 April, a clear, cold, windy day, the force left

Canseau, intending to arrive in the darkness of nine o'clock at night, as laid down in Shirley's orders and take Louisbourg 'while the enemy were asleep'. The wind was light and dropped altogether in the late afternoon so it was not until the following morning that the New Englanders saw their objective for the first time. They were not very impressed. Most of the buildings in the town were small and the ramparts surrounding them were nothing like as high as they expected. Vauban had not worried about the height of walls so much as the depth of the ditch in front of them. The ditch was eighty feet wide and thirty feet deep. The walls on the far side, of earth faced with masonry, were sixty feet thick, and on the enemy's side of the ditch a glacis (a parapet built in a long open slope to meet the natural surface of the ground) ran down into the marsh. Little of this could be seen from the sea.

The garrison, commanded by a brave but not very skilful soldier, du Chambon, who had taken over when du Quesnel died in the previous autumn, had been aware for a long time of the preparations being made to attack them. Indians who had been to Boston brought the story back to Canada though, as l'habitant de Louisbourg says, 'It was not believed and excited no alarm,' and when it reached Louisbourg in Acadia nobody seemed to know what to do. 'Nothing to the purpose was done, so that we were as much taken by surprise as if the enemy had pounced upon us unawares.'

Pepperrell's first task was one of the most difficult of military operations, an assault landing from small boats on an unknown coast, bedevilled by rocks and pounding surf, with the enemy waiting for him on the shore. He achieved it with remarkable success at Freshwater Cove, about two miles to the west of the fortress. At a cost of two New Englanders slightly wounded the first wave of troops got ashore, killed six of the enemy, captured six more, including an officer, and drove off the rest. By the following morning the whole force of 4,000 men had landed.

The first extraordinary stroke of luck was the discovery, on 2 May, that the Grand Battery was unoccupied. Pepperrell received a message from William Vaughan, now one of his officers, which read: 'May it please your Honour to be Informed that by the Grace of God and the Courage of thirteen Men I

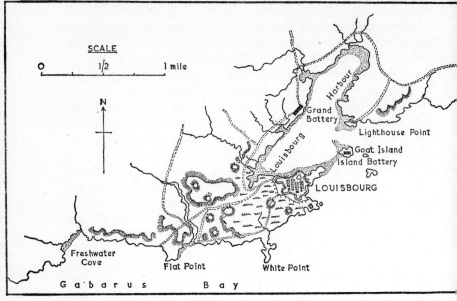

Louisbourg

entered the Royal Battery [*sic*] about 9 o'clock, and am waiting for a reinforcement and a Flag.'

Almost at once four boats filled with enemy approached from the town to reoccupy the Grand Battery, but Vaughan and his little section, standing on the open beach, kept them off with musketry until the arrival of the reinforcement he had asked for. The French then withdrew. Twenty-eight 42-pounder and two 18-pounder guns were taken in the battery. They had all been spiked but Major Seth Pomeroy, a gunsmith, and twenty 'soldier-mechanics' drilled them out and the guns were turned upon Louisbourg with inspiring effect.

This was the decisive event of the siege.

A New England battery was raised on Lighthouse Point on the other side of the entrance to the harbour, opposite Island Battery, which in due course was put out of action by a sustained cannonade. With prodigious labour some of the captured 42-pounders were dragged through the morass on the landward side of the town, to within 250 yards of the west gate. The walls began to crumble under the ceaseless pounding, the heaviest bastions gradually fell to pieces, every desperate sally from the town was thrown back, but du Chambon held on, waiting for the relief ship, the 60-gun *Vigilante*, to come to his aid. The end was near when Commodore Warren intercepted *Vigilante* and captured her. With the Island Battery out of action Warren could now sail into the inner harbour, destroy all the French shipping it contained, and bring the 386 guns of his fleet to bear on the town. The land forces were forming up into columns to storm over the shattered defences, and there was no more du Chambon could do. He raised the white flag and asked for terms.

In six weeks Pepperrell and his amateur army had achieved the impossible. He and his men marched into the town and to celebrate his victory he gave a banquet, attended by all the French officers and leading citizens. He was surprised to find nearly 5,000 people in the stronghold, and he arranged for them all to be returned to France. Parson Moody had a happy time smashing up the inside of the Roman Catholic church.

This was New England's hour. The honour and glory of this extraordinary achievement rest with New England alone. Commodore Warren's co-operation was obviously of enormous value but the muddy, bloody, exhausting work was done by the militia of the four provinces of New England.

The capture of Louisbourg was greeted with wild enthusiasm in London, where good news was very badly needed. The Duke of Cumberland had just fought the battle of Fontenoy, watched by Louis XV and the Dauphin, and the French claimed a major victory. Bonny Prince Charles had landed in Scotland and had routed the force opposed to him at Prestonpans.

To signify the royal pleasure, Commodore Warren was promoted to Admiral and Governor Shirley and General Pepperrell both received baronetcies. The New England colonies rejoiced, as well they might, and for the first time the British people realized that the American colonist was a fighting man in his own right.

To the French the loss of Louisbourg was an intolerable blow. The duc d'Anville was at once given command of a large force assembling at La Rochelle, consisting of thirty-nine warships and a large number of transports carrying some of the best regiments of Louis XV's magnificent army. The mission of this force was to recapture Louisbourg and Nova Scotia at all costs. Boston was to be sacked and all New England taken out of English hands. The plan was as ambitious as any made by Louis XIV, and like other great plans before it, took no account of certain unpalatable facts. All through the war the French Navy had deteriorated steadily, mainly because most of the money available for the war had been allotted to the successful army. Another factor was the capture of large numbers of French merchant seamen by the British, for the merchant navy was the first reserve of manpower for the warships, and wastage by battle casualties, sickness, desertion, and so on, could not be replaced by experienced men. The French Navy was not in a position to compete with that of Britain which, after the customary pause to shake off the effects of peacetime neglect, had gone from strength to strength.

The collection and preparation of the great French armament took time, and meanwhile Governor Shirley pressed on with another plan, to conquer Canada in 1746. In Whitehall the Secretary at War, the Duke of Newcastle, agreed to his proposals and in April 1746 three British regiments, the 29th, 30th and 45th Foot, arrived to occupy Louisbourg. Five more regiments under Lieutenant-General St Clair and a fleet commanded by Admiral Warren were promised. The British regiments and New England militia would sail up the St Lawrence in Warren's ships to attack Quebec while the usual land force went up the Hudson and Lake Champlain route to Montreal. The New England success against Louisbourg had fired many of the colonies with enthusiasm, and seven different Provincial Assemblies voted a total of 4,300 men for the attack on Montreal.

The French in Canada took fright and made feverish efforts to put their defences in order. They need not have bothered. At the last moment Newcastle diverted the promised force, and its General, in a particularly futile raid against the warehouses of the French East India Company at what was then called Port l'Orient (now Lorient) on the coast of Brittany. A landing was made on 1 October 1746 near Le Poldu, almost unopposed. The troops then plundered a small town as a punishment for the inhabitants who were believed to have fired on them during the march on the day after the landing. Port l'Orient was then besieged very half-heartedly despite the offer of the Deputy

Governor of the East India Company to surrender on good terms. Nothing was achieved. After a few days of digging and firing, and having lost about 100 men, killed and wounded, General St Clair re-embarked his men on 12 October and returned to England.

In Massachusetts, disappointed but not dismayed, Shirley turned his attention to the stone blockhouse the French had built at Crown Point, but had to abandon his plan to destroy it when he heard of the huge French force now apparently on its way to retake Louisbourg. This time it was New England's turn to become alarmed. Canada received the news with gladness and relief, and sent a land force of Canadian rangers down to Nova Scotia to co-operate with the French admiral d'Anville when he arrived.

Delayed by bad weather the fleet did not leave France until 20 June 1746; and damaged by storms in the Altantic, becalmed in the Azores, and decimated by a pestilence which swept through all the ships, it did not reach the coast of Nova Scotia until 14 September, making for the rendezvous in Chebucto Bay. Moving slowly for fear of the dangerous shoals off Sable Island, whose exact position they did not know, the ships' captains felt their way through thick fog until they were suddenly struck by a terrible storm. When d'Anville at last came into Chebucto Bay with two ships he found only one waiting out of a total of sixty-five which had sailed with him. According to one historian (Roberts) 'his mortification brought on a stroke of apoplexy which soon proved fatal'. A short while later his second-in-command, Admiral d'Estournelles, arrived. One report says he threw himself on his sword in despair, another that he was stricken with insanity and stabbed himself with his sword—there is very little difference.

Command of the ill-fated expedition now devolved upon another naval officer, Captaine de la Jonquière, who was on his way to take up the appointment of Governor-General of Canada. He waited until he had been joined by a few more ships of the scattered fleet and, feeling he ought to do something more energetic than merely take the remnants of the force back to France, set out to recover Annapolis. On the way he ran into another fearful storm. This time everybody gave up and went home.

During this series of calamities the Canadian land expedition, tired of waiting for ships that never came, began its own offensive, in the tradition of the Indian wars. The Canadian Rangers stole up to the peaceful border settlement of Grand Pré where there was a small garrison of one company of New England militia, commanded by Colonel Noble. It seems strange that after all the horrifying examples to illustrate what could happen during a border raid if sentries were not posted, or were not alert, it was still possible for a night attack to be so successful, yet the Canadians got in and murdered eighty of the inhabitants while they slept.

Despite the total failure of the duc d'Anville's expedition Louis XV was not disheartened and another force, commanded by de la Jonquière, was gathered together. In May 1747 a joint squadron, part of which was to regain Louisbourg and the remainder was to carry reinforcements to Dupleix in India, put to sea. It was met and engaged by Admiral Sir George Anson and Admiral Warren, and a fleet superior in every way, off La Rochelle. Six out of nine French battleships were taken and so were four out of eight armed East Indiamen. The victory put an end to any hope of further French offensives, for the time being, in either North America or India. One of the prisoners taken by the British admirals was de la Jonquière, still trying to get to Canada. The virtual destruction of the French Navy was completed in October of the following year when Admiral Hawke, off Belle Île, not far to the north of the Rochelle battle, attacked a fleet trying to guard a valuable convoy of merchantmen from the West Indies. Six of the French warships were destroyed.

It was just as well that the British Navy had cut the French supply lines to North America, for the Duke of Newcastle gave the colonies no more help. He sent 300 men to strengthen the garrison of Annapolis but more than half of them died on the voyage and the rest, being either Irish Papists or convicts who had bought freedom by enlistment, at once deserted to the French. The situation in Acadia was fraught with danger. Although the French population was not actually in arms against the English they had no love for the new administration, and the Canadians, particularly the Jesuit priests and missionaries, carried on a continuous campaign of subversion and incitement to revolt. Governor Shirley was the only man prepared to do something about it and he was supported by the people of Massachusetts. Indeed, throughout the story of the struggle with the French in North America, Massachusetts seems to have been the one state really prepared to fight for its existence. Thus it is logical enough that from Massachusetts came the spirit and the fire which, less than thirty years later, burnt up the ties with the mother-country and forged the United States—although they had to be guided by a Virginian.

It was Governor Shirley who decided that although the defence of Acadia was strictly a British Government responsibility, if the colonists did not protect it themselves it would have to be abandoned. It was because of his leadership that Acadia was still English at the end of the war.

By the end of 1747, after eight years of fighting, Europe wanted peace. France had, on the whole, been very successful. Dupleix was still dominant in India and the French had taken Madras. The armies of Louis XV were occupying Flanders, the boundaries of New York and Nova Scotia were as ill-defined as they had ever been, and none of the questions on which Britain had gone to war with France and Spain had been settled. Yet in the opinion of the French their gains in India and Europe were not balanced by the loss of Louisbourg, and during the negotiations for peace its recovery was the chief point at issue between England and France. Britain was in no mood to prolong an argument, for she was preoccupied and seriously embarrassed by civil war. Although on 16 April 1746 the Duke of Cumberland, making what the Highlanders considered to be extremely unsporting use of grape-shot, had defeated Prince Charles Edward Stuart at Culloden Moor, the Jacobite Rebellion was by no means crushed.

In English eyes the loss of Madras was of very great economic importance and the presence of the French in Flanders was an unacceptable threat. England needed no new gateway to North America, she already had one, guarded by New York, which had no winter ice problem. So, when the peace of Aix-la-Chapelle was signed the New Englanders, to their fury, discovered that their great conquest, their immortal achievement, had been handed back to France in return for Madras and a French evacuation of Flanders. The fact that they were carefully reimbursed for their expenditure on Pepperrell's expedition added insult to injury. The people of Massachusetts had long memories, and the handing over of Louisbourg was another milestone along the road which led to independence—and it was more than that. What was regarded in England as a remote stronghold of no commercial value, in an island most people had never heard of before Pepperrell's attack, was also a vital factor in the struggle for a colonial empire and the commerce of the world. France had got it back, and apart from England's gain of Annapolis Royal, everything in North America was as it had been before the War of the Austrian Succession began. It was now certain that the Peace of Aix-la-Chapelle would be nothing more than that: a brief peace, a breathing-space before the fighting started again, and continued until a decision was reached.

7 Jenkins' Ear

The Treaty of Ryswick in 1697 had had but little effect in the West Indies. The English gave back to the French their part of St Kitts, and Spain recognized the French occupation of western Hispaniola, but in home waters a new chapter in the colonial contest had begun when Admiral Russell and his Dutch ally defeated the French invasion fleet off Cap La Hogue. French naval superiority, so carefully built up by Jean-Baptiste Colbert, was destroyed, and thereafter it was England's command of the sea which had so inhibiting an effect on French expansion.

For twenty years before the outbreak of the War of the Spanish Succession Louis XIV had encouraged smuggling between his Caribbean colonies and the Spanish empire, and when he went back on his arrangement with William III and declared his grandson, Philip of Anjou, to be the rightful heir to the throne of Spain, as he said himself, *'le principal objet de la guerre présente est cela du commerce des Indes et des richesses qu'elles produisent'*. He therefore instructed his grandson to grant what he had never been able to obtain by any other means, the *Asiento*, or contract, which gave France the legal right to trade with the Spanish colonies. In 1702 the French Royal Guinea Company received this right and England and Holland both saw at once that it threatened their commercial existence. One fundamental fact was plain to both: if Louis XIV gained possession of the Spanish Indies he would at the same time acquire the resources with which to defeat his enemies. The figures for English trade with Cuba and the Spanish Main in the year 1700—representing only a tiny fraction of the market—give some idea of the size of these resources. Four thousand tons of shipping was employed and the sales of English goods realized nearly one and a half million pounds sterling.

In September 1701 Admiral Benbow sailed for the West

Indies with a squadron of ten ships of the line. He went first to Barbados and then by easy stages to Jamaica. He was followed, a few weeks later, by the largest fleet ever sent to the West Indies by the French, carrying 12,560 sailors and soldiers. Its objects were to protect the commercial interests of France and Spain and to gain the support of the Spanish colonies for France. It far outnumbered, in ships, men and guns, Benbow's fleet now anchored off Port Royal, Jamaica, but its advantages were considerably reduced by the inability of the French and Spanish to co-operate, or even agree, over anything, and an appalling death rate from disease in the French ships. Benbow, strengthened by reinforcements from England, prepared to defend Jamaica, but in 1702, the year the war began, the French fleet returned to Europe.

The English began the war with greater naval resources than those of the French or Spanish and increased them by the taking of Gibraltar, stormed in a combined operation led by Sir Cloudesley Shovell and Sir George Rooke on 4 August 1704. Three weeks later the French fleet came out of Toulon to recapture the Rock and was driven back to port after the battle of Malaga, the only major fleet action of the war. In the western Caribbean Admiral Benbow had a brief encounter with the French off Cartagena, and a cannon-ball removed one of his legs. He died in the following year. Perhaps the most notable event was the destruction of the Spanish bullion fleet off Cartagena in 1713, the last year of the war, when booty worth fifteen million pounds was taken to Kingston, Jamaica.

In the eastern Caribbean the Governor-General of the Lee-ward Islands, the son of Sir Christopher Codrington, attacked and took French St Kitts in the first year of the war—for the last time; the whole island became English under the terms of the Treaty of Utrecht. French privateers retaliated immediately. Operating from Martinique and Guadeloupe they did their best to cut off all contact between England and her possessions in the Lesser Antilles. In their own sphere of operations the privateers had very little opposition because it was against British policy to make use in war of men generally regarded as pirates. So the French, either in single vessels or small squad-rons, attacking only when conditions were favourable and run-ning away when they were not, had the Leewards at their mercy. They did an immense amount of damage, from which Montserrat and Nevis never really recovered.

Codrington had bold plans for offensives against the French islands but his first attack, on Guadeloupe, was a failure and since he could not get reinforcements from England on the scale he needed, he had to abandon his schemes. The Duke of Marlborough, busily shattering the military power of France in Europe, had his objectives clear in front of him and had no wish to waste any effort on side issues unlikely to affect them. It was his opinion, proved right on so many occasions later, that to send ships and men to the West Indies would be unnecessarily expensive and would ruin the regiments which had to go. Any regiment stationed for a year in the Caribbean was likely to lose ninety per cent of its men by sickness in that time, and this state of affairs had existed ever since Admiral Penn and General Venables had taken Jamaica from the Spaniards.

On the whole, the War of the Spanish Succession was a thoroughly nasty, destructive episode in the history of the West Indies, taking the forms of piracy, arson and murder rather than reasonably respectable open warfare, and it achieved very little except the ending of the arrangement made by Esnambuc and Warner and the loss by the French of their part of St Kitts. It was in Europe, through the genius of Marlborough, that the real results were gained. The territorial aspirations of Louis XIV were checked and there was no longer any fear that the Spanish Indies would become French.

One of the clauses of the Treaty of Utrecht granted the *Asiento* to the English slave-traders, thus giving them the right to supply the Spanish colonies with a stipulated number of slaves over a period of thirty years. To this was added a concession which allowed one ship of 600 tons to visit the great annual trade fair at Porto Bello. These 'privileges' were all very well, so far as they went, but the granting of them took no account of the enormous illicit trade traffic which had been going on throughout the Spanish Main ever since the days of Francis Drake. In the years since the Treaty of Ryswick this contraband trade had increased very considerably and although nothing much had been done about it during the seventeenth century—because Spain had been too exhausted and lethargic to cope with it—there were now signs that the deliberate violation of Spanish navigation laws by English merchants, which had been going on for so long as to have become almost a right, was to be challenged.

Soon after the signing of the Treaty of Utrecht there came into being a Spanish organization known as *Guarda Costas* whose task was to enforce the navigation laws by stopping and searching for contraband any English ship sailing in the Caribbean. It is more than likely there would have been trouble enough if these *guarda costas* had been a proper government service under regular administration and discipline, but they were nothing of the sort. They were privateers, that is to say, armed vessels owned and officered by private persons, operating under 'letters of marque' issued by the Spanish Government, and the ships were fitted out as a private commercial speculation. They searched British merchantmen, often many miles from the area in which their activities had been authorized, and arrested the ships if they found in them anything which might be of Spanish origin. The captors got the prize money, and if in a subsequent appeal by a shipowner to the authorities in Spain the judgment went against the privateer, it was impossible to obtain restitution. It was straightforward piracy under another name.

During the years of peace which followed the War of the Spanish Succession the activities of the *guarda costas* caused intense resentment in the mercantile communities of England and the English colonies in the Caribbean, and they had good cause for complaint. Yet it was a problem which might have been solved by negotiation, at least Sir Robert Walpole was convinced it could be sorted out round a conference table. Unfortunately for his political career there were two other aspects which encouraged the Opposition to clamour for war. One was the known fact that Spain, almost bankrupt and just as anxious as Walpole to avoid war, was in no position to defend her rich overseas possessions. War provided an opportunity for taking them by force. The other was national pride—or perhaps arrogance. By the end of the War of the Spanish Succession Spain had become a second-class power whereas Britain was beginning to feel the superiority that sea power confers. It was intolerable that Spanish pirates should prey unchecked upon the shipping of the greatest maritime nation.

Spain must be taught a lesson she would never forget. In the House of Commons there was much windy eloquence on great traditions, honour, the glorious days of Elizabeth, and so on, but this did no more than create an explosive atmosphere out of abstract principles. If the parliamentary Opposition, the war party, was to achieve its two-fold aim of war with Spain and the downfall of Walpole they needed a detonator.

In 1739 a certain Captain Jenkins, skipper of a small merchantman trading in the West Indies, was brought before the House of Commons carrying a bottle in which was a small unpleasant-looking mummified object which he claimed was his ear. His story was that while he had been about his lawful occasions on the high seas his ship had been stopped and searched by *guarda costas*. He had been arrested, strung up by the neck to his own yard-arm, lowered when half-strangled and then deprived of an ear.

'What did you do?' he was asked.

'I commended my soul to God and my cause to my country,' he replied, omitting to add that these stirring words had been put into his mouth by the Opposition. He went on to say that his assailants had handed him his bleeding ear and told him to take it back and give it to King George as a present.

There is a great deal of doubt about the story he told. He had certainly lost an ear but it may well have happened in some drunken brawl, and there was nothing to prove that the nastiness in the bottle was his. But, as Sir Winston Churchill wrote: 'Jenkins' ear caught the popular imagination and became the symbol of agitation.' War against Spain was declared on 19 October 1739. The bells of London rang out and shouting crowds filled the streets.

'They are ringing their bells now,' said Walpole, whose power as Prime Minister was at an end, 'but soon they will be wringing their hands.'

France came into the war on the side of Spain largely because Louis XV and his ministers were disturbed by the growing power and prosperity of England, and the amount of money she was making in the Spanish Main. The War of Jenkins' Ear grew into the War of the Austrian Succession, and in 1744 France sent two fleets to the Caribbean to attack and destroy the British fleet commanded by Admiral Edward Vernon.

The Admiral had been having an unlucky war. He had begun operations against Spain in the Caribbean by taking Porto Bello by surprise in 1739 and razing all its fortifications. This had gone reasonably well, but in 1741, with a force of 15,000 men, he launched a very muddled attack on Cartagena, was repulsed and went back to Jamaica with only 1,700 men fit for duty, two-thirds of his soldiers and sailors having died of fever. In the following year he had not succeeded in making a landing in an operation against Santiago de Cuba. He then made a second assault on Porto Rico, and that failed too. However, the English and French fleets did not meet, and in fact from 1744 until 1747 there were no large-scale operations because of a reluctance, on both sides, to acquire more territory in the sugar islands. More territory would mean more sugar, and a sudden expansion of the industry would bring down the price of the commodity—and no merchant wanted that to happen. The French were always short of labour, particularly in time of war when their slave ships were valuable targets for enemy warships and privateers, and so the object of their operations against the English islands was not to seize plantations but destroy them and carry off the slaves. The only exception to this was the capture of St Lucia in 1744 by a small French expedition from Martinique, for the strategical reason that the island protected French access to their possessions in the Leeward Islands.

In 1748, just before the end of the war, Admiral Knowles attacked and captured St Louis, the stronghold in Hispaniola, and secured the right for English warships to use the harbour.

Under the terms of the Treaty of Aix-la-Chapelle in 1748 French troops were made to leave St Lucia, and four of the islands in the Windward group—St Lucia, Dominica, St Vincent and Tobago—were declared neutral, in the sense that there was to be no competition for them in future wars. On all these islands except Tobago there were both French and English settlers, most of them being people who disliked living under the commercial pressures of the sugar islands, objected to government controls and all the restraints of so-called civilization and wanted to enjoy that mythical benefit, 'freedom'. The geographical position of the islands made them attractive. Tobago was an excellent base for any French attack on Barbados, and as the Governor of Barbados pointed out, 'the vicinity of Tobago is such that in times of war it will cut off the trade here by hostilities'. St Vincent was on the direct line of communication between Martinique and Grenada, and Dominica on that between Martinique and Guadeloupe. The strategic importance of St Lucia, lying in the triangle formed by Martinique, Barbados and St Vincent, was obvious.

There was no mention in the treaty of the smuggling trade, and British warships continued their overt protection of British merchantmen involved in it. Spanish *guarda costas* went on making a nuisance of themselves, and of the right of search, which had really started the War of Jenkins' Ear, nothing more was heard. Everything slipped back quietly to where it was before the war began, and since the Treaty of Aix-la-Chapelle had not solved any of the outstanding problems, England and France were at war again only eight years later.

The colonial contest between England and France—the outcome of the discoveries of Portuguese, Italian and Spanish mariners in the fifteenth century—was still unresolved. In the beginning the insecurity of the colonists and merchants in the West Indies and in India had led them to make local arrangements and to respect, up to a point, each other's neutrality. The first treaty of this sort, made by Esnambuc and Warner in 1627, was renewed regularly at intervals of about six years until 1655, and in 1659 the constant attacks by the cannibal Caribs—then described as 'daily invasions'—from their strongholds in Dominica and St Vincent, forced the English and French to make a mutual defence pact which was in fact a revival of the old treaty, ratified again in 1662. And so it appeared that, making allowances for occasional upsets, in the West Indies the colonists of the two nations were prepared to live alongside one another in peace. Unfortunately this fragile relationship could not withstand the dual pressure of war between the mother countries and the immense profits to be made from tobacco and sugar. Where there was so much money to be made there was bound to be trouble, and since the two sides involved had been enemies for six hundred years, there was bound to be war.

In India the story runs on much the same lines. In the period from 1689 until 1713 there was plenty of commercial rivalry but no actual fighting between English and French. Not until 1732, when Dost Ali, trying to get official approval for his claim to be Nawab of the Carnatic, brought the French Governor Dumas into local politics, did the hitherto purely commercial interests of the rival nations begin to expand into the potentially dangerous fields of local government and the acquisition of territory. By 1740, when the Mogul Empire had broken up, the Mahrattas were trying to carve out their own empire and the nawabs and rajahs, having cut themselves off from any central government, were losing their grip over their own provinces, the European traders had to decide whether to assert themselves and stay, or allow themselves to be swept out by the tide of anarchy. Once again, money was the deciding factor. The Eastern trade was too valuable to be abandoned, and for the next twenty years the story of the struggle in India was dominated by the figure of that great Frenchman, Joseph François Dupleix. Even his departure in disgrace in 1754 brought only a brief pause in the fighting in India, and it was in this year that the serious fighting began again in North America, in what was known as the French and Indian War.

On the continent of Europe the Seven Years' War began in 1756, bringing to an end a period of 'peace' in which Indian raids and frontier disputes had never ceased in North America, the fighting in India had continued as if there had never been any Treaty of Aix-la-Chapelle, and in the West Indies the war between slave-raiders and plantation owners, privateers and pirates had been as brisk as ever.

As so often before, the new war began disastrously for England. By 1757 it seemed as if all would be lost. No one could have foreseen that the war which had really begun in 1689 had reached the last round.

8 The Bleak Beginning

In North America the main effect of the Treaty of Aix-la-Chapelle seemed to be an intensification of the deep-rooted antagonism between the English colonists and the French Canadians, particularly in Nova Scotia and the Ohio valley.

There was a vague clause in the treaty which provided for the setting up of a boundary commission at some future date, but it proved impossible to reach agreement on the demarcation of Nova Scotia. The French insisted that when they had ceded territory under the terms of the Treaty of Utrecht in 1713 they had not parted with the whole peninsula to which the narrow neck of land at the head of the Bay of Fundy gives access. The British claimed all the land between the St Lawrence and the boundary of Maine. This was a difference too wide to be bridged by any boundary commission and so, when the commissioners assembled, and discovered almost at once that nothing could be achieved by peaceful negotiation, they lost heart.

Until 1749 the population of the disputed area, vaguely described as Acadia, was entirely French, and after the Treaty of Utrecht the British Government handled it with the greatest care, exempting the settlers from taxation and respecting their religion. In the thirty-five years following annexation they prospered greatly and increased three-fold, but during all this time the authorities in Canada never relaxed their efforts to win Acadia back for France. Chiefly through the mission stations the settlers were constantly urged to rebel against the 'enemy' government or, if they were not prepared to rise in armed revolt, to be entirely non-co-operative. But it was not easy to be actively non-co-operative with a government that made so few demands, and the constant propaganda had little success. However, the position changed radically when Louisbourg, taken with such glory by Pepperrell and his New Englanders, was handed back to France, and the British Government realized there was now a very real danger of losing Nova Scotia. Fortunately the means to counter French influence were readily to hand, and would solve another problem at the same time.

When the War of the Austrian Succession ended in 1748 the British, as usual, at once reduced the size of their armed forces; many ships were paid off and units were disbanded. A very large number of trained sailors and soldiers were put out on the street and created a virtually insoluble social problem. With no jobs, no pension and no future, many of them, like their forebears, had to take to crime as an alternative to starvation, and in the past many of them had died on the gallows simply because no provision was made for the men who often enough had saved their country. This time, the need for public security, and perhaps the stirrings of a new-found humanity, led to the making of an offer. All veterans who would emigrate as settlers to Nova Scotia would be given fifty acres of freehold land with an extra ten acres for every child, their outward passage would be paid, they would be provided with all they needed to make a start and they were guaranteed immunity from taxation for ten years.

Four thousand ex-servicemen accepted the offer, and under the command of Colonel Cornwallis, crossed the Atlantic and landed at Chebucto, thereafter named Halifax, in honour of George Dunk, Earl of Halifax and President of the Board of Trade and Plantations. Three companies of local rangers were formed for their protection and two battalions of regular troops were detailed for the garrisons of Nova Scotia and Newfoundland.

It at once became clear to the French that Halifax was to be the counterpoise to Louisbourg, and that the value of their fortress was greatly diminished by the existence of a rival. The French Governor-General of Canada, la Galissonière, sent many more religious and political agents and trouble-makers into Acadia to intensify the campaign of subversion and heighten the discontent already caused by the influx of immigrants. When Hopson took over from Cornwallis, the first Governor of Nova Scotia, he found he had to deal with another Indian War. By 1755 there was no peace in his province. Indian warriors from Canada, trained, armed and paid by the colonial government in Quebec, carried out frequent murderous raids, their victims being the English colonists and any Frenchmen who wanted to live in peace and did not object to the British control of Acadia.

Things got so bad that in 1755 the British took a step they had long considered and on which they had issued many warnings. They rounded up all the French settlers they could catch and shipped them off to centres in New England and the Middle colonies. To the howl of protest that went up from the French they responded with the unanswerable statement that the activities of the Quebec government had left them with no alternative. It was the only way to put an end to the present state of war which existed in time of peace and to prevent a foreign power from tampering with the allegiance of British subjects.

This severe measure introduced some stability in Nova Scotia, but there was no such solution to the problems in the Ohio valley. Ever since they had discovered the Mississippi and planted a colony in its delta the French had never lost sight of their plan to establish a highway—most of which would be a waterway—to link the Gulf of St Lawrence with the Gulf of Mexico. The most promising route appeared to be through Lake Ontario and Lake Erie, thence overland for fifty miles to the head-waters of the Allegheny river which flowed into the Ohio, then down the Ohio and into the Mississippi. It was to secure this route that Fort Frontenac was built at the northern end of Lake Ontario, guarding the entrance to the Great Lakes, and Fort Niagara protected the link between Lakes Ontario and Erie. Yet there was much more to all this than just connecting Canada to Louisiana. The French were well aware that England's sea power and her wealth had already raised her to a dominant position in the world. They believed, as one French government official said, that 'America will furnish England with the means of dictating to Europe', and therefore, since France was the only rival and the only country in a position to thwart the designs of her ancient enemy, it was up to her to save Europe from this fate by holding fast to North America.

To the English, North America was a vast continent which the Almighty had very obligingly placed at their disposal. The idea of any French monopoly, anywhere, could not be countenanced. It was because of this that Governor Burnet of New York had built Fort Oswego, midway between Forts Frontenac and Niagara. There was no question of any prior claim by the French to the Ohio valley, and traders from Pennsylvania and Virginia had been operating there since 1740. Eight years later, when the War of the Austrian Succession had ended, the Ohio Company, formed by leading merchants in London and Virginia, obtained a royal grant of half a million acres in the Ohio valley. A year later, in 1749, the newly constituted Loyal Company was given 800,000 acres to the west of Virginia and North Carolina, and two years after that the Greenbriar Company of Virginia was granted 100,000 acres on the Greenbriar river which flows into the Kanawha. The Allegheny mountains were no barrier to the restless spirits among the English colonists and they were determined to push on westwards.

La Galissonière, who in fact was only serving as Governor-General of Canada while de la Jonquière was a prisoner of war in England, determined to stop this westward flow. He proposed to settle 10,000 French colonists along the line of the Allegheny mountains, but Louis XV, whose victorious armies had been maintained at the cost of his navy and whose battle casualties in Europe had been so heavy, could not afford to depopulate his country any further. In 1749, disappointed in his plan to hold the frontier by settlements and forts, la Galissonière sent out a man named Céloron de Bienville to mark the boundary of French territory. This was done by fixing metal plates bearing the arms of France to trees at regular intervals, and a lead plate inscribed with a proclamation of French ownership was buried at the foot of each of the marked trees. The line was drawn along the Allegheny river on the eastern side of the Ohio valley. This enraged the people of Pennsylvania, who became more angry when the French told them they would not be allowed to trade to the west of the Allegheny mountains, in areas where they had been active for years.

This arbitrary demarcation of a long-disputed area forced the boundary commission set up under the Treaty of Aix-la-Chapelle to switch from the problem of Acadia to that of the Ohio valley. The French and English commissioners debated regularly over a period of three years, from 1750 until 1753, and then the English withdrew, convinced that no settlement could be reached without war.

It was Canada's misfortune that in 1750, released from captivity in England, de la Jonquière at last arrived in Quebec and became Governor-General. La Galissonière, capable and patriotic, had to stand down. De la Jonquière's only interest was money, and there is no doubt that the widespread corruption which he introduced into every field of public expenditure contributed to the final result of the contest against England. For instance, he appropriated all the revenue from liquor licences and sold licences to anyone who could pay for them until drunkenness became a major problem throughout the country. He acquired large sums of money from France ostensibly to finance exploration of the far West, but he used them on fur-trading ventures from which he made huge profits. When at last someone in Paris paid attention to the constant complaints made against him, and called him to account, the old miser died in time to save himself the expense of defending counsel at his trial. His place was taken by the marquis du Quesne who, following his example, enriched himself by defrauding the King and the Colony.

De la Jonquière was not the type of man to concern himself very deeply with territorial and boundary disputes and it seems that during his brief tenure of office much of the work was done by his deputy, la Galissonière. He realized that English settlers, in no way connected with any sort of military occupation, would soon establish themselves in such numbers in the Ohio valley that the chain of minor outposts, designed to shut them off, would be overrun, effectively dividing French America in two. Traders in the valley sent warnings to New York and Pennsylvania saying that French activity among the Indians on the border indicated that something unpleasant was going to happen, and Robert Dinwiddie, the Governor of Virginia, heard much the same thing from his own sources. He, with sound strategic insight, saw the significance of the confluence of the Allegheny and Monongahela rivers which formed the Ohio and he tried, without success, to obtain money from his Assembly for the building of a fort there. While he was doing this, in 1751, the French began arresting English traders in the Ohio valley and telling them to leave the area.

In the following year de la Jonquière died and du Quesne came out from France. He began, with great energy, to pursue the policy of driving the English out of the valley, and in the spring of 1753 sent an expedition of 1,500 men to the eastern shore of Lake Erie where they built a log fort at Presquile, or Presqu'île, the site of the present town of Erie. They then built a rough road southwards to Rivière aux Boeufs (now French Creek) where, when the water was high, they could launch canoes and go down the stream to the Allegheny and the Ohio. From the strongpoint they christened Fort le Boeuf they went down the creek with the two-fold object of intimidating the local Indians who were showing signs of favouring the English and of building a third fort where French Creek joins the Allegheny—on the site of the already existing English trading station of Venango. The plan had to be abandoned because so many of the troops were sick, and having left a garrison in Fort le Boeuf and Presquile the rest of the force went back to Montreal. Communications between the St Lawrence and the Ohio had been firmly established.

As soon as Governor Dinwiddie heard of all this he sent a summons to the French commanders of the two new forts, ordering them to withdraw immediately from territory which belonged to the King of England. The man chosen to deliver this message was the 21-year-old Adjutant-General of the Virginia Militia whose name was George Washington.

When he reached Venango, Washington found that the English traders had been driven out and the place had been converted into a French outpost. Since France and England were not at war he was hospitably received by the French commander. The Frenchman told Washington very politely that he had orders to take possession of the Ohio, this he intended to do and it would be most unfortunate if anyone got in his way. Washington went on, up to Fort le Boeuf, where he delivered Dinwiddie's summons. He returned to Virginia and told Dinwiddie that his letter was being forwarded to Montreal but there was no possibility of any withdrawal by the French garrisons until they received specific orders from their Governor-General.

Dinwiddie made another appeal to his Assembly for money to build forts on the Ohio. He explained in detail what the

French proposed to do and the effect their action would have on the future of the colony. He produced a letter he had received from the Board of Ordnance in London approving his plans and offering to supply all necessary arms and ammunition. He also showed a letter from King George II authorizing him to use force to repel force. The Assembly would not vote one penny.

One of Dinwiddie's greatest attributes was tenacity. In February 1754 he renewed his appeal and the Assembly reluctantly voted some money, but nothing like enough. Dinwiddie appealed to neighbouring colonies pointing out to their governors that when the trouble started they would all be involved. Those furthest away did not agree, those nearby would not give any help simply because their own governors asked them to. The need to assert their independence by defying the British Government, through its representatives, on every possible occasion was apparently far more important than their security. North Carolina was the exception and voted enough money to equip a force of three or four hundred men. Having obtained permission from England to use the two regular infantry companies, one in New York and the other in Carolina, Dinwiddie then recruited 300 men in Virginia and began to assemble his force. In the meantime he sent off a party of backwoodsmen to build a fort at the strategic point on the fork of the Ohio, on a site selected by George Washington.

Forty men were at work on the nearly completed structure when on 17 April 1754 a flotilla of small boats came down the Allegheny carrying 500 French troops. They landed, aligned their field pieces on the new stockade and invited the workmen to surrender. They had no option. The French then destroyed what they had made—which must have been infuriating—and built a much more imposing stronghold on the same site. They called it Fort Duquesne.

To a man of Dinwiddie's temperament this sort of thing was a challenge. Although no shots had been fired, the French, in time of peace, had used force to drive British citizens from British territory. He and Washington, with every justification, looked upon the French action as a declaration of war, and if the French wanted war, they would have it. Although only about half the force Dinwiddie was collecting was ready to move, Washington set off with all the men available, crossed the

Allegheny mountains and came to the Youghiogany, a tributary of the Monongahela. It was his intention to take Fort Duquesne and check any further inroads by the French, but here he met a small party sent out by the French commander of the fort to investigate rumours of Washington's approach and warn all Englishmen off French territory.

No one seems to know exactly how it all started but everyone agrees that the men in Washington's force fired first, and in so doing began the French and Indian War. It was a wild little battle; a skirmish in the wilderness between men whose real motivation was a boiling over of the hatred which had its roots in the hideous Indian massacres and murders over many years of frontier warfare. The French were cut to pieces and their commander was killed. French accounts of the affair describe it as '*un assassinat*'. No doubt it was murder, and after this unpleasant little episode Washington pitched his camp in a place called the Great Meadows and, rightly assuming that retribution would soon be on its way from Fort Duquesne, made haste to fortify it. He gave the name of Fort Necessity to the enclosure surrounded by a shallow trench and low bank, and he was just finishing the defences when he was joined by the detachment of regular troops from New York. They arrived in a disgraceful state. There were only a few of them because the muster rolls has been falsified by 'faggots' (people paid to fill the ranks on muster parades so that pay could be drawn for the full complement—that of the 'faggots' going into the pocket of the unit commander), they had no tents, bedding, equipment or ammunition. They brought with them nothing but their muskets and thirty women and children who added to the ration problem. The regulars from Carolina did not turn up at all. While on the march they had mutinied and gone home.

A few days later a party of Indians increased the strength of Washington's force to about 350, and then Capitaine de Villiers, the commander of the Fort Duquesne garrison, appeared, at the head of a much larger force. The battle of Great Meadows, fought in pouring rain, went on for nine hours, until the interior of Fort Necessity was a slough of mud and blood. Washington surrendered and was allowed to march out with the honours of war. He led his men, and the women and children, back over the mountains and de Villiers returned to Fort Duquesne happy in the thought that the British had been driven out of the Ohio valley.

The action at the Youghiogany stream and the defence of Fort Necessity were not minor incidents to be brushed aside while the dispute continued in the council chamber of the boundary commission and in polite correspondence. The war which was to decide the ownership of North America had begun, though no one could have guessed its real significance at that stage. Dinwiddie certainly did not underestimate the importance of the issues at stake. He saw that he had to halt the steady pressure of the French coming southwards from the Great Lakes. With their usual skill in dealing with natives, the emissaries of Governor du Quesne were creating a coalition of the tribes on the long western boundary of the English colonies, and their loyalty to the French had received much encouragement from Washington's defeat at Fort Necessity. Once again, and very soon, the feathered, painted warriors would be on the war-path and wretched settlers would be roasted alive to amuse the 'braves' after a massacre of the women and children. The danger was real and urgent, but the torpid English colonies remained indifferent. Only after a bitter struggle did the Assembly of Virginia vote a reasonable amount, not all, of the money Dinwiddie asked for. The people of Pennsylvania, being mostly Quakers and Germans whose only interests were peace and the quiet cultivation of their lands, refused to contribute anything. New York would not believe there had been any French intrusion until Washington had actually been defeated. Maryland with reluctance and after a long delay produced a small contribution and New Jersey, when approached, sent back a flat refusal. Only New England, led as usual by Massachusetts and the energetic Governor Sir William Shirley, showed real enthusiasm for the destruction of the Papists.

It was impossible to arouse any spirit of unity in the colonies or to arrange for any concerted action. Each colony regarded itself as an isolated entity, free, independent and autonomous, and therefore it was a remarkable achievement by the colonial Governors that, under pressure from the British Government, the representatives of Pennsylvania, New York, Maryland and the four states of New England were persuaded to meet round a table to discuss joint action for winning over the fickle Indians on the western borders. That great American, Benjamin Franklin, put forward a project for colonial union at this first provincial congress but it could make no headway against a wall of mutual jealousies.

On the question of Indian loyalty the French had the advantage. They pointed out to the Indians that Frenchmen wished only to hunt and trade, employing Indians as agents, trackers and allies on terms of great mutual benefit. On the other hand the English, as the Indians could see for themselves, were enemies. They destroyed the hunting grounds and drove away all the game in order to put land under the plough.

The Ohio Indians certainly feared the encroaching white man, and so those who did not remain neutral and kept out of the war became the consistent supporters of the French.

Disappointed but not surprised by the response to his appeals to the other colonies, Dinwiddie made an urgent application to England for warlike stores and two regiments of regular infantry. The British Prime Minister at this time was the Duke of Newcastle, whom Fortescue describes as 'the deplorable person who possessed no talent beyond an infinite capacity for such intrigue as lifts incompetence to high office, and was only less of a curse to England than Madame de Pompadour was to France'. This is perhaps a little harsh. Admiral Anson was at the head of the Admiralty, the wise and far-sighted Hardwicke was Lord Chancellor, with great influence in the Cabinet, and at the Paymaster's Office, fulfilling his duties with an honesty and integrity seldom if ever exercised before in that potentially lucrative position, was a man named William Pitt. The Secretary of State in charge of the colonies was Sir Thomas Robinson who was, according to Fortescue, 'a fool still greater than Newcastle'.

Despite Newcastle's alleged incompetence the government reacted swiftly to Dinwiddie's request. In July 1754 the sum of £10,000 in coin and 2,000 'stands' of arms (a stand being a complete set: musket, bayonet, ramrod and all associated equipment) were shipped to him, and on 30 September the 44th and 48th of Foot, then on the Irish Establishment, were ordered to embark at Cork for the colonies. In addition to this, orders were issued for the raising in America of two regiments, each

1,000 strong, to be taken into the pay of Great Britain and, while they were in existence, to be ranked as the 51st and 52nd of the Line. Sir William Shirley was to be the Colonel of the 51st and Sir William Pepperrell Colonel of the 52nd.

General Edward Braddock was chosen to be the commander of the force sailing from Cork, and he was to take over the command of operations in North America. His orders were not detailed; he was to drive the French from the Ohio, establish garrisons to prevent their return, and also expel them from Niagara, Crown Point and Fort Beauséjour, the latter being on the narrow isthmus joining Nova Scotia to the continent. Braddock had forty-five years' service, much of it in the Coldstream Guards. He was a rough, tough, rude martinet, intolerant of civilians, careful of his men, unusually brave and possessing plenty of experience and ability.

In April 1755 he and the two British regiments sailed up the Potomac to Alexandria where, on the 14th, a council assembled to decide how to tackle the tasks ahead. Everything seems to have been arranged rapidly and amicably. Braddock and the 44th and 48th regiments were to take Fort Duquesne; a young Irishman named William Johnson, who had distinguished himself in the Louisbourg campaign by his extraordinary influence over the Indians (he was married to Molly Brant, sister of Chief Brant of the Mohawks), was to lead a body of colonial troops, now called Provincials, against Crown Point; Shirley and Pepperrell, leading their own regiments, were to attack Niagara, and Lieutenant-Colonel Moncton was to march against Beauséjour.

Braddock, largely through faults in his temperament, began badly. He had the greatest difficulty in obtaining all the wagons and horses he needed for his force, and his bad temper and the attitude of arrogant superiority he adopted when dealing with what he described as 'these damned Americans' did nothing to overcome the apathy and reluctance of the Pennsylvanians who just wanted him to go away and not bother them. However, he made one move which showed he was neither as stupid nor as pig-headed as people throught. With a proper respect for local knowledge and experience, and with a becoming deference, he invited Colonel George Washington to join his staff.

The force which was to attack Fort Duquesne assembled at the beginning of May at the junction of Will's Creek with the Potomac river, where the former trading station had been replaced by an outpost built of logs and named Fort Cumberland, after the Duke whose character was in many ways so like that of Braddock. The place was nothing more than a clearing in a vast forest, and in it were encamped the two British regiments, each raised by recruits from Virginia to a strength of 700; a Royal Artillery detachment of 100 men; thirty sailors lent by Commodore Keppel who had escorted the transports across the Atlantic; 450 of the Virginia Militia and fifty Indian warriors, an auxiliary force entirely new, and therefore fascinating, to the British troops.

Braddock was well aware of the value of the Indians as scouts but he and his regular troops looked with scorn upon the Virginia Militia; yet, for the work that was to be done they were probably the best troops he had. They knew a great deal more about what we would today describe as jungle warfare than the British commander; they were accustomed to the deep, forbidding forests and they knew what to do if attacked in the woods.

Though Braddock himself reached Fort Cumberland on 10 May his cannon did not come up until a week later. He was not a very competent administrator and after more delay in collecting supplies it was not until 10 June that he was able to move his force out of Fort Cumberland and set off on the march through the forest.

In the world beyond this 'wilderness of leaves' much had been happening. As soon as the French learned of the reinforcements sent to Dinwiddie they equipped a fleet of eighteen ships and a force of 3,000 men to leave at once for Canada. Newcastle dispatched two naval squadrons to intercept them, but all but three ships, which had lagged behind, arrived safely at Louisbourg and Quebec. Admiral Boscawen caught up with the three stragglers off Cape Race on 7 June and captured two.

War had still not been declared, and in fact no state of war existed because it was generally recognized at the time that hostilities in the nature of the battle at Great Meadows, confined entirely to the colonies, did not necessarily entail a formal declaration of war in Europe. Boscawen's attack on French shipping was rather a different matter. But the French were in an awkward position: they had a very strong army and a weak navy. Without naval superiority they could not hope to hold their colonial possessions against determined British attack. On the other hand they knew how strongly George II of the House of Hanover felt about the State of Hanover and it did not take much strategic skill to work out that the easiest way to guard against colonial losses would be to invade Hanover. The only snag to this was that they could not trust Frederick the Great who was only their nominal ally; and Austria, their enemy on and off since the days of Louis XI, was still a threat they could not ignore.

The situation was no easier for Newcastle. An all-out attack on France would bring the other Bourbon power, Spain, in against him. This could to a certain extent be balanced by the defensive treaty recently concluded with the Dutch, but under the terms of this treaty one party would come to the assistance of the other only if it was attacked by a third power. Thus Newcastle had somehow to avoid being the technical aggressor. It could be argued that the activities of the French on the Ohio and Allegheny rivers constituted technical aggression— in which case, what was the technical significance of Washington's abortive advance on Fort Duquesne, which had led to casualties on both sides? The problem, at this stage, was far too complex to be solved by declaring war, and so both governments sent reinforcements to North America in much the same spirit as the man who applies a match to the blue paper without being at all sure whether there will be an almighty explosion or a damp fizz.

There was no road over the mountains from Fort Cumberland to Fort Duquesne, and to be able to move his supply wagons at all Braddock had to send 300 axemen in front to fell trees and clear a way only twelve feet wide. This, being filled with carts, pack-horses and artillery, was too narrow for marching troops and they had to move through the forest on either side. There is no doubt that Braddock took proper precautions against surprise: his Indians scouted ahead and flank guards protected the column on the march. Throughout the intolerably slow advance, discipline was never relaxed. Only thirty miles were covered in the first eight days. In that time many of the British troops fell sick and the horses, weak from lack of fodder before they started, were practically worn out. Braddock decided to take Washington's advice, leave the heavy baggage behind with a guard under Colonel Dunbar, to follow as best it could, and push on ahead. On 16 June a reduced force of 1,200 men, ten guns, thirty wagons and only a few packhorses, continued the march. Even then, progress was extraordinarily slow and despite the news that 500 Frenchmen were on their way to reinforce Fort Duquesne Braddock stuck rigidly to the rules laid down for marching through Flanders. As Washington said later, every molehill was levelled and a bridge was thrown over every stream. Only twelve miles were covered in the next four days.

On 7 July Braddock reached the mouth of Turtle Creek, a stream running into the Monongahela about eight miles from its junction with the Allegheny at Fort Duquesne. The direct route lay through difficult country and a dangerous defile, so Braddock decided to ford the Monongahela, swing round in a half circle, cross it again and come up on Fort Duquesne from a direction the French might not have anticipated.

Inside the fort the French were somewhat apprehensive. They had received accurate intelligence of Braddock's whereabouts on 5 July, and the commandant, who was now M. Contrecoeur, had only a few companies of regular troops, some 900 Indians and a body of Canadian rangers. He detailed Capitaine Beaujeu to take out a force of seventy regulars, 140 Canadian rangers and 650 Indians and lay an ambush, preferably in the area of the second ford across the Monongahela. This detachment left Fort Duquesne at first light on 8 July.

Braddock moved off from his camp at about the same time but it was nearly one o'clock in the afternoon before he came up to the second ford. Expecting to be attacked at this point he sent forward a strong advanced guard under Lieutenant-Colonel Thomas Gage with orders to cross the river, clear the opposite bank and protect the crossing of the main body. There was no sign of any enemy because Beaujeu had been delayed by trouble with his Indians. It was a boiling hot day, the sun shone from a clear sky and hardly a leaf moved in the forest. The

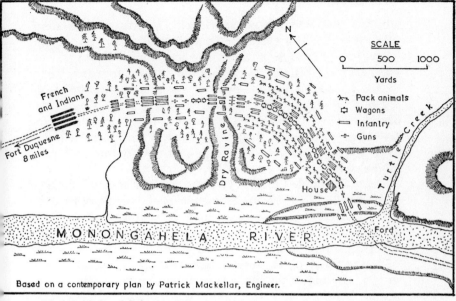

French
and Indians

Fort Duquesne
8 miles

Dry Ravine

Turtle Creek

Pack animals
Wagons
Infantry
Guns

House

M O N O N G A H E L A   R I V E R   Ford

Based on a contemporary plan by Patrick Mackellar, Engineer.

Monongahela   8 July 1755

main body formed up and crossed the river with perfect order
and regularity, as if the men were on the drill square. After the
disorder and fatigue of the long approach march it was quite
a relief to the soldiers to get back into proper formation on open
ground.

In many history books there is only a very brief account of
the events of the next hour or so and one is left with the impression that Braddock walked almost blindfold into an ambush,
and the result was a foregone conclusion. It was not quite as
straightforward as that.

When the whole force had crossed the Monongahela the
column halted for a rest. The sandy track it was now on ran
from the low bank of the river across a strip of marshy ground,
climbed up in a left-hand curve and disappeared into the forest,
running roughly parallel with the river on the left while close
beside it on the right rose a long steep ridge, thickly covered
with trees. It was ideal ambush country and Braddock took no
chances.

At the head of the column when it resumed the march were
several Indian guides supported by six mounted Virginians. A

musket shot (about 100 yards) behind them came a small advanced guard of Gage's vanguard, then the vanguard and after that, in succession, a road-clearing party of axemen, two guns with their ammunition limbers, and a rearguard. There was little or no interval between this and the main convoy led by light horsemen, more axemen and three guns. The wagons remained on the track while the marching troops and most of the pack-horses threaded their way through the trees on either side. Several flank guards were pushed right out on both sides of the column.

Just over a mile from the ford the track, now closely hedged in by trees, dropped down the steep bank of a ravine, crossed the wide floor of it and went up the high bank on the far side. Gage and his vanguard had crossed this ravine and the main body was just coming down into it when a man dressed in the feathers and war paint of an Indian but wearing an officer's silver gorget, glinting in the sun, was seen on the track immediately ahead. This was Beaujeu, and when he saw the English he swung round, took off his headdress and waved it. Fire was at once opened on the British from among the trees in front of them and for the first time the soldiers of the British Line regiments heard a wild war-whoop. They immediately deployed in perfect steadiness and under Gage's orders returned the fire in three controlled volleys, shooting in the general direction of the enemy musket smoke, towards an invisible foe. This precision musketry, which killed Beaujeu, so frightened his Canadians that they fled back to Fort Duquesne. Gage's two guns came into action and drove the enemy Indians away from the head of the British column. Gage's troops then advanced in formation, the men cheering and shouting 'God Save the King!' To Capitaine Dumas, Beaujeu's second-in-command, the battle appeared to be as good as over, but he and his small party of regular troops stood firm while his brother officers made great and successful efforts to rally their Indians. The French, opening fire by platoons, checked the advance of Gage's men while the Indians, filling the woods with their terrifying yells, slipped through the trees on either side of the column, always keeping out of sight.

Then, from their position on the flanks, they made use of every piece of cover to send a rain of bullets into the formation of redcoats out in the open. For a time the British kept their ranks, bravely returning the fire with volley after volley which hurt no one. At length they broke and fell back just as Braddock came up with the main body. This was thrown into disorder and all round them in the forest the shooting and the whooping never stopped. Only the Virginians knew what to do. They melted into the trees and returned the Indian fire in the Indian way, taking cover and shooting when they had a target. Some of the British tried to imitate them, and Braddock lost his temper completely. This was not war as it was supposed to be fought. There was nothing of this sort in the drill books; this was not how they had fought in Flanders, it was an abominable flouting of order and discipline. Purple in the face, utterly regardless of his own safety, he rode up and down, storming and cursing and beating Virginians and British back into the suicidal formation with the flat of his sword. Four horses were killed under him. After sixty out of his eighty-six officers had fallen and the slaughter had lasted for three hours—which must have seemed interminable—he realized that the day was lost and gave the order to retreat. He was trying to bring his force away in some sort of order when he fell from his horse, the fifth he had mounted since the fight began. A bullet had passed through one arm and both lungs. George Washington, his clothing ripped and tattered by countless bullets, was, by some miracle, unwounded, and he stood by his commander. The remnant of the force, seeing Braddock fall, turned and ran. Washington and some others tried desperately to rally them at the ford on the Monongahela, but, as Washington himself wrote in a letter ten days after the disaster, 'we might as well have tried to stop the wild bears of the mountains'.

Gage managed to rally about eighty at the next ford but the rest ran on, panic-stricken and terrified of being roasted by the Indians whose war-whoops rang in their ears. Much of their fear arose from the stories they had been told by the militiamen on the march up from Fort Cumberland. Braddock, mortally wounded, begged to be left on the battlefield but some officers carried him away. The attitude of the soldiers towards him is clearly indicated by their refusal to have anything to do with him.

The French made no attempt to follow up. A strange

omission, for their casualties were 43 against about 900 English killed and wounded. Braddock and Gage spent the night after the battle at the second ford of the Monongahela, among the few men who had rallied. Weak though Braddock was, in dreadful pain no doubt made worse by the distress of defeat, he remained in command and issued orders for the following day, when all that was left of his force began, in good order, to trudge back the sixty miles to Fort Cumberland. Braddock, in the agony of an unsprung cart, travelled only a little way, watched over by his faithful aide-de-camp Captain Orme, who recorded the final scenes. Throughout the long march on 10 July Braddock lay white and silent, knowing that his life's blood was oozing away. Not until the evening did he attempt to express his misery, not at his wound but at the bitterness of defeat, with the whispered remark, 'Who would have thought it?' The bully, the martinet whose voice had for so long terrified his soldiers, had but little speech left. All through the next day he made no sound until, towards sunset, he said gently, 'Another time we shall know better how to deal with them,' and died.

However, with certain notable exceptions—Brigadier Lord Howe, for example, as we shall see—it took a long time for the British, trained to the rigid Prussian style of warfare, to learn the lesson that the only way to combat guerrilla tactics is with guerrilla tactics. One cannot help feeling sorry for Braddock, an indomitably gallant man given a task so far beyond his training and powers of adjustment. He was incapable of improvising in a few moments and in the stress and dust and smoke and noise of battle an entirely new system of fighting, contrary to everything he had ever been taught or experienced, to cope with the unexpected behaviour of a strange enemy in a strange country. He remained unafraid, doing his duty as he saw it, until the very end. His body was carried a little way towards Fort Cumberland and buried in the road, so that the troops marching over his grave would obliterate all signs of it and so protect it from desecration by the Indians.

The battle for Fort Duquesne was an unmitigated disaster, a total, crushing defeat by any standards, but the Virginians, whose speed of reaction, courage and admirable behaviour had shown them to be splendid troops, emerged from it with credit. If only they had been allowed to show the British regulars what to do, the outcome might have been very different. Comte Dieskau, one of the senior French officers in Canada, expressed no surprise when he heard what had happened, for bitter experience had taught the French that regular troops, trained on European parade grounds and battlefields, could not be used in forest warfare without intensive retraining and an adequate force of rangers and Indians to shield them.

Not the least of the unfortunate aspects of the disaster on the Monongahela was the capture by the French of papers belonging to Braddock which contained details of all the plans to attack Crown Point, Niagara and Beauséjour.

There was a long delay, owing to inexperience and the usual jealousies, in collecting William Johnson's force for the attempt against Crown Point, but at length 3,000 Provincials and 300 Indians gathered together at Albany. Johnson had never been a soldier and knew nothing of war; his appointment was based solely on his knowledge of the Indians and his ability to handle them. His men were farmers and farmers' sons from New England and New Hampshire, undoubtedly excellent material but with no training of any sort. They wore their own clothes and brought their own weapons.

In August 1755 they began to move up the Hudson river towards Lake George, a new name bestowed by Johnson to honour George II. At the point on the Hudson where they had to take their canoes out of the water and go overland they began to build a strongpoint, named Fort Edward, and leaving 500 men to complete and garrison it Johnson went on to Lake George, fourteen miles away. On the south shore he built a fortified camp and christened it Fort George.

Warned by the documents captured at the Monongahela, the French had by this time sent 3,500 regular troops to reinforce Crown Point. They were under the command of comte Dieskau, an officer who had learned his soldiering under the great Marshal Saxe.

Johnson had a choice of two routes for his next advance: one straight up Lake George and the other along the stream called Wood Creek running parallel with Lake George and flowing into Lake Champlain. These routes converged at a point commanded by a promontory on the west shore of Lake Champlain, a key feature known to the French as Carillon but which became better known by its native name of Ticonderoga.

With a mixed force of 1,500 men Dieskau marched to Ticonderoga and pushed on from there to attack Johnson in his camp at Fort George. With some vague idea of cutting off Dieskau's retreat Johnson sent forward a detachment of 500 men. They were caught in an ambush, roughly handled and routed. Following this up, Dieskau now moved swiftly against Fort George, confident that he would achieve an even greater success than Capitaine Dumas at the Monongahela. He attacked Johnson's very strong position from two angles simultaneously, and lost about 600 men in the first assault. Although somewhat dismayed by so stubborn a resistance he persisted. He himself was badly wounded and taken into the English camp. His men fled. Johnson failed to exploit this success. Governor Shirley told him repeatedly to advance to Ticonderoga and secure it, but he replied that he could not move. Sickness, bad food, inadequate clothing and a complete lack of military discipline had brought his men to the brink of mutiny. He stayed where he was until the end of November, spending the time in rebuilding Fort George which he renamed Fort William Henry. He then withdrew to the Hudson. For his victory over Dieskau the British Parliament voted him the sum of £5,000 and George II rewarded him with a baronetcy, even though his expedition had failed to achieve its object. He had set out to take Crown Point and it was still firmly in the hands of the French.

Governor Shirley of Massachusetts decided that he personally would lead the undertaking against Niagara. He had planned in meticulous detail the campaign in which Louisbourg had been captured, but that had been only a plan; he now had a chance to put his military theories into practice. Like Johnson, he started from the town of Albany. His force consisted of his and Pepperrell's regiments and a regiment of militia from New Jersey—the Assembly of that colony apparently being prepared to co-operate with Massachusetts if not with Virginia. The men of the 51st and 52nd Foot wore the King's uniform and were part of the British Army though they were still raw Provincial recruits. This was probably no real drawback, for lacking the drill and discipline which were likely to make them a sitting target in forest warfare they could probably give a better account of themselves than Braddock's unfortunate regular soldiers on the Monongahela.

This force of 2,500 men started off up the Mohawk river in boats as far as the Great Carrying Place (where the city of Rome now stands). Thence the boats were drawn on sledges to a small creek which ran into Lake Oneida and from there they paddled downstream to Fort Oswego on the shore of Lake Ontario. Shirley and his troops arrived at Oswego long before his supplies and so there was a delay in which he could do nothing and there was not very much to eat. While he was waiting he discovered that the French knew all about his plans and had put strong reinforcements into Forts Niagara and Frontenac. A glance at the map showed him that unless he now changed his plan and took Fort Frontenac first, as soon as he left Oswego to move against Niagara the French could come across the lake behind him, take Oswego and cut him off from his base. Already running short of food although his rations had come up, Shirley had not the means to cope with this problem. He garrisoned Fort Oswego with 700 men in October 1755 and went back by the way he had come.

The only success in the great strategic plan for 1755 was gained by Colonel Moncton. On 1 June, with a force of 2,000 New England volunteers, he had anchored in the bay opposite Fort Beauséjour and after a siege lasting only two weeks its governor surrendered. This removed Acadia from the sphere of active operations.

Apart from the setback in Acadia, the French had had a good year. The reinforcements which Boscawen had been unable to intercept had put New France out of any real danger from the forces available to the English in America. The vital French outposts on the Great Lakes were secure, so were the communications to Louisiana, and the English had been driven out of the Ohio valley. Furthermore, in that area the French had gone over to the offensive. When the remnants of Braddock's force had left the frontier it had been followed up by war-party after war-party of Indians, many of them led by the French, flooding across the border into Virginia, Maryland and Pennsylvania bringing fire and slaughter to countless outlying settlements. Washington, commanding 1,500 of the Virginia

Militia, did everything he could to protect 300 miles of frontier, but the task was hopelessly beyond him, or anyone else. The extraordinary thing was that the Assembly of Pennsylvania not only refused to give him any reinforcements but paid no attention to the desperate appeals from their own settlers for arms and ammunition. They would not even consider legislation which would have set up some sort of defence organization. Apparently the only fighting in which the members were interested was between them and the Governor, and not until enemy raids had penetrated within sixty miles of Philadelphia did they grudgingly give him powers to check the Indian invasion. It was a ridiculous and a very dangerous situation. The French, noting the dissension, began to consider seriously the possibility of exploiting the impoverished element of the German and Irish settlers and recruiting them into the French service. In fact a start must have been made because in the campaign of 1759 Jeffery Amherst was surprised by the number of Germans serving in French regiments in Canada.

Although much blood had been shed in 1755 there was no declaration of war until the following year, and though not quite so disastrous, the year 1756 brought little improvement in the fortunes of the English in North America. On the western frontier the Indian raids and massacres continued unchecked, and the only way to put an end to persecution now becoming intolerable was to take Fort Duquesne, but the Pennsylvania pacifists refused to vote any money, and the Virginians, who reckoned they had already done enough, felt they could do no more. Only in New England was there still a healthy fighting spirit, fostered by Shirley who was quite undeterred by the disappointments of the previous year and busy with plans for operations against Frontenac, Niagara and Crown Point.

In June 1756 the 35th Foot and 42nd Highlanders disembarked in New York, and on 23 July Lord Loudoun arrived to fill the post of Commander-in-Chief. He found that the orders given to him in London were much the same as the plans Shirley had been working on independently. In fact Shirley, taking advantage of the lessons he had learned about supply in the previous year, had already arranged for stores to be dumped along the route to Fort Oswego and at Forts Edward and

William Henry. He had gone even further and earmarked troops for each enterprise.

For some reason or other Loudoun took an instant dislike to Governor Shirley and made no attempt to hide his contempt for him as a soldier, as an administrator and as an American. His antipathy was increased by the discovery that the allocation of money for military purposes had been spent, without very much to show for it; that Oswego—according to an engineer's report—was indefensible, and as a result of the indiscipline, inefficiency and generally filthy conditions in Fort William Henry, men were dying there at a rate of thirty a week. The Commander-in-Chief abandoned the Niagara project and turned his attention to Ticonderoga and Crown Point.

The French, encouraged by their progress in the previous year, were not sitting idle and waiting to be attacked. In May, two months before Loudoun reached America, Louis XV had sent out to Canada a number of veteran regiments and a new commander, Louis de St Veran, marquis de Montcalm, a soldier of forty-four who had already made a name for himself in Italy and Bohemia. On his staff were men who were to become familiar names in French history: de Lévis, Bougainville and Bourlamaque, a formidable team.

In August, reports reached Loudoun of a possible French attack on Oswego, so he sent Colonel Webb and the 44th Foot to reinforce it. He was not aware that on 9 August Montcalm had swept down on the fort with a force of 3,000 men, hammered it with his guns for three days and forced it to surrender. Webb heard about this when he got to the Great Carrying Place, and he also heard that the French were advancing upon New York. In some panic he burnt the small post at the Great Carrying Place and withdrew at full speed down the Mohawk river.

Montcalm destroyed Oswego and, with the 700 prisoners he had taken, retired to Ticonderoga. Here he deployed 5,000 men in a defensive position from which Loudoun, with the force at his disposal, could not hope to dislodge them. Loudoun therefore cancelled all plans for offensive operations and did no more than improve the defences of Fort Edward. In every way he was an unfortunate choice for the command he had been given. He inspired neither respect nor confidence; impatient, arrogant, rude and incapable of conciliation he could not even balance the defects in his character with a reasonable competence. He was in no position to despise or criticize the energetic Shirley. The only result of his first campaign was the loss of Oswego, the vital base for severing the encroaching chain of French posts and the only link between the English colonies and the immense Indian trade spreading out into the far west.

By the end of 1756 the French had once again improved their position while the English were at an even greater disadvantage. For the colonists on the Atlantic seaboard the outlook was indeed bleak.

9 The Turning of the Tide

In Europe the constantly changing pattern of political events had for a time concealed the embers of war which had been smouldering since the Treaty of Aix-la-Chapelle. During the War of the Austrian Succession the Empress Maria Theresa had made two attempts to recover lands taken from her by Prussia, and now, having won new support among the nations of Europe, she felt the time had come to try again.

Early in 1756 Newcastle had gained one major diplomatic success. He managed to keep Spain out of the trouble everyone knew was coming, and he had preserved his King's beloved Hanover by the Convention of Westminster, in January, under which Frederick the Great guaranteed its neutrality. With the Dutch, Newcastle made no progress, for they declined to 'come to assistance' under the terms of the defence treaty. This was serious because France had now decided that covert hostilities in North America and India had been going on for long enough. If war was as inevitable as everyone said it was it would be far better to bring it all out into the open, co-ordinate the national resources and those of her allies, and destroy England once and for all.

As soon as Louis XV took this decision Newcastle lost all control of what was in any case a very slippery situation. His incompetence gave rise to a strong movement against him and a series of misfortunes began.

The French had for some time been preparing for the war which was formally declared in May 1756, and their obvious target, one which would have the most effect on George II, if not on his subjects, was Hanover. For the moment, owing to the King of Prussia's guarantee, any attack in this direction had to be postponed, and so the activity at Toulon and Dunkirk, part of the general preparations, was intensified. It soon became known that the first two items on the French programme for the war

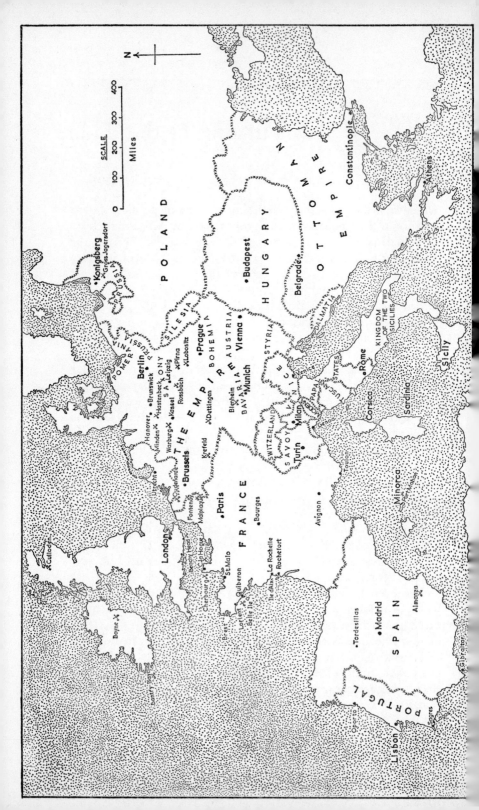

were an invasion of England and the capture of Minorca. This news was followed by information that 50,000 troops of the formidable French army were concentrated in the Channel ports —and this was only the first wave. Since the total strength of the British army, at home and abroad, was only 35,000, this caused a panic in London. However, the French realized, not for the first or the last time, that it was impossible to ferry an invasion force across the Channel without at least temporary command of the sea in the area of operations. France was a great military power but Great Britain was supreme at sea, and showed no sign of relinquishing that supremacy. Although, as always, the British navy and army had been dangerously neglected in the years of so-called peace, the French navy could not guarantee a safe passage for troop transports across the Channel. So the invasion of England had to be postponed too, for the time being.

As early as January 1756 intelligence reports received by Newcastle had given the most probable destination of the enemy fleet fitting out in Toulon, but it was not until 7 April that a fleet of ten ships, undermanned and ill-found, was sent to the Mediterranean under the command of Admiral John Byng. On the day after Byng had sailed from Portsmouth twelve French warships, commanded by Admiral de la Galissonière, recently returned from Canada, put out from Toulon with a convoy of transports carrying 16,000 troops led by the duc de Richelieu. This imposing armament anchored off the port of Ciudadela on the north-west end of Minorca on 18 April.

Warning of the impending attack had reached the Governor of Minorca, General Blakeney, about two days previously, but neither he nor his garrison were really in any condition to withstand the rigours of blockade and siege. The General was an experienced but somewhat elderly soldier, being over eighty. His resources amounted to four infantry regiments and a number of marines provided by Commodore Edgcumbe, whose squadron, far too weak to tackle the French invasion fleet, was lying off Port Mahon. This force, amounting to about 2,800 men, was unusually short of officers. The Lieutenant-Governor of the island, the Governor of Fort St Philip, the colonels of all four regiments and twenty-nine regimental officers were all absent for one reason or another. To add to his troubles, poor old Blakeney was crippled with gout.

193

Richelieu disembarked his troops on the day of arrival, 18 April, and Blakeney, unable to do anything to stop the French marching across the island, concentrated all his men in Fort St Philip, a large and elaborate fortress commanding the town and harbour of Mahon. Built to a design by Vauban it was one of the strongest in Europe, and had the advantage of large numbers of passages and galleries cut in the rock which protected the defenders as well as giving them mobility. Richelieu moved into Mahon on 19 April and began the siege. He was not an outstandingly competent commander, the fortress was defended with great spirit and progress against it was very slow. Not until 8 May did the besiegers' batteries begin to have any effect against the massive walls.

During this time Richelieu became very bored. He had only two real interests in life—women and food. In the occupied town of Mahon there were no women considered suitable for the duke's bed and so he had to be content with the pleasures of the table, but these were limited. His cook could find no butter or cream on the island and so, out of sheer necessity, he had to invent a new sauce using only eggs and oil. He called it Mahonaise.

Admiral Byng arrived at Gibraltar at the beginning of May. He carried the 7th Fusiliers as a reinforcement for Minorca and had orders to collect another battalion from General Fowke, commanding the Rock. Fowke had hardly enough men to find the normal guard duties, let alone defend Gibraltar against an assault which might be made at any time, and only with reluctance did he provide 250 men to replace the marines loaned by Commodore Edgcumbe to the Minorca garrison. Even Byng's fleet had so few men that he was forced to use the 7th Fusiliers as sailors. The shameful neglect of the fleet and the Mediterranean garrisons had become very evident. Blakeney had only just enough men to man the walls of Fort St Philip and dared not risk a sally against Richelieu.

On 19 May Byng arrived off Port Mahon and fought an indecisive action against la Galissonière. He then withdrew, basing his decision for this step subsequently so disastrous to the garrison of Minorca and himself, on what appeared to him to be two obvious facts. The strength of the enemy at Minorca was such that he could not save the place and Gibraltar was now so vulnerable it was his duty to reinforce General Fowke.

At his departure the defenders of Fort St Philip were greatly disheartened and the French much relieved. Byng's mere presence off the island could have made it very difficult for them to bring in supplies and more troops. Despite their depression the besieged troops continued to defend themselves with skill and determination, and Richelieu began to think there might be some truth in the story that the fortress was impregnable. Six more regiments were sent to him, new batteries were built and on 6 June one hundred guns and mortars put down a concentration of fire which made a large breach. The British repaired it and served their guns so well that Richelieu made no attempt to storm. Three days later the French opened an even more vigorous fire which caused two more breaches. On 14 June the garrison made a bold sortie, drove the French from several of their batteries with the bayonet and spiked the guns. In the euphoria of victory they pursued the enemy artillerymen too far. Suddenly surrounded, every man of this gallant little force was captured.

Not until 27 June did Richelieu decide to assault, and he attacked several different places simultaneously during the night. The valour and resolution of the defence surprised him, and though three bastions of the outworks were taken he did not gain his objective. His casualties were heavy. At one point the British fired a well-sited mine and blew three companies of French Grenadiers to bits. Blakeney, counting the cost of the defence, found he had not enough gunners left to work the guns, and on 28 June he capitulated with the honours of war. He and his troops were taken to Gibraltar. In the seventy days' siege Richelieu had lost nearly 2,000 men—French accounts give the figure as less than 600—whereas Blakeney's casualties were in the region of 400 killed and wounded.

The loss of Minorca—which brought no discredit on the regiments which had fought to defend it against great odds and without hope of relief—was directly attributable to Newcastle and his government. In spite of constant warnings and a developing situation which no one in their senses could misinterpret, they had neglected to make even the most obvious preparations. Nothing had been done about the Royal

Navy, on which all depended, and the Mediterranean garrisons had not been reinforced.

The news reached London on 14 July. The outcry was savage and spontaneous, and as usual the politicians who were really responsible outdid all in their furious demands for punishment of the 'guilty'. Newcastle, who could see all too clearly that this would bring down his government unless the blame could be transferred effectively, was determined to find a scapegoat. Every sort of bitter, cruel and vindictive attack was made against the service commanders involved. General Fowke was court martialled for refusing to send the battalion he had not got, and though found guilty only of an error of judgment and suspended for a year, he was dismissed the service by George II personally. Even old Blakeney, who had not taken his clothes off or gone properly to bed for ten weeks during the siege, was attacked in the press and accused of everything from incompetence to cowardice. Happily, when the real facts appeared through the fog of malice and anger, he was rightly lauded as a hero and elevated to the Irish peerage. In Admiral Byng, Newcastle saw the scapegoat he needed. Byng was tried by court martial, and although his personal courage was vindicated he was found guilty—with the court's unanimous recommendation for mercy—of 'failing to do his utmost against the enemy'. Pitt braved the storm of public opinion and tried to save him. Even the duc de Richelieu made a chivalrous appeal from Paris on his behalf, though this may have done more harm than good. As is so well known, Byng was executed by a firing squad of marines on the deck of his flagship in Portsmouth harbour, and almost as well known are the words of Voltaire in his satire *Candide*: 'Dans ce pays-ci il est bon de tuer de temps en temps un amiral pour encourager les autres.' Fortescue's comment is perhaps more accurate: 'the unfortunate Admiral was shot because Newcastle deserved to be hanged'.

Newcastle had saved himself and his incapable administration from one storm only to find himself in a deluge of disaster. There seemed to be bad news with every dispatch: Braddock's defeat and death at the Monongahela, Boscawen's failure to intercept the French reinforcements for Canada, Governor Shirley's withdrawal from the Lakes and then the loss of Oswego, and all the time, over all Britain hung the threat of invasion.

No one had any confidence in the government or in the ability of the armed services to protect either the country or its colonial possessions.

In Europe the efforts Newcastle had made to protect Hanover with Frederick's guarantee seemed to have been wasted. France, Austria, Saxony, Russia and Sweden had formed a League to crush Frederick the Great and partition Prussia. Far from being able to defend Hanover, Frederick would be hard put to it to defend himself. This rather strange coalition which seemed to ignore bitter enmities of the past had come about for a variety of reasons. France had come into it from the most trivial of causes: Madame de Pompadour, all-powerful at Versailles, hated Frederick for three reasons. She had sent him a friendly message, couched in the terms of one Head of State to another, and he had rejected it on the ground that he did not really wish to correspond with a French courtesan; he was wont to refer to her as *Fräulein Fisch*, which was not un-reasonable because her name, underneath the titles, was Mademoiselle Poisson; and he had given the name Pompadour to one of his bitches. France was to stake everything to soothe the pique of the King's mistress. In Russia, Catherine the Great was also smarting under one of Frederick's waspish epigrams; Maria Theresa of Austria was determined to recover Silesia, and she had brought Saxony in with promises of a share in defeated Prussia. Sweden had hopes of acquiring Pomerania.

Frederick did not wait for his enemies to unite and fall upon him. He applied through diplomatic channels for permission to march his troops through Saxony so that they could protect Hanover. It was refused, as he knew it would be, and so in September 1756 he launched the Prussian war machine and made himself master of Saxony by the battles of Pirna in September and Lobositz in October. He went on to invade Bohemia, and this Prussian involvement in Bohemia and Silesia left Hanover open to attack.

In the autumn of 1756 it seemed, to the rest of Europe, that England's star was setting. France was triumphant in North America, Minorca had gone, the Royal Navy was apparently no longer the bulwark of the nation, and in the tense atmosphere of permanent crisis the Duke of Newcastle, whose considered opinion was usually that of the last person to whom he had spoken, was useless. Unable to make a firm decision, fearful, irresolute, treating every breath of rumour as fact, he was in reality the fruit of seventy years of political corruption. George II, now seventy-three, shocked by the collision of events, was no help to him. Obsessed with Hanover, the King left Britain to look after herself. Yet in all the gloom and dismay of this supreme national crisis there was one light. The incorruptible William Pitt, heartily disliked by the King for his outspoken views on the differences to the people of Britain between the defence of Hanover and the defence of their own country, the remorseless critic of Newcastle, was perfectly convinced in his own mind that he, and only he, could save his country.

Eventually, as the autumn of 1756 turned into winter, the massive opposition to Newcastle's administration could no longer be held in check and, as Fortescue says, 'in November the shifty old jobber himself, after endless intrigues to retain office, reluctantly and ungracefully made way, nominally for the Duke of Devonshire, but in reality for William Pitt'.

Pitt took an uncomplicated view of the task facing his country. In him the centuries-old struggle against France, and all the varied and diverse causes and animosities which had fuelled the fires of enmity, had coalesced into a simple creed: France was the challenger of his country's supremacy, France must therefore be destroyed. He had no political axe to grind, no commercial ends to serve, no personal interest in trading ventures or public funds. He was, in simple terms, a patriot, and it was the very simplicity of his creed which lifted him so far above comtemporary politicians and endowed him with such clarity of purpose. On 15 November he was appointed Secretary of State, the equivalent of Premier, although on paper, as First Lord of the Treasury, the Duke of Devonshire was senior to him.

This recognition was a natural consequence of his efforts throughout the year. He had never ceased to hammer home the same points. The war was being fought for sea power and for America. Britain must spend her money on her fleet and her army in her colonies, even if, temporarily, Hanover was submerged in the tide of European war. For two years now his speeches had been upon this theme—to the embarrassment of the government and the fury of the King, who had dismissed him from the office of Paymaster, which had not carried a seat in the Cabinet.

Having attained high office on oft-repeated principles and policy he was not, for the moment, prepared to send troops to Europe, either to save Hanover or support Frederick. George II, slow to recognize genius, did not trust him, and there were other forces acting against him. He was the Great Commoner, not from the peerage but from the middle classes and representing them and their feelings. The great families of the aristocracy, which for generations had monopolized political power and at whose head was the Duke of Newcastle, trusted him even less than did the King. With a shrewd understanding of political tactics they made no attempt to oppose him, they simply refrained from supporting him and soon enough the blow fell, delivered not by the people but by the King.

In the spring of 1757 the Duke of Cumberland, 'Butcher' Cumberland to the Scots after Culloden Moor, before setting off to command the Hanoverian army against the French— whose army of 100,000 men had poured across the Rhine in March—told his father the King that Pitt could not be relied on over any aspect of Hanover, the country so dear to their hearts. It would be extremely unwise to depend on him for instructions and supplies, and if the needs of Hanover were to be sacrificed to those of Britain, any efforts Cumberland made were doomed to failure. George II reacted in the way his son hoped. On 6 April 1757 Pitt was dismissed. He had been in office for five months.

The value of the Funds (the stock of the National Debt, used for investment) fell sharply and there began what Walpole has described as 'the rain of golden boxes', practically all the principal towns sending Pitt the Freedom of their Corporations. The King called upon Newcastle to form a government. For eleven weeks, during the critical period of the campaigning season, the bargaining and negotiating went on, while the empire was without a government of any kind and the country shouted for Pitt. Since the only alternative was a complete national breakdown, George II had to give way, and on 27 July Pitt returned to office. In a compromise, Newcastle became the nominal head of the government and immersed himself in all the jobbery and patronage of internal politics.

Pitt, as Secretary of State for the southern department, was responsible for the armed forces, the colonies and foreign affairs. The northern secretaryship, dealing with the German powers, was filled by an inferior politician who did what Pitt told him to do. Anson went back to the Admiralty and Hardwicke became a general adviser.

With the country squarely behind him, Pitt was at last able to tackle its immense problems. 'I will borrow the Duke's majority,' he said, 'to carry on the Government. I am sure that I can save this country and that no one else can.'

This was the turning point of the war and of the battle for Empire.

There was much to be done. A great deal of valuable time had been lost during all the political wrangling and there was more bad news to add to Pitt's burdens. In North America the Earl of Loudoun had made plans for what he felt was the first step towards the conquest of Canada, the retaking of Louisbourg, which would open the way into the St Lawrence. With this intention he withdrew all the available troops from the frontier garrisons of New York and New England, then spent most of the summer drilling them and growing vegetables 'to keep the blood of the soldiers in good condition'. His soldiers, bored and discouraged by inactivity, complained that he would carry on the war with cabbages for cannon balls. Then he took them to Halifax at the beginning of July 1757 and not until he arrived there did he make any attempt to collect intelligence about Louisbourg, the object of his expedition. He discovered in due course that the French fleet in the harbour consisted of twenty-two ships of the line, that the garrison had been increased to 7,000 men, and in fact that the French naval and military strength was so much greater than his own that any assault he attempted would result in a far worse disaster than the Monongahela. He at once abandoned his plans and returned to New York.

In the meantime the stripping of the frontier posts had given Montcalm an opportunity he was quick to seize. By the end of July he had gathered 8,000 French troops, Canadians and Indians at Ticonderoga, and on 3 August this force laid siege to Fort William Henry at the southern end of Lake George. Bearing in mind Dieskau's defeat at the same place, Montcalm approached his task with caution. The fort, built of crossed logs forming walls packed with earth, roughly square, was fortified with bastions mounting a total of seventeen guns. The lake protected it on the north, there was a marsh to the east and the south and west sides were protected by *chevaux de frise*. The garrison, made up of regular troops, sailors, militia and mechanics under the command of a veteran Scot, Lieutenant-Colonel Monroe of the 35th Foot, amounted to 2,200 men.

On 4 August the besiegers started work on their trench system, and two days later the French batteries opened fire. The guns in the fort replied with speed and accuracy but the splintering of the wooden walls under the impact of heavy shot made it clear that without rapid relief the capture of the fort could only be a matter of time. Fourteen miles away General Webb was sitting in Fort Edward with 3,600 men, and Monroe sent an urgent appeal to him. Webb had already shown he was a coward by the way he scuttled back from the Great Carrying Place when he heard Montcalm had taken Oswego. He now provided further evidence by sending back a message to Monroe saying that it if was reinforcements Monroe wanted, he couldn't spare a man; and if Monroe was thinking that the whole garrison of Fort Edward ought to come up and fall upon Montcalm, the idea was ridiculous. He had good reason to believe that Montcalm had more than 12,000 men round Fort William Henry and it would be inviting suicide for his little garrison to attempt anything against such impossible odds.

Webb ended his letter with the advice that the most sensible thing Monroe could do would be to make the best terms he could. The messenger carrying the letter was intercepted by Montcalm's men. Montcalm read it and politely sent it on. Four days later, on 8 August, Monroe was in serious trouble. Three hundred of his men had been killed or wounded, all his guns except one or two light pieces had been knocked out and a fearful epidemic of smallpox had broken out in the fort. On the following day he surrendered.

He was given honourable terms for his capitulation and Montcalm undertook to protect the troops and families of the Fort William Henry garrison who were being allowed to join Webb at Fort Edward. Accordingly, the English laid down their arms, marched out of the ruined fort and set off through the woods. Montcalm's Indians, in a nasty mood because there had been so little plunder in the fort, were waiting for them and, as Roberts says, 'the wilderness became a shambles. The men were helpless having given up their arms to the victors. Women were snatched out of the ranks and scalped, children were dashed to pieces against the trees, the heads of men were split open with hatchets.' Unlike some of his countrymen in Canada, men like Baron St Castin, d'Iberville and du Vivier, Montcalm was no murderer. He and his officers did their best to stop the slaughter, 'some being wounded in the struggle with their butchering allies', but eighty of the English were killed and many others badly injured. It could have been just another Indian massacre, but the effect was far-reaching. Montcalm's inability to honour his undertaking in the surrender agreement not only destroyed all trust in him as a man of his word but aroused once more all the old bitterness, and this, in the end, was why the British insisted on the expulsion of all the French administration from Canada.

To Pitt, who really hated the French, the story of the broken pledge and the massacre merely confirmed his opinion of the nation as a whole, and he looked on the loss of the fort on Lake George as yet another serious setback for the British in North America.

The whole of the Hudson valley now lay open to Montcalm's victorious troops and there was nothing, militarily, to prevent a full-scale invasion of New York, but it was now, at the moment of crisis, that the essential difference between the English and French colonists proved to be so great an advantage to the English. Living primarily by hunting and fishing, the French produced barely enough food to feed themselves, and without additional supplies from France it was impossible for them to support all the regular troops who had recently arrived in Canada. Now, instead of being able to march through New England, Montcalm had to allow all his militia to return home for the harvest and so bring the campaign of 1757 to an end.

In Europe the Duke of Cumberland had demonstrated once again that he was not a great commander. While Frederick II (the Great) was fighting the Austrian armies in Bohemia, Cumberland organized a joint Anglo-Hanoverian army of

36,000 men to hold the line of the Weser against the threatened French invasion of Hanover. Louis XV sent Louis le Tellier, marquis de Courtanvaux (later duc d'Estrées) and 74,000 men to take the city of Hanover, and on 26 July 1757 the French vanguard came up to Cumberland's position at Hastenbeck, three miles to the south-east of Hameln. Both commanders seem to have lost control of the confused battle which followed and each thought he had been beaten. Victory, such as it was, was claimed by the French when Cumberland suddenly retreated to the Elbe. Six weeks later, on 5 September, Cumberland found that the authorities in Hanover had arranged for him to sign the Convention of Kloster-Zeven whereby he was bound to evacuate the country and leave Hanover and Westphalia in the hands of the French. Pitt repudiated the agreement, on the ground that Cumberland was not empowered to sign such a document, and George II relieved his son of his command. But the damage had been done. Frederick, defeated by the Austrians at Kolin on 18 June, had had to withdraw, and his western flank was now exposed to any further French advance. In July, while Frederick was still involved with the Austrians in the south and France in the west, a large Russian army under Marshal Count Stepan Apraksin crossed the eastern frontier of Prussia. General Hans von Lehwald and a Prussian force of 30,000 men tried to stop him and were overwhelmed at the battle of Gross Jägersdorf on 30 July. Just when it seemed that nothing could prevent Apraksin from crushing all Prussia by sheer weight of numbers, the traditional administrative inefficiency of the Russian War Office came to Frederick's rescue. Apraksin's whole supply system suddenly came to a halt, some of his regiments mutinied and he was forced to withdraw. This left Frederick free to concentrate on the far more serious menace in the south-west. In twelve days he marched 170 miles to confront a combined army of 30,000 French under the Prince de Soubise, and 11,000 Imperial troops led by the Prince of Saxe-Hildburghausen, at Rossbach, twenty-six miles to the south and west of Leipzig.

This was Frederick's greatest victory for he won it by sheer tactical skill with a force reduced by the long approach march to just under 21,000 men, and out-numbered by two to one. Frederick took up his position on the line of the Janus hills to the north-east of the village of Rossbach, and on 5 November the allied commanders decided that the easiest way to deal with him would be by a massive right hook against the Prussian left. Frederick, having divined their intention because it was what he would have done had he been in their position, pushed forward a covering screen across his front while his main body moved round, hidden by the high ground held by his screen, to meet the blow when it fell. The allied columns marching round to the right became disordered in trying to go too fast and suddenly were fired on by a concentration of Prussian artillery on the flank. Thrown into confusion by this unexpected pounding they were then charged by cavalry, with General Friedrich von Seydlitz galloping at the head of them. Following up the horsemen came seven battalions of the superb Prussian infantry, and in forty minutes it was all over. Soubise lost 7,500 men, most of them taken prisoner unwounded, and fled. For the loss of 600 casualties Frederick had removed, for the time being, the threat to his western borders. For the rest of the war his subordinate commander Ferdinand, Duke of Brunswick—one of the finest generals in military history—was made responsible for keeping the French in check.

During the autumn of this year (1757) Pitt did his best to relieve the pressure on Frederick and draw French troops away from Germany by launching a combined operation against Rochefort in the Bay of Biscay. On 8 September a fleet of sixteen warships commanded by Admiral Sir Edward Hawke, convoying transports in which there were ten excellent battalions of infantry, sailed from Portsmouth, and after some delay caused by flat calms and contrary winds dropped anchor in Basque Roads on the 23rd. On the same day the fortifications of the little Île d'Aix, built during the reign of Louis XIV to defend the mouth of the Charente and the approach to Rochefort, were reduced to rubble by the guns of the fleet, and the island was captured. It was then discovered that the French were fully prepared for an attack on Rochefort and that there was no hope of taking it by escalade. After a certain amount of rather acrimonious argument between Hawke and General Sir John Mordaunt, commander of the land forces, nothing more was done, and to the anger and shame of the ordinary sailors and soldiers, the whole fleet returned to England.

Mordaunt was tried by court martial and honourably acquitted; he had been suspected of trying to damage Pitt by making the expedition look ridiculous. But among his subordinate officers were men of outstanding ability—Wolfe, Conway and Cornwallis, for example—and it became clear that the army officers, most of whom had been against the project from the start because so little was known about Rochefort, had had their original doubts confirmed. Strangely enough it was Wolfe, always an aggressive commander, who wanted to attack, and this first brought him to Pitt's notice. The rest of the officers could see no point whatsoever in throwing away the lives of trained soldiers, of whom at this stage in the war there were all too few, in an operation which could not achieve anything. Least of all would it draw troops away from Central Europe. The fault for this minor fiasco really lay with Pitt, who obviously wanted to end the long series of disasters with a gesture which would restore the nation's morale. Fortunately England possessed generals who were not prepared to risk the country's slender resources on what might easily have turned out to be another calamity.

In India, after the departure of Dupleix in September 1754, the focus of events moved from the Carnatic north-east to Bengal. Here, all through the bitter struggle between Madras and Pondicherry which had been going on for ten years, the trading stations of France based on Chandernagore and those of England based on Calcutta, had carried on their business in an untroubled state of peace and prosperity. This was because, unlike the situation in southern India, the Nawab of Bengal, Alivardi Khan, was a strong ruler who would not tolerate the squabbling of Europeans in his territories. As his name indicates, he was one of the Pathans from the North-West Frontier who had come down from the hills to make his own kingdom out of some of the pieces of the Mogul empire, and during his rule, which had begun in 1742, there was no question of any European interference in local politics. Towards the end of his life he became concerned about the extent to which European influence was growing in his province, and he was aware that the long-standing privilege of tax-free trading, granted to the East India Company (British), was being abused. Natives were

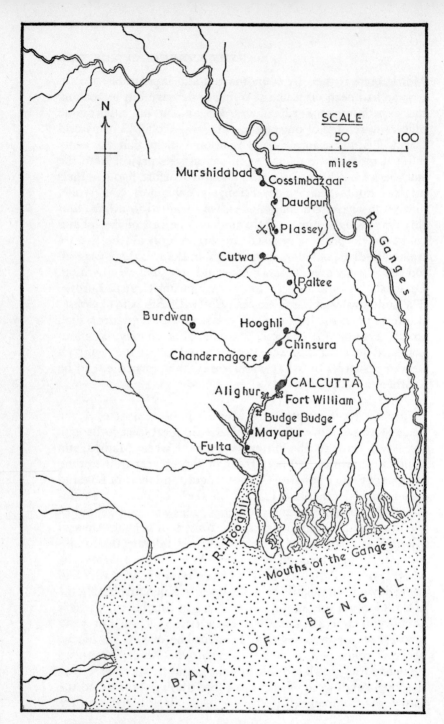

Sketch Map of the Bengal Area of Operations

trading under passes issued by the company, and the Nawab's revenues suffered accordingly. He had also been perturbed by news from the Carnatic which indicated clearly enough that the native rulers in that area were being reduced to the status of mere pawns on the chess board of Anglo-French commercial politics, and when he heard that the English were rebuilding the fortifications of Calcutta he might well have been apprehensive in case the same thing happened to him.

These were all new problems, and as he felt too old to cope with them he left them to his successor, his nephew Surajah Dowlah.

Alivardi Khan died in 1756, just at the time when the English in Calcutta, having heard rumours of impending war with France, were making belated attempts to defend themselves against a seaborne attack by the French. Surajah Dowlah was suspicious, and he sent his representative to find out what was going on. He was told the works were purely defensive and that all the new batteries were on the river frontage. This did nothing to calm the new Nawab who was now convinced that the English intended to take over his province in the same way as they had acquired the Carnatic. He wrote to the merchants of Calcutta stating categorically, 'if they do not fill up their ditch and raze their fortifications I will expel them totally out of my country'.

He sent a similar directive to the French at Chandernagore but they were far more skilful than the English at producing a soothing reply. The English, unwisely, paid no attention and to save his face Surajah Dowlah had to take action. Collecting a large army he first surrounded the small English factory at Cossimbazaar which was in no condition to offer any resistance. Having for years been protected against any military threat by the firm rule of Alivardi Khan, the English and French in Bengal had concentrated entirely upon their commercial affairs and neither were in any state to go to war. Accepting the surrender of Cossimbazaar on 9 May 1756, Surajah Dowlah then marched on Calcutta and discovered for himself that the merchants had spoken the truth. The walls on the landward side were in ruins and the fire of any guns that could be mounted on them was obstructed by buildings. He sent in his first attack on 18 June and was beaten back by the gallant defenders. On the following day his troops, who were not interested in military ethics, penetrated the defences under a flag of truce and captured the principal batteries. While this was going on the Governor decided to embark the women and children on ships in the Hooghli. Haste and disorganization led to panic and a rush to escape. The Governor, who hitherto had shown great firmness and courage, particularly when exposed to the fire of the enemy, yielded to a momentary fear and embarked with the rest. For three days the small party of soldiers and civilians left behind fought on behind broken walls against overwhelming odds. 'The men who did the fighting,' wrote Sir George Forrest, 'showed at the siege of Calcutta English courage at its very best.'

At length the garrison was forced to surrender, and the story of what followed is perhaps one of the best known incidents in the history of British India before the Mutiny. John Zephaniah Holwell, the leader, and 145 other Europeans were confined in a guard-house, in a room hardly twenty feet square intended for two or three prisoners. There were only two small windows. In the unbearable heat and humidity of a 'hot weather' night everyone except Holwell and twenty-three others died of suffocation in what became known as the Black Hole of Calcutta. Surajah Dowlah was not personally responsible, but he expressed no regret and made no attempt to punish the subordinate who was. With his Oriental attitude to life and death it probably never occurred to him that anything particularly unpleasant had happened, nor did he realize he had provided the English with a motive for revenge. He looted the city, installed a garrison of 3,000 men and on 2 July departed with his army for his capital at Murshidabad. On the way home he demanded large sums from the French factory at Chandernagore and the Dutch at Chinsura as the price of their immunity.

From his point of view he had dealt very satisfactorily with the merchants of Calcutta and had shown the French and the Dutch that he was master in his own country. He had kept his word, saved his face, expelled the English and, as he thought, solved all the problems his uncle had failed to tackle.

Clive had gone to England in 1753 because of bad health and he did not return to India until late in 1755. He was now a lieutenant-colonel in the East India Company's army and a Member of the Council of Madras. When he came back he went first to Bombay which was to be the base for operations against Bussy, still in control of most of the Deccan. He found that the company had a more pressing problem, and for the next few months, working in close co-operation with Admiral Watson, he attacked and destroyed the strongholds of pirates, and put an end to a menace which had seriously interfered with trade on the Malabar Coast. Clive then went to Madras, took his seat on the Council and soon afterwards was appointed Governor of Fort St David.

News of the fall of Calcutta reached Madras in August 1756 and in a prolonged session the Council debated what action should be taken. Many of the members argued that the real threat to British interests in India was not Surajah Dowlah, whose influence was confined to the eastern districts of Bengal, Orissa and Bihar, but Bussy in the Deccan. For the last five years he had, to all intents and purposes, been the viceroy of the huge province, ruling through the puppet Salabad Jang, and recently there had been a plan to send a British force to support the leader of the Mahrattas, Balaji Rao, who was at war with Salabad. The idea was that the defeat of Salabad by the Mahrattas, assisted by the British, would establish British influence in the court of the Deccan, to the discomfiture of Bussy. Like all Oriental intrigues it was elaborate and largely dependent on imponderables, and no doubt full of hidden snags. Fortunately for the plotters in Madras, before it could be set in motion, a parallel, far more local intrigue achieved almost the same result. Salabad was prevailed upon by conspirators in his own court to dismiss Bussy—whose finances had improved considerably during his stay—and get all the French troops out of Aurungabad.

Bussy still had his army, and his reputation as a soldier was equal to the renown he had gained for skill in coping with conspiracies. His enemies at Aurungabad were well aware it would not be easy to remove him, and when he was dismissed in May 1756 they asked the company at Madras for a British force to help them expel him. The request had been received with gratification, and a force of 1,800 men was nearly ready to set off when the fall of Calcutta became known.

This raised the immediate question of whether or not to deal with Bussy while there was still time; and Bussy was not the only problem. At any moment there might be another formal declaration of war between England and France (news of the actual declaration in May 1756 did not reach India until December of that year) and the English possessions in the south of India would probably need every available man to hold off attacks by Bussy, coming from the interior, and the large French expedition which, according to various reports, was being assembled at Brest with the Carnatic as its objective.

These somewhat parochial views did not prevail and it was decided to send every ship and man that could be spared to recover Calcutta. Clive was given a force of 900 Europeans (of which 250 were of the 39th Foot) and 1,500 sepoys. His mission was to take Calcutta and obtain reparations for all losses and the restitution of all former privileges. In command status he was junior to Admiral Watson whose squadron of four warships was to escort the troop transports and take an active part in the operations.

Although the expedition sailed on 15 October from Madras it was delayed by foul winds and it was not until 29 December, in the middle of the cold weather, that the fleet dropped anchor off Mayapur in the Hooghli river. This anchorage was about two miles below the fort at Budge-Budge, to the south-west of Calcutta. Watson could not pass the fort until it had been taken and he was reluctant to make any attempt against it from the river, so the troops were disembarked in order to approach and storm it from the landward side. In their camp on the first night they were attacked by Mohnichand, one of Surajah Dowlah's officers who had been made Governor of Calcutta, and because Clive had failed to post sentries there was very nearly a panic among the men rudely awakened from sleep by the enemy. Clive, as imperturbable as ever, rallied his men, organized a counter-attack, brought his guns into action and formed his line for a general advance—all in the dark. Just at that moment a cannon shot grazed Mohnichand's *pagri* (turban) and he at once gave the order to retreat.

H.M.S. *Kent* then sailed up the river and silenced the guns of the fort. On the next night a drunken sailor wandering about, no doubt hoping to find a woman, stumbled into the fort and found it had been abandoned by the enemy. On 31 December the fleet moved on up the river to Alighur where Clive again disembarked to attack Calcutta. To cover his movements the ships bombarded Fort William, and Surajah Dowlah's troops fled from the city and the fort before Clive could reach either. The fort was occupied by a detachment of the 39th Foot under the command of Captain Eyre Coote. Following up these rapid gains Clive determined to recover the town of Hooghli, where there had been a British factory, before Surajah Dowlah could advance upon it from Murshidabad. It was stormed and taken by the 39th Foot and a detachment of sepoys with the loss of a few men wounded, on 12 January 1757.

Meanwhile the news that Britain and France were at war had been received by Clive and Watson in Calcutta, and their immediate concern was that the French troops at Chandernagore—about 300 Europeans and a train of artillery—might join Surajah Dowlah's army and add considerably to the problem of re-establishing the British East India Company in Bengal. The Nawab had collected 40,000 men and was advancing steadily on Calcutta. His advanced guard was first seen by the sentries on the walls on 2 February but the French made no attempt to join him. On the contrary, there was some talk by them about Anglo-French neutrality, as in former wars, but this came to nothing, for one good reason. When Surajah Dowlah had threatened Calcutta in the previous June the British Governor made frantic appeals for help to the French and the Dutch. The Dutch said they could not, and the French with calculated rudeness said they would not. Clive was not prepared to make any 'arrangements' with the enemies of his country.

On 3 February the Nawab's army moved into camp under the walls of Calcutta, along the line of an entrenchment known as the Mahratta Ditch. Clive attacked at first light on the following day, but as the light grew stronger everything was obscured by a thick fog. In the fearful muddle which ensued, Clive's troops found themselves under fire from their own artillery and surrounded on the other three sides by enemy cavalry. With difficulty, and great skill, Clive extricated his force and withdrew. He had lost 100 Europeans and fifty sepoys, killed and wounded, for no apparent gain; indeed, his men were open in their complaints of his rashness. They, however, were only temporarily discouraged; the effect on Surajah Dowlah was far more profound. His losses were 600 men and 500 horses, he had advanced confidently to expel the English once again and instead of winning an easy victory he had been given a most unpleasant surprise. He made proposals for peace.

Clive was relieved, but cautious. He was worried about the defencelessness of Madras and the need to deal with the French in Chandernagore before they could make the Nawab change his mind. Five days later, on 9 February, he agreed to a treaty and thereby gained all the objectives of his mission except compensation for the losses of individuals when Calcutta had been sacked. Having thus, as he hoped, disposed of Surajah Dowlah, Clive resolved to attack the French in Chandernagore, despite the insistence of the Nawab that he should do nothing of the sort. With a reinforcement of more artillery and three infantry companies from Bombay he began to advance up the river on 7 March, moving as rapidly as possible because there were reports that Bussy was on his way from the Deccan to help the garrison in Chandernagore. The siege began on 14 March and though the small garrison put up a desperate fight the place was taken. Surajah Dowlah was furious at this deliberate disregard of his authority but the threat of Afghan invaders on his vulnerable north-western border was giving him much concern and he did not feel strong enough to tear up the treaty and fight the English. He got in touch with Bussy, he made overtures to the Mahrattas, sometimes he threatened the English, sometimes he apologized; it became obvious to Clive and Watson that he was totally unreliable and would snatch the first opportunity to go back on all his undertakings. In these circumstances there could be no question of returning to Madras for the time being and it seemed probable that the force needed for the defence of the Carnatic might have to remain in Bengal indefinitely.

Then, without any warning an apparent solution to the whole problem appeared from an unexpected source. The lesser nobility at Surajah Dowlah's court decided they could no longer tolerate a Nawab whose debauchery, cruelty and rapaciousness were setting new standards even for Oriental despots. The conspirators made covert approaches to the British commanders in Calcutta suggesting they might like to join in a plot to overthrow Surajah Dowlah and replace him by his Commander-in-Chief, Mir Jaffir, now one of the ringleaders in the scheme. The complicated negotiations which followed are remarkable chiefly for the stain they have left on the character of Clive, although the exact truth will probably never be known.

The go-between, acting as the contact-man between the conspirators at Surajah Dowlah's court and the British in Calcutta, was a shifty character named Ormichand who, when all seemed to be going well, suddenly demanded the sum of about £1 million, to be provided from the Bengal treasury when it came into Mir Jaffir's hands, or he would reveal the whole plot to Surajah Dowlah and arrange for the murder of the English envoys at his court. Clive, so the story goes, arranged for two versions of the proposed agreement with Mir Jaffir to be drawn up. The genuine one made no mention of Ormichand's 'reward', the other, which was to be disclaimed as a forgery when Surajah Dowlah had been overthrown, referred to it in a special clause. Ormichand, shown only the false agreement, on which some of the signatures were certainly forgeries (that of Admiral Watson in particular, who would have nothing to do with the counterfeit document), was satisfied.

On 4 June Mir Jaffir signed the genuine agreement under which the British promised to place him on the throne of Bengal, Orissa and Bihar, and in return he undertook to make over to them all the French factories in those provinces, make a grant of land surrounding Calcutta and provide compensation for the losses of individuals when Surajah Dowlah sacked the city. The situation then began to develop all the complexities inherent in Oriental intrigue, since there was always a tendency for those involved to play both ends against the middle. Mir Jaffir began to waver, and details of the conspiracy began to leak out. Surajah Dowlah, realizing something was in the wind, first sent his emissaries to negotiate with his former subordinate and then went himself, begging abjectly for a settlement of any differences. Mir Jaffir submitted and both swore friendship on the Koran.

In the meantime, having a very shrewd idea of what was going on, Clive decided that the only way to hold Mir Jaffir to his agreement was by taking immediate action. On 13 June 1757 he led his troops out of Chandernagore and set off for Murshidabad. On the next day he sent a letter to Surajah Dowlah which was tantamount to a declaration of war. Surajah Dowlah, vastly reassured by his reconciliation with Mir Jaffir, replied defiantly and ordered his army to assemble at the little mud-hutted village of Plassey, some twelve miles south of Murshidabad.

Clive's force, consisting of 900 Europeans, 200 half-caste Portuguese, 2,100 sepoys and ten guns, arrived at Paltee, on the Cossimbazaar river near its junction with the Jelingir, on 16 June. Here it halted, and Clive sent Major Eyre Coote forward with a detachment of the 39th Foot to seize the fort at Cutwa, twelve miles upstream. Although the garrison commander was one of the Mir Jaffir faction in the conspiracy he refused Coote's invitation to surrender, but withdrew, setting fire to the fort, as soon as Coote deployed his troops for an attack. The whole force camped that night on the Cutwa Plain. Clive, disturbed by the behaviour of the commander of the fort, was made even more uneasy by a vague message from Mir Jaffir saying that though he personally had been reconciled to the Nawab he had every intention of meeting his obligations under the treaty he had signed.

On 20 June further messages arrived from Mir Jaffir professing loyalty to the British but implying that he would not be able to give much active assistance in the battle which was likely to be fought. With these messages was a note from one of Clive's agents indicating that Mir Jaffir could not be trusted. All this was very disquieting. Clive called a Council of War, put the facts to the twenty officers who assembled and asked for their opinion whether it would be better to cross the river and attack the Nawab's army, or to remain at Cutwa until the end of the monsoon and send to the Mahrattas for help. Thirteen voted to remain at Cutwa, Coote and six others voted for immediate attack or return to Calcutta. Clive went away by himself to the river bank, thought it all over, and when he returned he gave orders for the crossing of the river on the following day.

By four o'clock in the afternoon of 22 June the army had crossed to the east bank of the river, and another letter arrived from Mir Jaffir giving details of Surajah Dowlah's intentions. Clive, no doubt becoming bored with all the correspondence, sent back a message saying he was moving at once to Plassey and then on to Daudpur six miles beyond, on the next morning. If Mir Jaffir failed to meet him at Daudpur he would make peace with the Nawab and give up the whole plan.

Moving all his supply boats upstream against the current was a slow, laborious business and it was not until one o'clock in the morning of 23 June that the British force reached the village of Plassey, fifteen miles from Cutwa. The men, tired by their exertions on a hot, muggy night, moved into a large grove of mango trees and lay down, but they found it difficult to get to sleep because of the continuous noise of cymbals and drums from the Nawab's army encamped close by. Its presence took Clive rather by surprise for he had thought the enemy were much further away to the north.

Next morning the Nawab's army, full of confidence, deployed from a camp about two miles to the north of the mango grove, and Clive, standing on the roof of a hunting lodge built some time ago by Surajah Dowlah beside the river, watched the enemy form up in battle order. His own little army of 3,200 men was being pinned against the river by 35,000 infantry, 18,000 cavalry and fifty pieces of artillery. In addition a party of about fifty French soldiers and adventurers, led by M. Saint-Frais, who had been part of the garrison of Chandernagore and had now joined Surajah Dowlah, brought four light field guns into action. Knowing how much depended on showing a bold front, Clive brought his men out of the grove, which was surrounded by a thick mud wall, and drew them up in a single line facing the direction from which he thought the main attack would come. He felt sure it would be made by a force of 5,000 cavalry and 7,000 infantry in a division led by Mir Murdin, the one commander Surajah Dowlah could really trust. The rest of the enemy army lay in a huge curve right round the right flank of Clive's tiny little force. It must have been obvious to every man in the British force that their position was virtually hopeless. They could not advance, even if they were able to, against Mir Murdin's formation immediately to their front

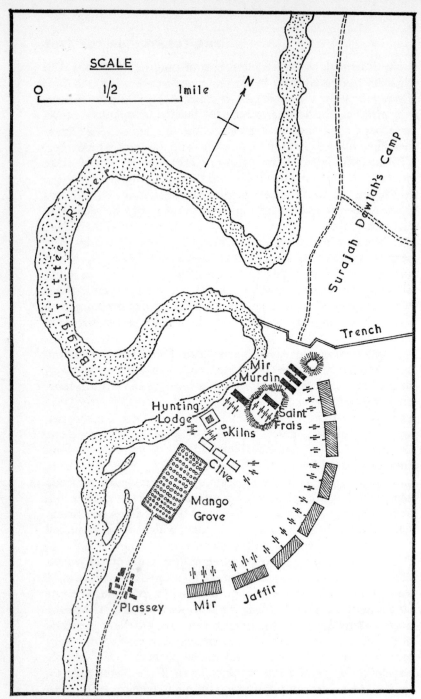

SCALE

0   1/2   1mile

N

Bhagiruttee River

Surajah Dowlah's Camp

Trench

Mir Murdin

Hunting Lodge

Kilns

Saint Frais

Clive

Mango Grove

Mir   Jaffir

Plassey

Plassey   23 June 1757

without inviting an overwhelming attack on the right flank. On their left and behind them lay the river, on the other two sides the whole plain was covered with the dense mass of the enemy.

Clive placed his guns with care. Three 6-pounders, manned by fifty men of the Royal Artillery and fifty seamen loaned by Admiral Watson, protected each flank of his line of battle, and two field guns and two howitzers were posted out on his left front under cover of two kilns which had provided the bricks for the hunting lodge. He was out-numbered by about seventeen to one, and though, as Fortescue points out, it was the first time the British had faced such odds, it was not to be the last.

The French began the battle at eight o'clock on the morning of 23 June, by firing a field gun, and the shot killed one man of the grenadier company of Coote's regiment, and wounded another. At this signal the whole line of enemy artillery, in front and all along the great flanking curve, opened a thunderous fire at their maximum rate. The British guns replied with considerable effect, but having lost thirty men in the first half-hour of the cannonade, which says little for the accuracy of the enemy, Clive withdrew his whole force behind the walls of the mango grove. Seeing the redcoats disappear among the trees the enemy yelled with triumph and pressed forward, closing in on the grove and doing their best to increase the rate of cannon fire. Little damage was done because Clive told his men to lie down and take cover, and his guns, firing through embrasures dug through the mud walls, cut down swathes of the enemy now only a little distance away. At eleven o'clock, after the cannonade had been going on for three hours, Clive called another council, and in the roar of gunfire and crackle of musketry it was decided to stay where they were until dark and then attack the enemy camp.

Then, a sudden rainstorm changed the whole situation. In the grove of mango trees the British had tarpaulins folded and ready beside their ammunition to keep it dry. Out in the open the French and native artillerymen had nothing. Both armies were drenched; the fire of Surajah Dowlah's gunners fell away at once while that of the British did not slacken at all. Even so, Mir Murdin at once assumed the British had the same ammunition problem as he had, and he ordered his division to move forward and clear the British out of the mango grove. His troops were met by a storm of grape shot, he himself was mortally wounded, his cavalry were dispersed and his infantry fell back. Surajah Dowlah, seeing this repulse, sent for Mir Jaffir, who was away at the far end of the flanking force, to ask what should be done. Mir Jaffir, realizing there was now a chance that the plot might work out satisfactorily, galloped up, swore to defend the Nawab with his life's blood, returned to his troops and tried to get a message through to Clive telling him to attack the Nawab at once. His messenger, watching the effect of the fire coming from the mango grove, very sensibly made no attempt to deliver the letter, but in the meantime Surajah Dowlah had asked another of his generals for advice. This man, being one of the conspirators, said that the best thing for the Nawab to do would be to withdraw the army behind the entrenchments of the previous night's camp and himself to return to Murshidabad, leaving his generals to mop up the little British force. The Nawab took this in good faith, mounted a camel and with an escort of 2,000 cavalry went back to Murshidabad.

At about half-past two in the afternoon the Nawab's artillery limbered up and began to withdraw to the camp, followed by a general movement of the huge disorderly host. Major Kilpatrick, one of Clive's officers, saw what was happening and noted that Saint-Frais and his little band were still in their forward position on the bank of a *jheel** about 600 yards in front of the mango grove. This was the perfect place from which to take the enormous native army in enfilade as it fell back, and Kilpatrick resolved to attack, drive the French off and bring guns into action in the new position. He therefore sent a message to this effect to Clive who, having decided not to take the offensive until nightfall, was fast asleep in the hunting lodge. Clive got up at once, told Kilpatrick to bring up the rest of the force, and he himself took command of Kilpatrick's two companies detailed for the attack. Saint-Frais, seeing the assault coming in, hitched the teams to his field guns, withdrew to a redoubt at the corner of the Nawab's camp and came into action again. Clive and the two companies occupied the position on the banks of the *jheel* and opened fire.

* A tank containing water, made by throwing up earth banks sometimes 15–20 feet high round a spring.

While this attack was going in, the division commanded by Mir Jaffir was seen to be advancing towards the mango grove, presumably—since no message had been received from Mir Jaffir—with the object of capturing the boats and baggage stacked in the grove. Three platoons and one gun were detached to hold them off, whereupon they withdrew slowly, but it was clear that the division had separated itself from the rest of the army. The significance of this was not immediately appreciated, largely because when the British guns on the *jheel* opened fire a great many of the Nawab's infantry, withdrawing to the camp, turned about, moved out on the plain again and began shooting industriously. The native artillery wheeled about too, and although Surajah Dowlah himself was well on his way home, his best general was dying and the army had no commander, it was at this moment that the real battle began.

In Clive's view the situation was now extremely dangerous— he of course did not know there was no co-ordinating command. He could see there was a certain amount of confusion in the enemy's camp and so he determined to attack before they could sort themselves out. He therefore deployed all his available troops as far forward as possible, and their gunfire and musketry at close range was so effective against the enemy's gun teams that most of their guns could not be brought into action. Yet all the time Clive was anxious about the enemy division threatening the mango grove behind him, until it suddenly occurred to him that it must be the one commanded by Mir Jaffir. This meant that his rear and right flank were secure and he could concentrate on the enemy to his front. He still had no easy task. Every mound and ditch and fold in the ground was crowded with enemy infantry busily firing away, while beyond them a great mass of cavalry was hovering about waiting to charge as soon as there was any slackening of fire from the British guns. Saint-Frais's guns in the redoubt were still firing with considerable effect and this disorganized battle seemed likely to continue indefinitely, if only because of the enemy's immense superiority in numbers.

In spite of all the noise and smoke and confusion Clive 'read' the battle with cool detachment and saw what had to be done. He sent out a party on either flank, one to drive Saint-Frais out of the redoubt on the left and the other to drive the enemy from a hillock on the right. He himself advanced with his main body in the centre. The enemy on the hillock ran away before the attackers could fire a shot, and Saint-Frais, now isolated in the redoubt, had to abandon his guns and retreat. By five o'clock in the afternoon the British force had occupied the Nawab's camp and entrenchments, and the Battle of Plassey was over. Clive had gained the provinces of Bengal, Bihar and Orissa at a cost of seven Europeans and sixteen sepoys killed, and thirteen Europeans and thirty-six sepoys wounded. It was an extraordinary battle and perhaps the really outstanding feature of it was the ability of one man not only to hold a force of 3,000 men in perfect steadiness in the face of 50,000 enemies, but to attack—much as Henry V had attacked at Agincourt—and drive from the battlefield an enemy force so much larger than his own.

Having taken the enemy camp Clive immediately sent Eyre Coote forward to keep the enemy on the move, and the 39th Foot pursued as far as Daudpur, where the British force spent the night. On the next day, when Mir Jaffir rode in to congratulate the victors of Plassey, Clive saluted him as the Nawab of the three provinces. Mir Jaffir then hastened off with his division to Murshidabad, reaching the city that evening (24 June). He at once sent out search parties to bring in Surajah Dowlah who had fled as Mir Jaffir approached his capital. A few days later he was betrayed, captured, brought back and promptly assassinated by Mir Jaffir's son, before the British could intervene. Clive entered the city on 29 June and formally installed Mir Jaffir on the throne. The negotiator Ormichand then appeared, demanding his share of the loot, and was told the story of the false treaty. He got nothing, and in fact Surajah Dowlah's treasury contained only a small fraction of what was believed to be in it. Clive, who could now have followed the example of Dupleix, refrained from making himself Nawab and took none of the loot of Murshidabad. Instead he accepted a 'present' of £200,000 and 'stood astonished at his own moderation'.

In the context of the battle for empire the main effect of the battle of Plassey was that it completely destroyed French influence in the three provinces of eastern India.

It was soon apparent that Mir Jaffir could continue to be Nawab only if supported by British arms and, as Clive had always intended, he was only the puppet of the East India Company, in whom the true sovereignty was vested. Clive emphasized the need for an agent of the company to live permanently at Mir Jaffir's court, and for this task he chose a young man of twenty-five whose name was Warren Hastings. Placing Mir Jaffir firmly on his throne, protecting the interests of the company and setting up a garrison in Cossimbazaar—to protect Murshidabad—all entailed a great deal of work, and so it was not until May 1758 that Clive was able to return to Calcutta. While he had been so busy in Bengal, where the threat of large-scale intervention by the French had never materialized, a successor to Dupleix had been making as much trouble as possible for the British in south India.

10 1758 The Year of Achievement

In the period from April 1758 until January 1761 the chief
character in the story of Anglo-French rivalry in India is the
comte de Lally de Tollendal or, to give him his proper name,
O'Mullally of Tullindally, the son of an exiled Irish Jacobite.
Lally was a professional soldier who had served in the Irish
Brigade in the French army, and before he went out to India
he was chiefly famous for having suggested the redeployment
of the artillery which then shattered the British column at
Fontenoy. He also had a reputation for being entirely fearless.
He cherished a deep abiding hatred of the English; in character
he was impulsive, choleric and passionate, with a tendency to
leap to conclusions. Honest himself and scornful of dishonesty in
others he was apt to suspect the motives of anyone who did not
share his views. Contemptuous of native customs, he made no
attempt to acquire any knowledge of Indian political methods,
and although he was a man of great gifts and had an excellent
military record in French campaigns in Europe, he was not a
worthy successor to the great Dupleix.

Lally was fifty-four when the Seven Years' War began, and
from the time in 1755 when the renewal of hostilities became
imminent he had been regarded as possibly the right man to
lead a strong expedition to India to recover all that had been
lost. For two years the French Government played with the
idea and did no more, and it was not until May 1757 that he
left France, bound for Pondicherry, bearing the titles of
Governor, Commander-in-Chief and Director of the French
East India Company.

At least six months of this delay had been the fault of Admiral
d'Aché, in charge of the naval force, who having once set out,
turned back to port for no good reason and thus gave his

government an opportunity to withdraw two ships from the expedition and send them to North America. The real voyage, when it at last began, took twelve months, to the fury of the military commander who was outspoken in his opinion of the Admiral's professional qualities, and it was not until the end of April 1758 that the nine ships carrying 2,000 regular troops anchored off Pondicherry.

This was the force that had caused so much conern to the Council of Madras when the question of what to do about Surajah Dowlah and the fall of Calcutta was being discussed. Had Lally been able to arrive a year earlier, when Clive and most of the available military resources were committed in Bengal, it might have prevented the British conquest of the eastern provinces.

The orders given to Lally before he left Versailles were clear-cut. His task was to destroy the English strongholds and influence in India. He was not to get involved in the interior and he was to keep right away from native politics and the sort of alliances and intrigues which had been the very breath of life to Dupleix and Bussy; if necessary, Bussy was to be recalled from the Deccan. Lally was also warned of the appalling corruption in Pondicherry—largely the result of Dupleix's policy that the servants of the company were at liberty to amass their own private fortunes if they were lucky enough to have the opportunity, and he had been told to devise and introduce reforms which would put a stop to it.

He arrived in a cantankerous mood, bored and frustrated by the delays of the long voyage. It had taken Admiral d'Aché just over three months to cover the 3,000 miles from Mauritius to the Coromandel coast. Lally found only what he expected to find. M. de Leyrit, the Governor of Pondicherry, had no plans for any campaign against the English, he knew nothing of the English forts, garrisons or defences, or even where they were, and worse still, in Lally's opinion, there was no money in the treasury. The officials in Pondicherry disliked Lally on sight and were resolved to thwart him if they could, no matter what harm this might do to the French cause in India. Lally, with some justification, regarded them as rogues and traitors, and made no attempt to hide his feelings.

In these circumstances it was hardly surprising that the

French campaign to expel the English from India began badly. In his orders Lally had been told that his first objective was to be Fort St David, so as soon as he arrived in Pondicherry he sent d'Aché and his squadron to anchor off Cuddalore and await his arrival with the land force he proposed to muster in Pondicherry. What he did not know was that Commodore Stevens, who had left England with four ships of the line some three months after d'Aché had sailed from Brest, had reached Madras five weeks previously. Stevens had joined Admiral Pocock (who had just relieved Admiral Watson on the East India station) in the Hooghli, and both squadrons, amounting to seven ships, had left Bengal on 17 April to intercept and destroy d'Aché's fleet. While on a southerly course Pocock missed the French ships and so went about and stood in to the Coromandel coast. On the morning of 29 April 1758 he sighted d'Aché at his moorings off Cuddalore. D'Aché put to sea at once and it was not until the afternoon that the English came up to him. The battle was a success more than a victory for Pocock. Six hundred of the French were killed or wounded—a very serious loss among crews already weakened by the long voyage from France—and one of d'Aché's ships was so badly damaged she had to be run ashore and abandoned. The casualties in Pocock's fleet were just over one hundred, but the French chain-shot had made such a mess of his rigging that he could not pursue the enemy and had to return to Madras to refit. D'Aché took refuge in a roadstead twenty miles north of Pondicherry where he was of no use at all to Lally.

On the day of the naval battle the force Lally had collected, led by le comte d'Estaing, came up to Fort St David. On 30 April d'Estaing was joined by M. de Soupire and a train of siege artillery. Lally himself appeared on 1 May. In less than a week he had managed to extinguish all the admiration and affection for France built up in southern India by the labours of Dumas, Dupleix and Bussy. While fitting out his army in Pondicherry he had demanded transport and a labour force to get the guns to Fort St David, thus providing the hostile officials with an excellent opportunity to disappoint him. To someone with his determination and energy the non-co-operation of a handful of civilians was a challenge. He rounded up every dark-skinned man he could catch and ignoring all differences of status or caste forced all of them, whether Brahmin or Untouchable, to drag the artillery to Fort St David.

His initial successes obscured for the moment the damage that had been done and seemed to justify his zeal. He sent d'Estaing to take Cuddalore which had only a weak garrison of five sepoy companies, somewhat inhibited by having to guard fifty French prisoners of war. Cuddalore surrendered on 4 May. Two days later Admiral d'Aché appeared again and landed all the troops he had left after the sea fight with Admiral Pocock. On 15 May, with a force of 5,000 men—half of them Europeans —Lally began the formal siege of Fort St David. The garrison, commanded by Major Polier who made the mistake of trying to defend all the outworks with too few men instead of concentrating his resources in the main fortress, capitulated on 2 June, even before the walls had been breached.

This loss caused great alarm at Madras, and Clive, when he heard of it, expressed himself freely on the cowardice of the defenders. Their excuse was that the bombardment of the siege guns had destroyed their water supply, and in any case they were short of powder. Major Polier had previously proved himself to be a gallant soldier and he must have had good reasons for hauling down the flag on one of the strongest fortresses in India.

On the day of Polier's surrender Lally sent d'Estaing off again on another mission, to capture Devicotah. Being little more than a factory, the town was indefensible against the pressure Lally's force could apply, and the British abandoned it as the French approached.

Full of enthusiasm for a task which was turning out to be much easier than he had imagined, Lally now marked down Madras as his next objective, to be followed by the invasion and conquest of Bengal; but there was no money to pay for his great schemes. His first set-back was the departure of d'Aché who went off to wage a private war, for his own pecuniary advantage, against British merchantmen in the waters off Ceylon, and without him, and without funds, there was no hope of doing what Louis XV had said must be done. In this difficult situation Governor de Leyrit and a Jesuit priest named Lavaur, an old friend and disciple of Dupleix, produced a plan for raising money. Once again, as in the days of Murzaffar

Jang, Chunda Sahib and Dupleix, the kingdom of Tanjore was involved. One of the prisoners taken at Fort St David was an Indian apparently entangled in the usual complications of succession to the throne. Lavaur's suggestion was that the present Rajah should be told that unless he paid the sum of 56 lacs of rupees (approximately £56,000), said to be a still outstanding debt to the French East India Company under a bond signed in 1750, French arms would put this rival claimant on the throne of Tanjore.

Lally did not like this idea at all. His orders stated specifically that he was not to get involved in local politics, but he had to have money and there seemed to be no alternative.

On 18 July he started to march south to Tanjore at the head of an army of 1,600 Europeans and about 2,000 sepoys, and entirely through his own fault the whole adventure was ill-fated from the start.

The method he had used for bringing the guns to Fort St David had alienated every native for miles around. None would join his army and so he had to set off without transport. Because of the looting, raping and generally shocking behaviour of his troops in the villages round about, the local natives had hidden all their cattle and food, so there were no supplies either. Each night, when the force camped, the soldiers were allowed to go off and forage for themselves. Discipline, always in short supply, became non-existent. At Devicotah the troops, who had not eaten for more than twelve hours, set fire to huts in the fort when the only food they could find was rice in the husk, and they would have blown themselves to pieces had not someone put out the fire before it reached the ammunition magazine. The Dutch settlements at Negapatam and Tranquebar were forced to provide ammunition, and two temples of particular sanctity beside the road to Karical were plundered, for no purpose or advantage, and the priests who remonstrated where tied in front of the muzzles of cannon and murdered in a revoltingly messy and dishonourable way. At Karical, after a march of 100 miles, the troops had their first meal on a reasonably organized basis, and moved on to Tanjore and began the siege on 2 August.

The Rajah was in a mood to compromise and would no doubt have come to some arrangement, but Lally, with his unfailing tactlessness, threatened to send him as a slave to Mauritius; and the English provided him with a reinforcement of 1,000 sepoys and ten British gunners. With this future awaiting him, and with the British behind him, the Rajah decided to fight to the end.

On 8 August news reached Lally of another sea battle between d'Aché and Pocock, fought on 2 August. In an action lasting two hours the British seamen had done so much damage to their ancient enemies that the French ships broke away and sought refuge under the guns of Pondicherry. This second defeat so discouraged d'Aché that he made up his mind not to attempt any further engagements with the British Navy and to return to Mauritius. Lally was wildly indignant when he heard of this, and he sent the comte d'Estaing to protest—in vain. D'Aché sailed for Mauritius on 2 September, but before he left he took as prizes, quite illegally, two Dutch ships in Pondicherry roads, and from them obtained £30,000 which— rather surprisingly—he handed over to the company's treasury to enable Lally to continue the war.

To Lally, sitting under the walls of Tanjore, the news of the naval defeat came as an unpleasant shock, and to make matters worse it was followed by the information that the British had occupied Karical, the only port from which his unfortunate army, always hungry and now running out of ammunition, could be supplied or evacuated. On 10 August the garrison of Tanjore made a determined sally from the town, and having just managed, after a savage little battle, to beat off the attack, he decided to raise the siege and withdraw to Karical. He had to leave three of his heavy guns behind. The Tanjore native cavalry came after him, making his retreat as difficult as possible by hovering on his flanks all the time, chopping down stragglers—of which there were many—and cutting off supplies. Lally, who had led nearly 4,000 men on an expedition more han a hundred miles from his base without making the simplest and most obvious administrative arrangements, or attempting to maintain discipline, did redeem a little of his reputation by bringing his force back to Karical, only to see Pocock's squadron at anchor in the mouth of the river. If the French force was ever to return to Pondicherry it would have to walk.

A less determined man might at this stage have cut his

losses and gone straight back to Pondicherry. Nothing had been achieved by the raid on Tanjore except the destruction of the health and discipline of the troops. There was now enough money at Pondicherry to finance an operation against the next major objective, Madras, and this should perhaps have been foremost in Lally's mind. Yet he delayed. While he had been besieging Tanjore the British in Madras had taken the opportunity to reoccupy some of the scattered forts in the Carnatic. Lally resolved to deal with them on his way to Madras. He therefore sent off three separate columns to recapture the forts of Trinomalee, Caranghooly and Trivatore, thereby opening the route to Arcot, and he ordered them to converge on Wandiwash, thirty-five miles south-east of Arcot.

Having completed their missions the columns met at the rendezvous, where he joined them and then led the united force against Arcot. Since there was no British garrison in Arcot the town and fort surrendered without a shot being fired, and there were now only two obstacles between him and Madras. One was the fort of Conjeveram on the Arcot–Madras road, and the other was Chingleput on the Paliar river. Both were weakly garrisoned and could have been taken without difficulty, and it could be said that in failing to appreciate their importance, and failing to deal with them there and then, Lally lost his chance of establishing the French as a power in India.

On 4 October he put his troops into cantonments and being short of money returned to Pondicherry to collect more. Here he met Bussy to whom he had sent orders, in June, to abandon the Deccan and join him for the attack on Madras. He had also told Bussy to leave a small detachment under the marquis de Conflans in the Masulipatam area for the defence of the Northern Circars.

By recalling Bussy he had of course removed Britain's most dangerous enemy from the one place where he could do the most harm, but Lally was not a strategist. He had been told to take Madras and, blind to all side-effects and long-term issues, everything had to be subordinated to the single mission. Bussy was well aware of the damage done and that all Dupleix's skilful machinations had been brought to ruin. He begged to be sent back. Lally privately regarded him as just as big a rogue as all the others, with secret financial reasons for wanting to return. Coldly and angrily he refused to change his mind. Bussy, in despair at the wilful sacrifice of years of hard, successful work in the cause of France, came to the conclusion his superior was mad. Lally was further enraged by a petition submitted by the officers of the force at Pondicherry, many of whom were senior to Bussy, asking that since Bussy was an officer of outstanding merit and ability he should take precedence over them and rank as the second-in-command of the army. With great reluctance Lally agreed.

His army now consisted of 2,300 Europeans and 5,000 sepoys, and because of his previous activities the collection of transport caused endless difficulties. Not until the end of November could the march on Madras begin.

The British authorities in Madras had been resigned to the loss of many of their possessions in the Carnatic as the direct result of the fall of Fort St David. In August they appealed to Clive in Bengal for assistance, but he had plans for a diversion which would take the pressure off the Carnatic and had no troops to spare for southern India. They therefore called in all the European troops that could be spared from garrisons such as Trichinopoly, and in September were greatly heartened by the arrival of Colonel Draper's regiment, 850 strong, from England. At the beginning of December the defending force in Madras amounted to 1,750 Europeans and 2,200 sepoys commanded by the veteran Colonel Stringer Lawrence.* The Governor was George Pigot, just as resourceful and intelligent as his predecessor Thomas Saunders in the days when Clive had been a very young officer, and since Lally's intentions had been known for months, adequate preparations had been made for a long siege. The French were not optimistic and

---

* It was in the following year, 1759, that Stringer Lawrence earned for himself the title of 'Father of the Indian Army'. He raised seven battalions of sepoys on the same establishment as the British army, and to each of them he attached two British subalterns and three sergeants, many of them volunteers from the 39th Foot who had much experience of Indian troops and knew their value, when properly led. Lally himself, who was not in the habit of complimenting anyone on anything, commented on this arrangement: 'Their sepoys will venture to attack our white troops, while ours will not even look at their black ones.' The first native troops enlisted in India to fight for the British seem to have been the two companies of Rajputs raised for the defence of Bombay in 1684.

morale was low, but one French officer wrote that it was probably better to be killed by a bullet on the glacis of Madras than to die of starvation in Pondicherry. It was unfortunate for them that Lally had made himself so unpopular, for an army which has no liking or respect for its commander has no confidence either and is half-beaten before it goes into battle. Clive, writing to Pitt from Bengal, had forecast the total failure of Lally's campaign 'unless some very unforeseen event interpose in his favour'.

Lally's army moved out of Arcot in two columns, one taking the road to Madras which went past Conjeveram, and the other going along the bank of the Paliar river towards Chingleput. Lally himself joined the Chingleput column on 4 December, and having reconnoitred the fort decided not to waste his resources on reducing it. Leaving it intact in his rear he marched on northwards to Madras. Stringer Lawrence had already exploited Lally's failure to take either of the forts at the end of September. He had withdrawn the troops in Conjeveram to the garrison of Chingleput, thus raising it to a strength of 100 Europeans and 1,200 sepoys, and made arrangements to hire a force of Mahratta and Tanjore cavalry to harass French road convoys and disrupt their communications during the siege. Lally seems to have been a soldier who made things unnecessarily difficult for himself. He rejected the wise advice of more gifted men, such as Bussy, implying that when he wanted their help he would ask for it.

Colonel Lawrence took his army into the field to see what Lally was doing and fell back slowly on Madras as the enemy advanced. On 13 December the French army camped on the plain about a mile to the south-west of Fort St George. Lally then moved up, established himself in what was known as the Black Town, and with his right flank resting on the town and his left on the beach, on the north side of the fort, prepared to open the siege. His troops were not particularly interested in his plans while the riches of the Black Town lay open to them. Within a short time they had disappeared among the buildings and, rapidly rendering themselves unfit for duty, lay or reeled drunkenly about the streets.

To take advantage of this, at eleven o'clock on the following morning Colonel Draper made a sortie with 500 men and two guns, but unaccountably was deserted by his men at a moment when it seemed possible he might put an end to the siege before it had begun. The incident brought no credit to either side, for Bussy had a chance to cut off Draper's retreat and failed to take it, either to spite Lally or because his men were too drunk to move. Draper got back into the fort but he had lost 200 men, killed, wounded and taken prisoner. The French had the same number of casualties but they claimed a victory, while the English were demoralized by their abortive attack.

Thus, at the end of 1758, Lally, sitting down round the walls of Fort St George, seemed to have a chance of doing what he had come to do.

In Bengal, Clive had many difficulties of his own in the year 1758. Mir Jaffir, the Nawab he had created, was by no means peacefully resigned to being a mere puppet; there was much dissension and intrigue in the court at Murshidabad, the treasury was empty and there was a threat of invasion across the northern frontier with Oudh. The population of the Nawab's three provinces was vast; the people, unwarlike and hard-working, were ruled by officials who were mainly Mohammedan adventurers from the north, and in the country, but separate from the indigenous peoples, were thousands of professional soldiers from the martial races of India who had been recruited for the armies of Alivardi Khan and Surajah Dowlah. These armies had now been disbanded, putting out of work men who lived by civil war and whose presence was a constant menace to internal security.

At Plassey, Clive had in effect destroyed the prestige of the native government and brought about a situation in which the British could not now revert to their former status of merchants dependent upon the Nawab's favour, since the immediate result would be anarchy. Law and order, of a sort, could only be maintained by strong British support of the Nawab's rule; an unsatisfactory situation which, as Clive realized, could only lead in the end to full British sovereignty. He spent the year enforcing the authority of the court at Murshidabad on local chieftains who showed signs of setting up an opposition.

Even when beset by complex political problems Clive found time to plan his counter-stroke against the French. Though, as

231

he knew, this was hardly the time to think of reducing or deploying the small force on which British influence in the eastern provinces depended, he was determined to seize the opportunity presented to him when Lally recalled Bussy from the Deccan. If he acted swiftly he might be able to replace the former French influence at the court of the Deccan with that of the English.

In the Northern Circars a ruler named Anunderaj had already rebelled against the French, seized Vizagapatam and asked the East India Company at Madras for military aid. At the end of September, Clive, to whom the request had been passed, sent him a force commanded by Lieutenant-Colonel Francis Forde and consisting of 500 Europeans, infantrymen and gunners, about 2,000 sepoys, six field guns and the same number of siege guns. Forde reached Vizagapatam on 20 October 1758 and at once marched to join Anunderaj's army at Cossimcotah. After a certain amount of argument on whether or not the Rajah would honour his undertaking to meet the cost of the British force which had come to help him, the army set off on 1 December, and on 3 December made contact with the force commanded by the marquis de Conflans, not far from Peddapur.

Conflans had 500 Europeans, 6,000 sepoys and a number of local native levies. Forde's expeditionary force had been augmented by the Rajah's army of 5,000 infantry—armed with pikes, bows and arrows—and about 500 horsemen; it was a disorganized rabble. After some delay, because each commander thought the other too strong to attack, the battle of Condore was fought on 9 December. Conflans was deceived by the uniforms of the sepoys from Bengal who, like the European troops, wore scarlet tunics instead of the white uniforms of the British sepoys in southern India. Forde, aware of this, ordered his sepoy units to furl their Colours, which might have been identified, so that the deception might be complete. Yet it was not the uniform and Colours of the sepoys that confused the French, so much as their drill, discipline and coolness under fire. Condore was an overwhelming victory for Forde, whose casualties amounted to a total of 250. Conflans lost seventy-six European officers and men killed, fifty-six taken prisoner and an uncounted number of wounded. Thirty cannon, seven mortars and all his baggage and transport were captured. The French losses would have been far greater if the Rajah's cavalry had had the courage to pursue a defeated enemy, but as it was, Forde was able to follow up his success by capturing Rajahmundry, the gateway to the district of Vizagapatam, on 11 December. He was eager to move on from here to Masulipatam, the centre of French influence in the province and the base from which Conflans would undoubtedly attempt to recover what he had lost, but the Rajah went back on his word, refused to pay Forde the promised money for his troops and withdrew his 'army'. Fifty days were wasted in negotiation while Forde watched his opportunity of taking Masulipatam slipping away. Thus, at the end of 1758 he was still arguing with Anunderaj, whom Fortescue describes as 'a deplorable potentate'.

At home, Pitt had given careful consideration to his plans for the year 1758 and the general policy was clear in his mind. He would keep the French busy in Europe by giving all possible support to Frederick the Great and the Hanoverians, and by nuisance raids on the French coast. A strong naval blockade would keep the French navy in its harbours and this would leave him reasonably free to achieve his principal aim, the conquest of Canada. To meet the requirements of this policy he agreed to the employment of British troops in Hanover under the command of a Prussian general, Ferdinand of Brunswick, and to the payment of subsidies to Hanover. This brought about a reconciliation with the ageing George II who, for the remaining two years of his life, put his trust in his Minister.

Pitt's genius, now allowed full rein, began to produce results which were a reassuring contrast to the mismanagement of the Duke of Newcastle. In Hanover, Ferdinand of Brunswick regained practically all that the Duke of Cumberland had signed away. He pursued the French across the Rhine and won a great victory over them at Krefeld on 23 June.

The first British raid on the coast of France in 1758 was launched from the Isle of Wight against the port of St Malo. Two squadrons, a total of twenty-four ships of the line, commanded by Lord Anson, Sir Edward Hawke and Commodore Howe, escorted transports containing 13,000 men led by the

second Duke of Marlborough with Lord George Sackville as his
second-in-command. This imposing force arrived in Cancalle
Bay, eight miles from St Malo, on 5 June; the battery guarding
the bay was put out of action by naval gunnery and the land
force was disembarked. The main result of the raid was the
destruction in St Malo harbour of over 100 ships, mostly
privateers and merchantmen, and though Granville, Le Havre
and Cherbourg were on the list for attack, the foul weather so
often encountered in the English Channel in June prevented
anything more than a show of force. The fleet went home, and
in August returned to Cherbourg, captured the town, destroyed
the docks and harbour defences and burnt all the shipping, but
in trying to add to this success and going again to St Malo
everything went wrong and 750 officers and men were lost.
Nevertheless, these raids and the constant threat of more,
caused continuous alarm along the French coast and tied down
large numbers of French troops and resources which were
badly needed elsewhere. Pitt claimed that the combined force
had kept three times its number committed to coastal defence
duties in France.

The naval blockade was equally effective. A French fleet
carrying reinforcements and supplies for Canada was encountered by Admiral Osborne off Cartagena in the Mediterranean,
defeated and forced to turn back to Toulon. In the Bay of Biscay
Admiral Hawke defeated another fleet which put out from
Rochefort, making for Louisbourg.

In North America Lord Loudoun was recalled by Pitt in
a letter dated 20 December 1757, and General James
Abercromby, originally sent out to America by Newcastle, was
selected to replace him. It was an unhappy choice. Pitt then
summoned from Germany an officer who for the last eighteen
months had been employed as Commissary to the Hessian
troops serving as mercenaries in the pay of the British Government. He was a Guardsman, named Colonel Jeffrey Amherst.
Pitt made him a general and appointed the newly-promoted
Brigadiers Lawrence, Whitmore and James Wolfe to serve
under him.

Pitt's plan for the 1758 campaign in Canada had three
phases. First, Louisbourg was to be taken. The task was given
to Amherst and he was allotted 14,000 regular troops. The

second phase was to be an advance, concurrently with the siege of Louisbourg, to Crown Point and then on to Montreal and Quebec if possible. This was to be Abercromby's responsibility and he was given Brigadier Lord Howe, 10,000 regular troops and 20,000 Provincials. Finally, Brigadier General John Forbes, with 1,900 regulars and 5,000 Provincials, was to wipe out the stain of Braddock's defeat and capture Fort Duquesne.

The regular troops were to be escorted to America by Admiral Boscawen and a fleet strong enough to deal with any French naval force on the other side of the Atlantic. The transports, accompanied by twenty-three ships of the line, sailed from Portsmouth on 19 February, but it was not until 2 June that Boscawen and Amherst, with 157 ships and 11,000 troops, sailed into Gabarus Bay, where William Pepperrell and Parson Moody had landed thirteen years before.

It was planned that James Wolfe and his brigade would land at Freshwater Cove which was no longer as it had been when the New Englanders landed there. The 400 yards of beach were defended by 1,000 Frenchmen well entrenched behind abatis and supported by cannon in positions camouflaged by growing shrubs; the lessons Pepperrell and his men had taught had not been forgotten. For five days the transports lay offshore, unable even to lower the landing craft because of fog and storms. At length, on 8 June, at two o'clock in the morning, the attack went in, covered by an intense bombardment of the enemy shore positions by the warships.

The French lay low, waiting for the boats to come close in before they opened fire with everything they had, and Wolfe realized no one could get ashore in that tempest of shot. He signalled to the boats to bear away, but three of them, on the extreme right and sheltered by rocks from the fury of the fire, pulled in behind a craggy spit, and led by Major Scott a few men of the Light Infantry managed to scramble ashore from their stoved-in boat. Wolfe, armed as usual with a light cane, went after them, and he was followed by waves of infantry who formed up and took the nearest French battery with the bayonet. Lawrence's brigade then came in on the left and landed without difficulty while the French were preoccupied with Wolfe and his men. Amherst followed, the shore defences of Freshwater Cove were overwhelmed and the French,

235

hotly pursued, fled back to the town fortress. The cost of the landing was 100 killed, wounded and drowned. The French casualties were about the same.

Amherst's main task now was to bring up his heavy artillery on the landward side—in fact he followed Pepperrell's plan almost exactly—and being an extremely efficient, thorough man with large forces at his disposal, he built a road through the morass. His task of reducing the fortress by gunfire was made easier by the crumbling of the masonry under the shock of the defenders' own guns. On 26 July the last enemy gun was silenced and a large breach had been made in the walls. Boscawen had dealt with all the French shipping in the harbour, and when the French Governor Drucour offered to negotiate Amherst replied there was nothing to discuss. The garrison either surrendered as prisoners of war or accepted the consequences of an assault. On the following day the British occupied Louisbourg and the task of dismantling it went on for months. Writing in 1898 Roberts says, 'the vast lines of the earthworks are still to be traced, covered with a mantle of green turf; and the bells of pasturing sheep tinkle softly over the tomb of the vanished fortress'. All the inhabitants of Louisbourg were deported to Europe, and Prince Edward's Island and Cape Breton Island passed into British hands.

The Chevalier de Drucour's gallant defence had at least secured one advantage: it had prevented Amherst from co-operating with Abercromby in his attack up the Hudson route, and when Amherst suggested going on from Louisbourg to Quebec, Boscawen, who knew the coast well, said the idea was not feasible. In any case, as things turned out, even if Amherst had been able to keep to Pitt's timings for the three phases of the campaign, he could not have done much to help Abercromby. Amherst left the 22nd, 28th, 40th and 45th Regiments of Foot to garrison and at the same time demolish Louisbourg while he and the remainder of his force sailed for Boston. He arrived on 14 September and was received with much rejoicing; as he wrote to Pitt, 'I could not prevent the men from being filled with rum by the inhabitants', and he was doubly welcome because of what had happened to Abercromby.

The task of the land forces bound for Lakes George and

Champlain and the forts of Ticonderoga and Crown Point had at first seemed simple enough, even though the French had apparently had plenty of warning. Vaudreuil, the Governor-General, had suggested that the best defence of Canada would be an attack along the line of the Mohawk river, but he was notoriously corrupt and inspired no confidence, and his plan was impracticable and vague. It was dropped, and Montcalm, stationed at Ticonderoga with about 4,000 men, was ordered to hold the approaches to Montreal. This force, which had no support from other French posts higher up Lake Champlain, was therefore isolated and in a vulnerable position. Abercromby moved against it with 7,000 regulars and 9,000 Provincials. Never before had the British in Canada had so great an opportunity and advantage.

One of Abercromby's greatest assets, though possibly he may not have realized it, was his second-in-command, Brigadier Lord Howe, a man of thirty-four who had arrived in America with his regiment, the 55th Foot, in 1757. Unlike the school of soldiers typified by men like Braddock, Howe had taken great trouble to study the arts of forest warfare from the great ranger Robert Rogers, the most famous of all the Provincial irregulars. Howe went out with these irregulars on their raids and scouting parties, wearing what they wore and eating what they ate; and having purged himself of all the rigid practices and prejudices of the barrack squares of Europe he set about teaching his men. First he did his best to equip them for the work they had to do. All unnecessary accoutrements were cast aside and their then practically empty knapsacks were filled with enough corn-meal to make them independent of supply columns for many days. The long skirts of their coats were cut off, and instead of stockings and thin breeches they were issued with stout leggings to protect them from thorns. Their well-greased queues were shorn off and their powdered hair cut short and washed clean. The gleaming barrels of muskets and the flashing blades of bayonets were browned. They were taught to paddle canoes, to move silently and independently, to make use of ground and cover and to shoot at snap targets. The men soon realized who was going to benefit from all this, and that they were not to be paraded like a row of targets on a battlefield. It is no wonder that Howe was able to keep so sure a hold on their affections, and yet he wrought all these fundamental changes* without for one moment relaxing the firm discipline which he instilled in regulars and Provincials alike. He must have been a remarkable man, but he was not alone in his ideas. Colonel Bouquet of the Royal American Regiment (later the 60th) wanted to dress his men like Indians, and Brigadier John Forbes agreed with him. George Washington, in a letter to Bouquet in July 1758, wrote that if he had any say in the matter he would put all officers and men into Indian dress and be the first to set an example.

By the end of June Abercromby's force with all its artillery, supplies and water transport had concentrated in the area of Fort William Henry on Lake George. The move up to the assembly area had gone remarkably smoothly because Howe had been responsible for it. On 4 July the stores were shipped and on the following day the men embarked. Fortescue has described the scene:

> Overhead the sky was blue and cloudless; the sun had just climbed above the mountain tops, and his rays slanted down over the vast rolling slope of forest to the lake. Not a breath of air was moving to ruffle the still blue water or stir the banks of green leaves around it, as the twelve hundred boats swept over the glassy surface.

Robert Rogers and his rangers led the way. By daybreak on 6 July the flotilla reached the narrow entrance to the waterway that leads into Lake Champlain past the headland of Ticonderoga. The garrison of a French outpost on the shore of Lake George was driven off and disembarkation began. By midday the whole army had landed on the west shore of Lake George.

---

* It must not be presumed that all these reforms were at once accepted by all professional soldiers. They were not. Howe's officers were most upset to find they had to wash their own clothes, carry their own knife, fork and spoon and mess-tin and forgo all the amenities of an Officers' Mess while on operations. Many of the men, most of them German soldiers serving in the 60th Regiment, deeply resented the loss of their queues and the cropping of their long hair.

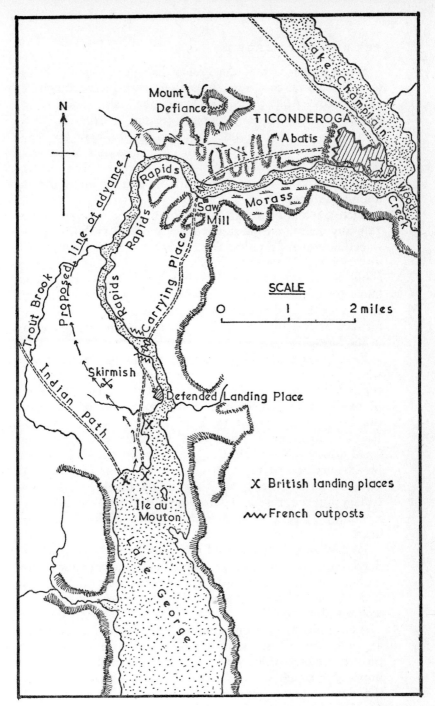

N

Mount
Defiance

TICONDEROGA

Abatis

Lake Champlain

Wood Creek

Rapids

Rapids

Rapids

Saw
Mill

Morass

Carrying Place

Proposed line of advance

Trout Brook

Indian Path

Rapids

Skirmish

Defended Landing Place

X

X   X

Ile au
Mouton

Lake George

SCALE

0   1   2 miles

X British landing places

ᨆᨆ French outposts

Ticonderoga

Scouts reported that the French had destroyed the bridge over the channel connecting Lake George with Lake Champlain and therefore Abercromby decided to move along the west bank of this channel and come upon Ticonderoga from the north-west. The way led through trackless forest where the dense undergrowth was entangled with the trunks and branches of fallen trees. Rogers was sent forward to reconnoitre and the assaulting troops were formed up in four columns for the approach march.

Such a march, through virgin forest without being able to gain any direction from sun or wind and with visibility limited sometimes to only a few feet, is at any time a formidable undertaking. The march on Ticonderoga became the utmost confusion crowned by one disastrous event. The guides did not know where they were, the columns became mixed up, and all semblance of order was lost as the men forced their way forward as best they could. In a short time the army was lost in the forest.

Exactly the same thing happened to the 350 French troops who had been driven out of the outpost on the lake shore. In trying to get back through the forest to Ticonderoga they began blundering round in circles until they suddenly ran into one of the British columns led by Lord Howe and some rangers. In the sharp, blind little battle that followed, the rangers stood firm and Rogers, hearing the shooting, turned back with his advanced guard, came up on the French from their rear and virtually annihilated them. In numbers the British loss was trifling, but the tragedy, fatal to the expedition, was that Lord Howe lay dead in the undergrowth with a bullet through his heart.

He had been the very soul and spirit of the army, and his death had a shattering effect. Abercromby spent much of that night in trying to collect his force together and at first light he withdrew to the landing-place where he found the rest of his troops waiting for him.

A few miles away Montcalm was expecting to be attacked at any moment. He had assumed the British would come down the track along which boats had to be carried to avoid the impassable rapids in the channel between the lakes. This was the usual route to Ticonderoga which went past some saw-mills at the foot of the rapids and across the bridge he had destroyed. It was on the west bank of the channel, over-looking the portage and the site of the bridge, that he had decided to make his stand. When various outposts came in to report on the size of the armada they had seen on Lake George he allowed himself to be persuaded by two of his staff officers that his only hope lay in falling back on Fort Ticonderoga. He therefore withdrew on the evening of 6 July, and as soon as it was light on the following morning his men set to work feverishly to strengthen the defences.

On 7 July Abercromby sent Rogers forward to occupy the saw-mills. The bridge was rebuilt and by dusk the whole army was in the camp Montcalm had just abandoned, two miles away from Ticonderoga.

The fort itself had been sited almost at the end of the blunt peninsula which, on the east, forms the west shore of Lake Champlain, and on the west flanks the channel between the Lakes. It was built on a small plateau which could be approached easily only from the north-west because on the other sides there were steep banks on the edge of the water. It was on the vulnerable side, thickly covered with trees, that Montcalm set his men to work. Just beyond the outer earthworks, dug along the line of a ridge, the ground sloped away, and on this incline, below the ridge, trees were felled, the tops were lopped off, and the logs piled in a carefully loop-holed breast-work nearly nine feet high. In front of the breast-work, among the stumps of the felled trees, the ground was covered with the lopped tree-tops and heavy branches, facing outwards and with all their points sharpened. This interlaced mass presented an almost impenetrable obstacle, and as one eye-witness said, the forest looked as though it had been laid low by a hurricane. The French officers in the fort were astonished that so much had been done in one day.

It all looked very impressive, but the sort of guns which could batter a way through the massive masonry of Louisbourg could make light work of such timber defences. In fact there were several options open to Abercromby. He could mount his guns on a position called Mount Defiance which commanded the fort and rake the breast-work from one end to the other; he could bring his artillery closer and with its concentrated fire drive a gap the width of a carriage road through the wooden structure and the abatis in front of it; or he could storm the virtually undefended flanks. Furthermore, there was no need to attack the place at all. He could leave part of his force to contain the French in their stronghold and take the rest northwards up Lake Champlain to cut off Montcalm's supplies and his retreat. The French general had only 3,600 men and rations for eight days. However, Abercromby's intelligence service had told him that the enemy garrison was 6,000 strong and that a reinforcement of half that number was on its way from Montreal. He thought he had good reason to attack before this fictitious force arrived.

At sunrise on 8 July he sent his chief engineer, Lieutenant-Colonel Clark, to reconnoitre the enemy position from the top of Mount Defiance. Clark, inefficient or idle, came back and said that the enemy's defence works could be carried by a frontal assault. One can be sure that Howe, had he lived, would not have agreed with him, but Howe would have looked at the ground himself. Abercromby left all his artillery at the landing-place by Lake George and gave orders that the abatis and breast-work were to be carried with the bayonet. He then withdrew to the saw-mills by the rebuilt bridge, and refused to stir from there all day. When reports of the fearful slaughter of his men came back, as they did at frequent intervals, each time he merely gave the order to attack again.

The assault was hopeless from the start. It began just after midday and went on until six in the evening. Nearly 2,000 heroic men died in the tangle of the abatis, and when Captain John Campbell and a few of his Highlanders scaled the breast-work and dropped down inside, each fell upon a bed of bayonets. The mind is sickened by the thought of what that battle must have been like. The French had 350 casualties. The murderous incompetence and stupidity of Abercromby—who was relieved of his command at the end of the campaign—had put off the conquest of Canada for at least a year. He withdrew to Fort William Henry and camped there for the rest of July and the beginning of August, doing nothing, while his men died of dysentery. At length, after much argument, he was persuaded to agree to a plan devised by Colonel Bradstreet for an attack on Fort Frontenac, for this would sever all communications between Canada and the Great Lakes and the Ohio valley.

With reluctance he gave Bradstreet 2,500 men, most of them Provincials. This little force went down the river to Albany, along the Mohawk river and across Lake Oneida to the site of Fort Oswego. From here, on the south shore of Lake Ontario, Bradstreet set off on his voyage of nearly 100 miles across the lake and landed near Fort Frontenac three days later, on 25 August. There were only 100 men in the fort. On 27 August they surrendered and at the same time handed over nine boats which constituted the French naval force on the lake. Bradstreet demolished the fort, burned seven of the vessels and took the other two back with him in triumph to Albany. The effects of his expedition were out of all proportion to its size. The French had lost their command of Lake Ontario, the highway from the Lakes to the Mississippi had been cut, Indian tribes which had been wavering in their loyalty now came over to the English and lastly, Fort Duquesne, the objective in the third phase of Pitt's plan, had been isolated.

Amherst, landing at Boston in the middle of September on his way back from Louisbourg, heard all about the disaster at Ticonderoga and set out to join Abercromby, but it was October before he reached Fort William Henry. By this time it was too late in the year for any attempt to be made against Montreal and so the troops were sent into winter quarters to await the next campaigning season in the following year.

Brigadier Forbes, who had the task of taking Fort Duquesne, arrived in Philadelphia at the beginning of April and found nothing ready. The troops allotted to him from Pennsylvania, Virginia, Maryland and North Carolina had not even been enlisted. Only half Colonel Bouquet's battalion of the 60th was available and Colonel Montgomery's Highlanders were away in the south. Even so, although the majority of his force was untrained, he was ready to move by the end of June.

His plan was to take a more direct route than that used by Braddock, advancing from Pennsylvania by short stages and setting up a properly defended supply point every forty miles. When in reach of his destination he would approach it with his whole force, leaving behind such encumbrances as the wagon train which had so hampered Braddock on the march. Forbes and Bouquet had already agreed to dress their men like Indians, and Bouquet invented a new drill for moving through densely wooded country. His units were divided into small columns moving two abreast which could form into line, facing any direction, in a matter of moments. He knew only too well the value of marksmanship in forest fighting, where a soldier only got a fleeting glimpse of a target, and he managed to obtain a number of rifled carbines for some of the men in his own battalion. They were the forerunners of the famous riflemen of the 60th.

In the beginning of July, Bouquet and an advanced party camped at Raystown (later Bedford) on the eastern side of the Allegheny mountains, and Forbes moved the main body first to the village of Carlisle and then the frontier post of Shippensburg. Here he became the victim of some extremely painful intestinal complaint and could move no further forward until September. Meanwhile Bouquet was slowly building a road over the Alleghenies, through wild and desolate country which presented him with every conceivable difficulty. Forbes, writing to Pitt, described it as 'an immense uninhabited wilderness, overgrown everywhere with trees and brushwood, so that nowhere can one see twenty yards'.

The first supply point was built at Raystown and named Fort Bedford; the next was made at Loyalhannon Creek, to the west of the Allegheny river, but progress was slow. Forbes had one good reason for not hurrying. He knew the French had enlisted a large number of Indians for the defence of Fort Duquesne and he also knew that if nothing happened for some time, these fickle allies would lose interest and go home. He took a lot of trouble to win the Indians over and his emissaries were successful in persuading the larger tribes to support the English.

Although things were going slowly they were also going well, until the unaccountable behaviour of Major Grant of the Highlanders.

This officer asked Forbes for permission to go forward with a small detachment, reconnoitre Fort Duquesne, take a few prisoners, collect some up-to-date information and if possible do something to alarm and discourage the garrison. He was given

800 men, some of the 60th, some Highlanders and the remainder Provincial troops. Grant led them out of Loyalhannon and in the darkness just before dawn on 14 September arrived within half a mile of the fort, on a position overlooking it, later known as Grant's Hill. According to Forbes, Grant then appears to 'have lost his wits'. He left a quarter of his force to guard the baggage, sent one small party out to the right and another to the left, moved forward with another himself, and then sent a company of Highlanders out on the open plain before the fort as escort to an officer who was to make a sketch of the defences. The splitting up of his force into these penny packets was bad enough but he added madness to his folly by ordering the beating of Reveille with all possible pomp and circumstance.

Not surprisingly the French and Indians erupted from the fort and with terrifying yells drove the parties hither and thither and back upon one another in the greatest disorder. The Highlanders lost their nerve, for the moment, when the hideous shrieking started, and turned and ran, and had it not been for the steadiness of the Virginians* who formed the baggage guard, there might have been no survivors. In this nonsensical affair Grant himself was taken prisoner and nearly 300 of his men were killed, wounded or captured.

This little French success could not save the fort. Bradstreet's destruction of Fort Frontenac had cut the supply route to Duquesne, and the French commander, unable to feed all but a handful of men, had to dismiss the larger part of them. Yet it seemed that in the end the English would be defeated by the weather. Heavy rain began to fall in the last week of September and continued well into October, when it turned into snow. Bouquet's road became a river of mud, preventing all movement, and at the beginning of November, when Forbes, now desperately ill, was carried to Loyalhannon, he decided that no attack could be launched that year. He was then told by his Indian scouts that the garrison in the fort was now too weak to defend the place, and so on 18 November a force of 2,300 specially picked men marched off, leaving all their tents and

---

* Virginians have a well-established reputation for resolution and steadiness under fire—witness the famous remark of the Confederate General Bernard E. Bee at the first Battle of Bull Run on 12 July 1861: 'There is Jackson, standing like a stone wall! *Rally behind the Virginians!*'

baggage behind and carrying Forbes in a litter at their head. Just before midnight on 24 November the sentries on the night bivouac heard an explosion in the distance, and on the following evening the column came up to the blackened ruins of what had been the fort. All the defence works had been blown up, stores and barrack huts had been burnt and there was only one grisly sign of human habitation—the heads of the Highlanders killed by Grant's folly had been stuck on poles and the kilts nailed up below them. Their comrades now had no hope of revenge, for the French had left the Ohio valley for ever. Forbes put a stockade round the cluster of huts that had not been destroyed and named it Pittsburg.

One task yet remained. Major Halket, an officer on Forbes's staff, led a party of Pennsylvanians through the forest until they came to the scene of Braddock's defeat on the Monongahela. Among all the skeletons Halket found two, lying close together beneath a tree, and of these, one was that of his father, Sir Peter Halket of the 44th Foot, recognizable by a peculiarity of the teeth, and the other could have been that of Major Halket's brother. Wrapped in the plaid of a Highlander the bones were laid in one grave, and over it the Pennsylvanians fired one volley in salute. The remains of all the other dead were gathered up and buried in a deep trench.

Suffering a great deal, Forbes was carried back to Philadelphia where he lingered through the rest of the winter and died in the following March.

So ended the great campaign of 1758 in North America. The flanks of the French, at Louisbourg and in the Ohio valley, had been destroyed; two out of three of Pitt's phases had been successful, but in the centre the French held firm. Vaudreuil called out all the remaining militia reserves and concentrated them in the area of Quebec, where Montcalm set up his headquarters. To Bourlamaque, one of his ablest officers, he gave the task of holding Lake Champlain and the Richelieu river against any British advance on Montreal. As Roberts says, 'both sides now seemed to realize that the death grapple was fairly begun'. The people of Canada waited in trepidation for the next blow to fall.

In India the power and the glory of France were slipping

through Lally's fingers. In the West Indies, where the year 1758 had slid away almost without the sound of gunfire, the merchants of both nations knew that the riches of the sugar islands must soon attract invasion fleets.

Now, in 1758, Pitt's relentless war against the French touched the French settlements in West Africa where, for the past five years, the merchants of the British Royal African Company had been complaining that the French on the Senegal river and the island of Goree were building forts and stirring up the natives against them. During his first brief ministry Pitt had been approached by a merchant named Thomas Cumming, known as the Fighting Quaker—somewhat of a contradiction in terms—who had great plans for the capture of Fort Louis in the Senegal river, and Goree. Their loss to France would affect her position in the whole Altantic trading area, and it was for supremacy in this area that Pitt was fighting. Pitt had listened. Cumming, who had been in close touch with local native chiefs, was confident his design could not fail, but not until 1758 could the project be undertaken. In the spring a small expedition was fitted out, and Cumming and Captain Marsh of the Royal Navy captured Fort Louis with little bloodshed. They turned south, reconnoitred Goree and decided that their resources were inadequate to cope with it. In November Pitt gave secret instructions to Captain Keppel, and at the end of the year he came down the coast of West Africa with five warships to finish the task Cumming and Captain Marsh had begun.

Now, nearly at the end of the second hundred years of war between England and France, England stood, for the first time, on the threshold of final victory.

11 1759 The Year of Victories

Fort Louis, in the Senegal river on the West Coast of Africa, had surrendered to Captain Marsh of the Royal Navy on 23 April 1758, but his force of 200 marines and twenty-five gunners was too small to attack the island of Goree, the main French slaving station. Another expedition had to be mounted, and at the end of the year Lieutenant-Colonel Worge was given command of the 76th Foot and two companies of the 66th. He was ordered to embark his force at Kinsale in the south of Ireland, in the squadron commanded by Captain Keppel. On 28 December the expedition arrived off Cape Verde and on the following day the naval guns opened fire on the French batteries on the island of Goree. After a brief bombardment the French surrendered, yielding over 300 prisoners and 100 guns, and thus the new year began with the acquisition by Britain of the French settlements in West Africa.

While Keppel was sailing south with his armament another expedition was on its way to the West Indies. This consisted of six battalions, commanded by Major-General Peregrine Hopson who had been the Governor of Nova Scotia in the troubled years just before the war began, and Colonel Barrington, a young and comparatively junior officer, was his second-in-command. The transports were escorted by eight warships under Commodore Hughes, and they reached Barbados, the normal base for all British operations in the West Indies, on 3 January 1759. Here they were joined by two more men-of-war and Commodore Moore took over the command of the fleet. On 13 January Moore set his course to the north-west, running before the trade wind, and two days later came into the Bay of Fort Royal (now Fort de France) in the island of Martinique. A French battery on Negro Point fired a few rounds to indicate that the garrison was ready to receive visitors, and at dawn on 16 January the warships stood in and silenced the coast guns.

That afternoon the troops landed unopposed in a small cove nearby and spent the night under arms, formed up in a square, ready for any French attack.

Next morning Hopson's outposts were fired on and they fell back, reporting that the enemy were coming up and that they were fortifying a house only a short distance away. Hopson sent his grenadiers forward, and they drove the French off after a brisk engagement which Hopson hoped would be the prelude to a general advance. But the enemy had disappeared into the dense tangle of trees and undergrowth.

'Never was such a country,' wrote the General; 'the Highlands of Scotland for woods, mountains and continued ravines are nothing to it.'

He soon discovered there was no hope of dragging heavy artillery through such country to attack Fort Royal and so decided to re-embark and try to find a more suitable place. About 100 of his men had been killed or wounded in the battle in the woods that morning, and although the French were waiting to take advantage of any move he made, he managed to get his men off without losing any more. On 18 January the fleet began to sail round the island, northwards, and in the evening arrived off St Pierre, the second largest place in Martinique. Moore moved in next morning to take a look at the town's defences and was met by so fierce a fire from batteries on the high ground that he came to the conclusion an assault landing was not feasible. At a Council of War it was resolved to postpone the taking of Martinique and attack Guadeloupe instead, an island which was the richest of all French possessions in the Caribbean and used as a base by most of the French privateers.

Passing Dominica, still held by the French, the fleet sailed north, preceded by a frigate carrying the chief military engineer whose task was to reconnoitre and report on the town of Basseterre in the south-west of the island. He came back with a gloomy tale of impregnable fortifications which Commodore Moore refused to believe, and at ten o'clock on the morning of 23 January he began to bombard the fort and the coastal batteries. Every warehouse in the town was full of sugar and rum, the produce of the recent harvest, and in a few hours a thick pall of smoke hung over the blazing buildings. By nightfall

all the enemy batteries were out of action and the town was in ruins. Next morning the troops went ashore and found all the elaborate defence works abandoned and the guns spiked, but random shooting from the sugar cane indicated that the enemy had not gone far. The British force occupied what was left of Basseterre and then the French began to harass the invasion force with constant sniping and skirmishing. Hopson sent a summons to the French Governor, demanding his surrender, and received only a rude reply. The Governor had withdrawn his main force about six miles from Basseterre to a virtually impregnable position on high ground protected by impenetrable forest on either flank and a river across his front. The only approach to it was along a narrow, heavily defended track. Refusing to deploy his troops for a proper battle the Governor stayed where he was and sent out small parties to make as much of a nuisance of themselves as possible. He was confident that in due course sickness and the climate would drive the invaders away.

He had good reason to be hopeful. By the end of January one-quarter of the British force was unfit for duty, and apart from sending 600 invalids to Antigua in the hope that some might survive, Hopson did not seem to know what to do next. Commodore Moore, who was free to conduct his own naval operations, sailed round to Grande Terre, the most fertile part of the island, attacked Fort Louis, guarding the excellent harbour of Point à Pitre, and battered it into surrender with his guns. He then installed a garrison of 300 Highlanders and Marines, and suggested to Hopson that the best thing to do would be to move to this new base and start his land operations all over again. But Hopson would not move, and he was too ill to cope with any new plan. He died on 27 February, and there is no doubt that his death saved the force from total destruction, for the command devolved upon Colonel Barrington. He had been unable to persuade Hopson to do anything, while the men were going sick and dying at an appalling rate, and he at once brought this period of fatal inaction to an end.

Barrington was a man of great energy and resource, and he had had time to think out a possible solution to the strategic and tactical problems that had been too much for Hopson. He came to the conclusion that in so wild and mountainous an island the French settlements could only be at the mouths of valleys which were in communication with other parts of the island either by sea or coastal roads. He then discovered, by a reconnaissance made in a small boat, that the French had set up a mass of batteries and trench systems to protect these settlements, and it was clear that the holding of these defences meant that all the available French troops were widely dispersed in little detachments dotted all over the place. By applying the principle of concentration of force these scattered defences could be destroyed in detail in a series of sea-borne raids.

Leaving a garrison in Basseterre, Barrington moved to Fort Louis, spent a fortnight in repairing its defences, and on 27 March began to put his plan into effect. Six hundred men under the command of Colonel Crump were sent off to the south coast with orders to land between the towns of St Anne and St François and destroy both, with all their defences. The operation was a complete success and did much to restore the morale of troops who had reached the stage of sitting down and waiting for death. Unable to guess when the next hammer blow would come, or where it would be delivered, the French lost heart, and on 19 April, when the British entered the district of Capesterre, reckoned to be the richest area in the whole of the West Indies, and were about to destroy it, a deputation begged Barrington for terms. On 1 May the capitulation was signed and the British Crown acquired Guadeloupe, with a harbour large enough to provide shelter from hurricanes for the whole British Navy.

Since trading interests had no voice in the councils of Louis XV these losses in the West Indies and West Africa were regarded only as minor military incidents, of little importance in relation to the war in Europe or events in India and North America. France would take her revenge in the coming invasion of England.

For some time there had been a great stir and bustle along the French coast, centred on Le Havre, and flat-bottomed boats to convey cavalry, infantry and artillery were being collected in many harbours and inlets. In England the Militia was embodied and 24,000 French prisoners of war, placed under stronger guards, were marched away inland from the southern counties, where they might have been able to assist an invasion force. In an attempt to meet and disperse the storm before it could break, Admiral Rodney bombarded Le Havre in the early summer, set fire to the town and did much damage. Any destruction of naval stores was an advantage to the British because the French Marine was in a deplorable state, having had five different Ministers in the past six years, each more incompetent than the last, and losses could not be replaced. In 1759 the Minister was M. Berryer, a protégé of Madame de Pompadour, held in contempt by all regular French naval officers.

In the Mediterranean, Admiral Boscawen attacked the outer harbour of Toulon. He withdrew after this show of strength and the commander of the Toulon fleet, Admiral de la Clue, seized what appeared to be a chance to break the tight British blockade, slip through the Straits of Gibraltar and join the Brest fleet commanded by the Marshal de Conflans, a move vital to the success of the invasion of England. Boscawen's watchful frigates saw him go, and on 18 August the British battle fleet fell upon the French off Cape Lagos on the coast of Portugal. Admiral de la Clue, fighting with great gallantry, was mortally wounded. His ship and three other first-rates (with an armament of more than 100 guns) struck to Boscawen and a fifth was driven ashore and burnt. This defeat added to the invasion problems, and though the French had hitherto regarded the junction of the Toulon and Brest fleets as essential if the passage of the land forces was to be adequately protected, they did not abandon their plan.

In November, winter storms forced Admiral Sir Edward Hawke's fleet off its task of blockading Conflans in Brest. Hawke returned on 20 November to learn that Conflans, who was now responsible for convoying the military transports across the Channel, had escaped. He also learned that the French fleet, sheltering from the storm then raging, had anchored in Quiberon Bay, away to the south-east. Ignoring the storm and the dangers of a lee shore notorious for its uncharted reefs and shoals, Hawke led his ships into an action deemed by Conflans to be impossible. Lying among rocks and sandbanks the French felt safe from any attack, until the British men-of-war came at them through narrow and dangerous passes. Commodore

Howe—now Lord Howe after the death of his elder brother in the woods near Ticonderoga—drove in so close to the great French ship *Formidable* that her prow struck the waist of his ship and smashed in the lower tier of guns. Of the French fleet of twenty-one ships, two—one of them the flagship of Marshal de Conflans—grounded on rocks and were burnt, two more were sunk, one was taken, and another struck her Colours but managed to get away because British sailors were unable to board her in the storm. Seven others escaped up a small inlet where the last one did not work herself free for two years. The remainder fled south and took refuge in Rochefort.

Admiral Hawke had a fleet of twenty-three ships, but in the howling wind and the gloom of that short November day less than half were able to take up station with him. No more than ten came into action. Two of these were wrecked but the crews were saved. This decisive victory, coming so soon after Boscawen's success, put an end for a time to all reasonably large-scale French naval operations.

Another result of Admiral Hawke's great battle was that for the rest of the war the little fishing port of Quiberon in Brittany was a British naval base where the sailors tilled French soil and grew vegetables to supplement their victuals.

After all the threats and preparations for an invasion, so long dreaded by the civilian population of England who were often ready to shout for war but usually reluctant to pay for or take part in it, the actual event, when it came about, had a touch of *opéra bouffe*.

In February 1760 a French privateer named Thurot landed 1,000 troops from five ships which came into Carrickfergus on the north side of Belfast Lough in Northern Ireland. After a mild skirmish the local garrison surrendered. Contrary to the terms of the capitulation Thurot then plundered the town; his troops acquired a little booty and enjoyed, rather hastily, some of the girls, and re-embarked. On the way home his squadron encountered three British warships, and in the brisk battle Thurot himself was killed and all his ships captured. As an 'invasion' it was an anticlimax, but at least it relieved the tension.

In the land operations in Europe Louis XV's vengeance on Frederick the Great for the insults to Madame de Pompadour was proving expensive, and it is significant that whereas the French King sent hundreds of thousands of French soldiers into Germany on this ridiculous mission, he left his colonies to take their chance. His colonial governors were forced to carry on the war as best they could with little hope of any effective aid from France.

Defeated at Krefeld by Ferdinand, Duke of Brunswick, in 1758, the French recrossed the Rhine in April 1759, moved up the valley of the Main and occupied Bergen. Here, on 13 April, Ferdinand attacked them again, but was defeated, and he had to withdraw north to hold the line of the river Weser which was his main supply route from Germany and England. He resolved to make his stand at Minden where the river flows through the narrow gap in the line of hills on the southern edge of the Hanoverian plain. His force of 45,000 men included six regiments of British infantry (the 12th, 20th, 23rd, 25th, 37th and 51st) and a detachment of fifteen squadrons of British cavalry (the Blues, the 1st and 3rd Dragoon Guards, the Scots Greys and the 10th Dragoons). Lord George Sackville was in charge of this body of Horse.

The French army, 60,000 strong, commanded by the Marshal duc Louis de Contades, followed up Ferdinand's withdrawal, making for Hanover. During the night of 31 July Contades sent his army across the Weser to battle positions on the plain of Minden, and early in the morning of 1 August it drew up in the unusual and unorthodox formation of a centre of cavalry and two wings of infantry.

Ferdinand's army was formed into eight columns. Of these, the first, or right-hand, column consisted of twenty-four cavalry squadrons under Sackville, the second of German artillery, and the third, commanded by Major General von Spörcke, was British infantry. The remaining columns were Prussian, Hessian and Hanoverian troops. When he saw the French moving into position Ferdinand ordered his army to occupy prearranged locations with the cavalry on the flanks and infantry in the centre. Seven out of the eight columns marched off at once. In Sackville's column all was confusion; some of the units were ready to move, some were not. Sackville himself could not be found.

While the British infantry regiments were deploying from

column into line, Ferdinand sent a message saying that when the time came for the advance it should be made with drums beating, but somebody got the message wrong or misunderstood it, and the ranks of scarlet, joined now by Hardenberg's Hanoverian battalion and two battalions of Hanoverian Guards, began to move forward immediately. With drums rolling, with perfect dressing and steadiness the Line Regiments, unsupported by the rest of Ferdinand's army, marched forward into the crossfire of more than sixty enemy cannon to attack the French cavalry, drawn up in three lines. As they advanced across two hundred yards of open ground great gaps were torn in the British ranks by the French guns, but nothing could stop this measured approach to the huge mass of enemy Horse. Suddenly this wall of cavalry came to life. Eleven squadrons detached themselves and charged the oncoming infantry. The battalions halted to receive them; standing motionless until the horsemen were only ten yards away. Then one volley strewed the ground with dead and wounded men and animals, breaking and hurling back the charge—and the advance continued.

The enemy cavalry rallied. Contades sent forward four brigades of infantry and thirty-two guns to take the British and Hanoverians in enfilade. The second line of Horse, eager to retrieve the first repulse, thundered down upon the nine isolated battalions. Under this triple attack of Horse, Foot and Guns the British and Hanoverian infantry seemed for a moment to waver, but they were merely closing their ranks before meeting the squadrons with a storm of musketry which swept them from the field. Turning then upon the French infantry they beat them back with appalling loss and Ferdinand realized that he had an opportunity to annihilate the French army. He sent an aide-de-camp to Sackville to tell him to charge with the whole of his column.

Sackville, who already had a reputation for reluctance either to obey orders or to expose himself to enemy shot or sabre, did not move. Ferdinand sent four messengers, one after another. Finally a fifth was dispatched direct to the gallant Marquis of Granby, commanding the squadrons of Sackville's second line. He was just moving off when Sackville rode up and forbade him to advance. The moment passed. Contades, who had lost

7,000 men and forty-three guns, was able to withdraw in good order. Sackville was subsequently court martialled and found unfit ever again to hold the King's Commission. Although he was cashiered it had little effect on his career. Changing his name to Lord George Germaine he later became Secretary at War in George III's government and played a conspicuous part in losing the Colonies in the American War of Independence.

The battle of Minden, which cost the Allies 3,000 men, mostly from the six British infantry regiments, did not end the Continental war. It dragged on until November 1762, and the next major action in which British troops were engaged was the battle of Warburg in July 1760. Here the cavalry redeemed themselves after Sackville's disgraceful behaviour, for the valley below the castle was the scene of that splendid charge of twenty-two squadrons led by the Marquis of Granby at the head of his own regiment, the Blues. As the trot became a gallop the wind snatched away Granby's hat, and with his bald head gleaming in the sun he bore down upon the French with the British squadrons in two lines thundering behind him.

Only three out of all the French squadrons were brave enough to stand and await the shock, but they were cut to pieces by the Blues and the King's Dragoon Guards. The French infantry, attacked on both flanks, broke and fled. The British artillery came down to the bank of the river Diemal at the gallop, unlimbered at a speed which amazed even the French gunners and brought so destructive a fire upon the fleeing enemy that they could not rally or reform. Granby crossed the river with ten of his squadrons and continued the pursuit. There was never any doubt about who won the battle of Warburg.

Other battles were fought: at Kloster-Kampen in October 1760, when the allies were defeated; at Vellinghausen in July 1761, where Ferdinand with 50,000 men defeated the French commanders de Broglie and Soubise who had 100,000; at Wilhelmsthal in June 1762 where the French were again defeated; and finally at the Brückemühle in September of the same year, another allied success. The war came to an end when the town of Kassel fell to Ferdinand on 1 November 1762. In five consecutive and successful campaigns the Duke of Brunswick, commanding the British and German troops, had established himself as one of history's great generals. Yet, despite the loss of casualties, nothing had really been achieved by either side. Louis XV's magnificent army had been convincingly defeated, Frederick the Great retained all the territory in Silesia which he had taken from Austria, and he was certainly never made to apologize to *Fräulein Fisch.*

In India, at the end of the year 1758, Colonel Forde and his invaluable subordinate Captain Knox were at Rajahmundry, arguing with Anunderaj over the payment of the troops, and longing to push on to capture Masulipatam, while the comte de Lally sat outside Madras and prayed the town would fall before the British Navy could relieve it.

After six weeks of negotiation Forde at last persuaded Anunderaj to honour his undertaking, and the campaign could go on, but the French had been given time to recover themselves. Moving from Rajahmundry on 28 January 1759, Forde occupied Ellore, forty-eight miles north of Masulipatam, on 6 February. Learning that the French commander, Conflans, had put garrisons into the two forts of Narsipur and Concal, to the north of Masulipatam, he sent Captain Knox forward to take Narsipur, but it was evacuated before he got there. On 3 March Forde took Concal, gallantly defended by a French sergeant, and three days later came in sight of the fortifications of Masulipatam. These had been considerably strengthened by the French during their years of occupation since 1751.

Conflans had disposed his force in a strong position in front of the town and it seemed as if he was prepared to seek a decision in battle in the open, but having little faith in his troops after their defeat at Condore he changed his mind and went inside the walls. The siege lasted for a month. In the middle of it, on 27 March, Forde received the alarming news that Salabad Jang, Nawab of the Deccan, had arrived at the river Kistna, hardly forty miles away, and he had brought with him an army of 40,000 men to expel the British invasion force operating in territory which was under his control. Anunderaj at once became panic-stricken and was just setting off to return to his own country when Forde persuaded him that his only chance of survival lay in staying with the British. An emissary was sent to Salabad who cannot have been very eager to attack the British for he undertook to remain where he was for the moment. Thus, on 1 April, when the emissary returned, Forde knew he had a brief respite.

For the past seven days the batteries erected to bombard the defence works had been doing a considerable amount of damage, although the garrison of the town had been repairing at night much of what had been done during the day. By this time three of the bastions had been reduced to the state where it would be possible for storming parties to climb them, but on 5 April the southern monsoon broke in a deluge of rain which turned the low ground round the fort into a swamp. On the following day, although the rain ceased, which was something to be thankful for, Colonel Forde had little else to cheer him. News came that Salabad was advancing from the Kistna and that Conflans's compatriot and subordinate, du Rocher, had collected a force of 250 Europeans and 2,000 sepoys and was about to join the Nawab's army. To make matters worse, Forde's artillery officers reported that the siege batteries had only enough ammunition left for two days.

Faced by a stronghold garrisoned with a force larger than his own, and threatened in the rear with an army out-numbering his by at least ten to one, running out of ammunition and with no money left to pay his troops, Forde had the choice of two options: either to raise the siege and embark on the supporting naval vessels lying off the coast, or to risk everything in one desperate endeavour. He resolved to take Masulipatam by storm.

He divided his force into four parties. One, under Captain Knox, was to launch a feint attack while two others, under Captains Callendar and Yorke, were to assault the north-east bastion named Chameleon. The fourth party was to be a reserve under Forde himself. One of the real problems was the quagmire surrounding the defences, but several of the local inhabitants were seen crossing it, and when Captain Knox investigated he found it was not more than knee-deep. On 7 April the siege batteries kept up a heavy fire all day until it was too dark to see, and at ten o'clock that night the assaulting columns began to move forward, trying to squelch through the mud as silently as possible. Knox made his feint attack exactly on time, the other two columns, with Forde close behind, carried the walls, and after several hours of confused fighting in the darkness Conflans sent a messenger to Forde offering to surrender on terms. Forde, knowing Conflans's strength in manpower, and his own weakness, demanded surrender, and Conflans, assuming that his own position was now hopeless, complied. Five hundred French troops and 2,000 sepoys laid down their arms and Forde had achieved his aim for the loss of eighty-six Europeans and 200 sepoys killed and wounded.

Salabad Jang was now only fifteen miles away and du Rocher even closer, but news of the fall of Masulipatam brought them both to a halt. Salabad reopened negotiations, which he managed to draw out over a whole month, but in the end he granted eighty miles of the coast to the British and undertook not only never to harbour or employ French troops again but to force any that still remained to leave the Circars. Thus Colonel Forde, against all the odds and faced by problems few men would have had the boldness to solve by his methods, had acquired the whole district formerly held by the French and destroyed, for ever, their influence at the court of the Deccan.

Outside Madras the batteries Lally had constructed opposite the north and north-west fronts of the fortifications opened fire for the first time on 2 January 1759. They went on shooting spasmodically throughout the month, but with little effect, and largely because Lally seemed incapable of maintaining any discipline in the troops under his command everything was slow and inefficient and nothing was done without reluctance. Meanwhile the British had sent Captain Caillaud down to Tanjore to hire troops from the Rajah, but he encountered all sorts of difficulties in the negotiations and it was not until 7 February that he came back with 1,300 Tanjore infantry and 2,000 Horse and joined Captain Preston who was commanding the fort at Chingleput. Lally had much cause to regret his failure to reduce this stronghold before moving against Madras, for Preston harassed him incessantly, raiding his camp at night and disrupting his communications.

On 30 January a British ship came into Madras and unloaded badly needed money and ammunition. It also brought news that Admiral Pocock was on his way from Bombay. Lally heard this too, and when he also learned of the Tanjore reinforcement in Chingleput he decided to do what he should have done months before. Detaching a force of 900 Europeans, 1,200 sepoys, 500 native cavalry and eight field guns he set out to deal with Preston, Caillaud and Chingleput. In a close and hard-fought battle the French were repulsed, so the menace of Chingleput remained and Lally's fortunes were at their lowest ebb. He had very nearly run out of supplies, ammunition and money; his troops were deserting by dozens every day, and though he had succeeded in battering a breach in the walls of Madras he could not persuade anyone to attack.

At length, on 16 February Admiral Pocock's squadron arrived to relieve Madras and threaten Pondicherry. On the morning of the 17th, just as it was getting light, the watchers on the walls of Madras saw Lally's rearguard marching away down the road to Arcot. Left behind were fifty-two guns, all Lally's stores and ammunition and forty sick and wounded men.

The siege of Madras was the last offensive operation under-taken by the French in India. It had cost the British a total of 613 European and 300 sepoy casualties—made good so far as Europeans were concerned by reinforcements carried by Pocock. There is no record of the French losses. Lally, embittered and angered by his failure, blamed it on the authorities at Pondi-cherry who, with all the pettiness of small minds, had done all they could to frustrate him and had succeeded. With their loyal support, things obviously would have been much easier for him, but his military defeat was very largely his own fault and stemmed from two major errors. He failed to take Chingle-put when it would not have been difficult to do so, and it became a fatal thorn in his side. Secondly, he failed to enforce discipline. Although the French cause in India was not yet entirely lost it had little hope of survival in the hands of such a man.

With his unpaid troops yet again in a state of mutiny Lally concentrated his force at Conjeveram, and on 6 April Stringer Lawrence set out from Madras to attack him, taking a force of 6,000 men of whom 1,156 were Europeans, and ten field guns. For three weeks the rival armies lay encamped within sight of one another, and then Lawrence moved south to the French station of Wandiwash, entered the town and began to besiege the fort. Lally hurried to defend the place whereupon Lawrence, gratified by the success of his plan, evaded him, slipped back and took the far more valuable fort of Conjeveram.

On 28 May both commanders put their troops in cantonments for the hot weather. Madras had been saved, the French troops were utterly dispirited and French influence along the Coromandel coast had been destroyed.

Admiral Pocock left Madras on 20 August and sailed for Trincomalee in Ceylon where he found his old adversary d'Aché whose morale had suffered badly from previous meetings. This time d'Aché had the advantage, with eleven ships of the line and four frigates against Pocock's nine men-of-war, one frigate, two East Indiamen and a fireship. This gave the French a superiority of 174 guns. Pocock at once offered battle but wind and currents prevented any real engagements for several days. He caught the French at last on 10 September, but after two hours d'Aché broke off and fled back to Pondicherry. By now he had lost all hope of ever being able to compete with British sea power and British sailors.

Pitt's plan of campaign in North America for 1759 was only slightly less ambitious than the one for the previous year. A direct attack was to be made on Quebec, Wolfe was to be responsible for it, and Amherst was to transfer ten battalions to his command. At the same time there was to be an advance by way of Ticonderoga and Crown Point under Amherst's direction—Abercromby having been recalled in disgrace— with the object of either joining Wolfe in the attack on Quebec or forcing the French to divert troops from the defence of the capital. There were too many imponderables for so vast a plan to have been a complete success, but the great measure of it that was achieved was due very largely to the brilliance of a young officer of Pitt's own choice. James Wolfe, now thirty-two, recently promoted on Pitt's instructions to the rank of lieutenant-general, had held a commission since the age of fourteen. He had distinguished himself as a brigade-major in Flanders but he had really caught the public eye by his behaviour at Louisbourg, leaping ashore at Freshwater Cove with his cane in his hand. He was an admirable soldier:

imperturbable under fire, competent, enthusiastic, devoted to his men and trusted by them—a fine, aggressive commander.

His task against Quebec was to be part of a co-ordinated design involving two other expeditions, and when worked out in detail it was all rather more complicated than had at first been envisaged. General Jeffrey Amherst was to occupy Crown Point, reduce Fort Ticonderoga, cross Lake Champlain and go straight down the St Lawrence to join Wolfe at Quebec. While Amherst was going down the great waterway, a third force under the command of General Prideaux and containing a considerable number of unpredictable Indians, was to take Fort Niagara, embark on Lake Ontario, pass the ruins of Fort Frontenac, capture Montreal and then join Wolfe and Amherst for the final assault on Quebec. The plan was not in fact quite so unworldly as it sounds, as Amherst was to prove in the following year.

Wolfe's relations with Amherst were not particularly happy, and they were made rather worse by Wolfe's return to England after the fall of Louisbourg without formal permission and probably because of a misunderstanding over his posting order. Thus Wolfe was at home when the campaign was being planned. He left England in the middle of February 1759, in *Neptune*, the flag-ship of a fleet of twenty-one ships under the command of Admirals Saunders, Holmes and Durell, and in May the Quebec assault force began to assemble at Louisbourg. Wolfe had been told he would have a total of 12,000 men but units which were to come from the West Indies were still on operations in Guadeloupe and those from Nova Scotia were well below strength because of sickness during the winter. In the end he had about 8,500, all excellent troops, and he divided them into three brigades led by Brigadiers Moncton, Townshend and Murray, who were all young, energetic and able. By 6 June all was ready, and the warships and transports left Louisbourg for the St Lawrence.

Despite Montcalm's success at Ticonderoga in the previous year the French commanders in Canada were under no illusions about what was likely to happen in the next campaigning season. They anticipated a two-pronged attack, from the south along Lake Champlain and down the Richelieu river, and from the west from Lake Ontario—the tasks in fact allotted to

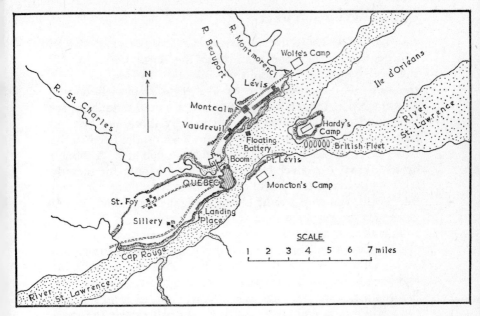

The Siege of Quebec 1759

Amherst and Prideaux—and they had made their dispositions accordingly. They then heard of the third approach, up the St Lawrence, and this upset all their arrangements. Five regular battalions, the militia from all over Canada and 1,000 Indians were concentrated at Quebec, and after much deliberation Montcalm worked out his plan of defence. The fortified town of Quebec stood on a rocky headland which is the north-west limit of a high plateau rising steeply from the river on its southern side. The headland marks the point where the river suddenly narrows from a width of fifteen to twenty miles down to a narrow strait barely 2,000 yards across. Immediately to the north of the plateau the St Charles river flows into the St Lawrence, and seven miles to the east, along the bank of the St Lawrence there is the rocky gorge of the Montmorenci. Midway between the St Charles and the Montmorenci rivers is the Beauport river, flowing out into mudflats between it and the St Charles. Westward, from the Beauport to the Montmorenci are steep and rocky cliffs.

In his appreciation, Montcalm reckoned that any sea-borne enemy attacking Quebec would try to come ashore on the north

263

side of the St Lawrence, between the Beauport and the St Charles, and attack the town from the north and east. He therefore determined to hold the bank of the St Lawrence with the right of his line on the St Charles and his left on the Montmorenci. Trenches were dug, batteries and redoubts were built, and the whole area was covered by shore and floating batteries and the hundred guns of the town on the heights, the entire defensive system being manned by 14,000 men. Although he took great care over his defence works Montcalm secretly felt they were rather a waste of time because he was confident that no foreign ship would try to navigate the unknown and extremely dangerous waters of the St Lawrence.

The mastheads of British ships were first seen by the garrison of Quebec on 21 June, despite the fact that on Montcalm's orders all the buoys and markers that made the river usable had been removed. There was, however, a junior Master in the British fleet, of the same age as Wolfe, who was to become one of the world's great explorers, and James Cook's early career as a navigator very nearly came to an abrupt end one night while he was taking soundings close to the bank of the St Lawrence. A party of Indians armed with tomahawks and scalping knives jumped into the stern of his boat while he leapt out from the bow. It was he who made a chart of the St Lawrence river, so accurate that it was not superseded for more than a century, and as a result of his work, ships of the line passed where the French had not dared to take a coasting schooner. By 26 June the whole fleet and all the transports lay safely at anchor off the Île d'Orleans, which Jacques Cartier's men had named the Île de Bacchus, a few miles below Quebec.

The British troops landed on the island on the following day, and on 28 June the French launched fireships down the river against the British fleet. The attempt literally misfired because the British sailors rowed out, grappled the burning vessels and towed them ashore where they blazed away harmlessly to the water line. A second attempt to burn the fleet was made a month later on 28 July, with exactly the same result. These were the only offensive moves made by the French, and Montcalm saw no reason why he should do anything more. All he had to do was defend his lines against attack and wait for winter to force the British out of the river.

Wolfe, after a long and careful reconnaissance of the French defences, found himself coming to much the same conclusion for he could find no opening for an attack. He sent Moncton's brigade up on to the heights of Point Lévis, on the south side of the river and almost opposite Quebec, where batteries were erected and the guns played havoc with the buildings in the town, but he knew this would do no more than upset the townspeople. He then sent Townshend's and Murray's brigades to dig in on the east bank of the Montmorenci, to threaten Montcalm's left flank and perhaps find a way round it, but this achieved nothing. There seemed to be nothing he could do.

Then, on the night of 18 July, the Royal Navy disturbed the state of deadlock by penetrating further up the river. The French were confident that no ship could sail past the guns of Quebec without being blown to pieces, but the *Sutherland*, 50 guns, slipped past in the darkness, followed by several smaller vessels, and destroyed some French craft moored above the town. This posed a serious threat to Montcalm who saw for the first time the danger that Quebec might be taken from the rear, or south-east, and he deployed 600 men from the camp at Beauport to defend possible landing places between the town and Cap Rouge, eight miles above it. The ability of the naval vessels to move up and down the river constantly threatening raids in sparsely held places was a perpetual worry to the French, and exhausted the troops who were kept moving up and down the north bank of the river, all to little purpose.

On 31 July Wolfe made one attempt at a landing near the mouth of the Montmorenci, but it failed, with the loss of 500 casualties. In August more ships under Admiral Holmes braved the batteries and passed up river, taking with them a flotilla of landing craft, and Brigadier Murray marched up the south bank with a force of 1,200 men to man them. This compelled Montcalm to detach another 1,500 men from the Beauport camp, and under the command of Bougainville—who later became almost as famous as James Cook for his voyages in the South Seas—this small force wore itself out trying to guard nearly twenty miles of shore. Yet, more important than the threat of sudden landings was the fact that the British fleet had found one way of reducing the city; by the blockade of the river. Cut off from all supplies up and down the river it now became a question of whether winter ice could save Quebec before the defenders starved.

Meanwhile the other British expeditions were on the move. General Prideaux had collected his force at Schenectady on the Mohawk river, moved upstream on 15 June and by way of the Great Carrying-Place, Lake Oneida and the Onandaga river came to Oswego. From here he sailed along the shore of Lake Ontario until he reached Fort Niagara, garrisoned by 600 men. He laid siege in form and very soon after his batteries opened fire he was killed by the premature explosion of a shell from one of his own guns. Sir William Johnson, who had joined the column with a party of Indians, took over the command, beat off a force of 1,300 French rangers and Indians trying to relieve the fort, accepted the surrender of Fort Niagara on 24 July, and by so doing secured the whole region of the upper Ohio and cut off from Canada all the French posts in the west. This opened the way for the advance on Montreal by Lake Ontario, and Amherst at once sent General Gage up to take over from Johnson and attack the French fort of La Galette at the entrance to the St Lawrence rapids, thereafter to push on to Montreal. Gage seems to have been unable to get the force moving at all and by the middle of August his operations had come to a halt.

Amherst set sail on Lake George with a force of 11,500 men on 21 July and followed Abercromby's route to Ticonderoga. He found all the outer defence works, built by Montcalm, had been repaired but were deserted. The French commander, Bourlamaque, had pulled his small force of 3,500 men back into the main fort. Unlike Abercromby, Amherst brought up all his artillery and prepared for a siege, but during the night of 26 July the French blew up a bastion and withdrew, falling back through Crown Point, which was also evacuated, to the strong outpost on Île aux Noix at the northern end of Lake Champlain. Although Amherst had achieved the first part of his mission, and taken both Ticonderoga and Crown Point, he could now get no further because the French had four armed vessels on the lake and he had none. By the time he had built similar craft for the protection of his own flotilla the season was too far advanced into winter for any further operations.

The loss of Niagara, Ticonderoga and Crown Point had

little effect on the Quebec garrison except for a higher rate of desertion among faint-hearted militiamen who wanted to go home and did not mind very much who ruled Canada.

Wolfe was discouraged by the news that he could no longer count on any support coming down the St Lawrence. He was faced with an apparently insoluble problem, for if he was to take Quebec he had to force Montcalm to give battle, and Montcalm had no intention of doing any such thing. The only possible battlefield was the open ground known as the Plains of Abraham on the plateau under the walls of the town, at the top of unscalable cliffs 200 feet high. The story of the solution to his problem is a familiar one.

Wolfe learned of a path up to the heights. At two o'clock on the morning of 13 September two signal lanterns were hoisted to the maintop shrouds of H.M.S. *Sutherland* and the chilly night was filled with quiet movement. Wolfe handed to Captain John Jervis of the *Porcupine* (afterwards Lord St Vincent) the portrait of the girl to whom he was betrothed, asking Jervis to return it to her if he was killed—he seemed to have a strong premonition of death. He and his staff then stepped into their boat and, with the rest of the force, moved silently upriver on the flood tide. At sunrise 4,500 men had climbed the cliff and were drawn up on the Plains of Abraham.

Montcalm seems to have lost his head. Though there was plenty of time for him to assemble all his troops and artillery he hurried into battle with 5,000 men of the town garrison and did not wait until he had been joined by Bougainville and seven more battalions which had been deployed to guard the banks of the river. Shortly before ten o'clock, with loud shouts and in somewhat ragged order, his line advanced to the attack. While still 200 yards from the British force the French opened fire, although the effective range of a musket was little more than fifty yards. Wolfe was hit in the wrist. He bandaged the wound and called on his men to stand steady and hold their fire. When the opposing armies were only thirty-five yards apart the British fired their first volley which Fortescue describes as 'the most perfect ever fired on any battlefield, which burst forth as if from a single monstrous weapon, from end to end of the British line'. It shattered the French. One more volley was fired and Wolfe gave the order to charge with bayonet, sword and claymore. He led, at the head of the 28th Foot. A bullet struck him in the groin but he did not even pause. Moments later another passed through his lungs.

'Support me, support me!' he gasped to an officer beside him, 'lest my gallant fellows should see me fall.'

Two or three men carried him, dying, to the rear, just as Montcalm, shot through the body but supported in the saddle by an aide-de-camp, rode back through the gates of the town and women screamed at the sight of blood on his white uniform. He was taken to the house of a surgeon. Wolfe refused to see one.

'There is no need,' he said. 'It is all over with me.'

His eyes closed.

'How they run,' called out one of the men near him, watching the fleeing French as they tumbled back into the town.

'Who run?' asked Wolfe, rousing himself.

'The enemy, sir. They give way everywhere.'

'Go one of you to General Burton,' said Wolfe, making a great effort, 'and tell him to march Webb's Regiment [28th Foot] down to Charles river to cut off the retreat from the bridge.' He paused, turned painfully over on his side, whispered, 'Now, God be praised, I will die in peace,' and died.

The year of Victories drew to a close. Britain had made great gains in the West Indies and West Africa. Her arms were triumphant in Europe and her navy supreme on all the oceans of the world. But in Canada and India there was still work to be done.

12 The End of the Struggle

Wolfe's victory on the Plains of Abraham did not decide the fate of Quebec. Immediately after the battle Montcalm lay dying in the house of a surgeon, Wolfe's body was carried on board the flagship of Admiral Saunders, and inevitably there was a brief hiatus while both sides tried to adjust to what had happened.

In the English lines General Townshend took over the command—the senior Brigadier-General, Moncton, had been wounded—and at once found the rear of his army threatened by Bougainville and the force that had been guarding the river bank above the town. Deploying two battalions and two field guns Townshend drove the French off and, feeling exposed and vulnerable on the open plain, began to entrench himself on the battlefield in anticipation of the massive counter-attack he had every reason to expect.

In Quebec, in the absence of de Lévis who was in Montreal and awaiting Amherst's approach, the command devolved upon the Governor-General, Vaudreuil. Being frightened as well as incapable he was in no state to make up his own mind, and so he called a Council of War. This developed into furious and incoherent argument over which Vaudreuil had so little control that in the end a messenger was sent to Montcalm to ask for his advice. He offered the three choices which must have been obvious to everyone: to retreat up the St Lawrence, to stay and fight again, or surrender the whole colony. The obvious course was to stay and fight again. Townshend's force was in a precarious position and considerably out-numbered by the troops under Bougainville's command. Quebec was still defensible, but the totally unexpected appearance of the redcoats that morning, the shattering effect of their musketry and the loss of the Commander-in-Chief had robbed the French of all resolution. At nine o'clock that night,

13 September 1759, Vaudreuil ordered a retreat, and the whole French army, except the local garrison of Quebec, began a disorderly flight to an outpost named after Jacques Cartier, thirty miles up the river. The instructions left for the garrison were that they should surrender when their provisions ran out.

The marquis de Montcalm died of his wound on the following morning. He was buried in a crudely-made coffin under the floor of the Ursuline convent, his grave being the crater of an English shell. Wolfe's body was eventually laid beside that of his father in Greenwich church and Parliament voted him a monument in Westminster Abbey.

Outside Quebec Townshend was now energetically directing his trenches towards the walls; though how he was still able to get work out of troops who had scaled the Heights of Abraham, fought a battle and dug themselves in, with very little food and no rest at all for over thirty hours, is something of a mystery. Part of their endurance must have stemmed from a very real fear of a French sortie in strength which could have driven them off the plateau if it caught them in the open.

The pressure on them was relaxed somewhat when they heard of Vaudreuil's retreat, but Townshend was aware of two factors which affected his planning. One was the possibility that the demoralized French would soon become an effective force again when they joined de Lévis's army and came under the influence of that extremely able commander. The other was the need to take all possible advantage of the present state of morale inside Quebec, whose inhabitants felt they had been abandoned, and occupy it for his own protection. He therefore sent a summons to the French Governor, M. Ramesay, saying that unless the town was surrendered at once he would come and take it. Ramesay hesitated, feeling certain that de Lévis would relieve him, and so, on 17 September, Townshend took action.

The British warships in the river began to close in to the effective range of their guns, the batteries on Point Lévis were manned, and an assault column of redcoats began to move up the road from the St Charles river towards the walls. French drummers sounded the alarm but the French militia, who were in fact the citizens of the town, refused to answer the call to arms. The French flag was lowered on the citadel, only to be raised again by a party of officers determined to save their honour by resistance; but it was hauled down at the insistence of the townspeople and replaced by the white flag. An officer was sent to Townshend with the object of gaining time by prolonged negotiations but the British commander was peremptory: either the town was surrendered by eleven o'clock or he would take it by storm. Ramesay signed the capitulation —from Townshend's point of view, only just in time. The signed documents were actually on their way back to Townshend from the Governor's office when a party of Canadian horsemen rode into the town carrying provisions and encouraging messages of help on the way. On the next morning, 18 September, de Lévis marched out of Jacques Cartier with a relieving force, only to learn he was too late. The British had occupied the town on the previous afternoon and were now putting its defences in order.

At the end of October Admiral Saunders took his fleet down the river and Townshend returned to England with him, leaving Brigadier-General Murray in command of Quebec with a garrison of 7,500 men. The first stage in the conquest of Canada had been completed.

Wolfe's great achievement in bringing Montcalm to battle outside the walls, and the death of the British commander at the very moment of victory, have tended to cloud over certain aspects of this campaign. The capture of Quebec is synonymous with the name of Wolfe, yet Wolfe did not take the town and the real credit for its fall belongs not to the army but to the Royal Navy. The work of James Cook, the master, has been much obscured by the work of Captain James Cook the navigator and explorer. The name of Admiral Saunders is almost forgotten and few have heard of Admiral Holmes, yet it was the constant defiance of the batteries of Quebec by Holmes and his squadron and the incessant movement of British ships up and down the river, above the town, threatening sudden landings here, there and everywhere, that wore out the French and forced Montcalm to weaken his army by detaching Bougainville's force for bank protection. It was the navy who made it possible for the army to get ashore at all, though it was the drill and discipline of the army, once it was on the plateau, that won the battle—practically with one volley. The whole operation must rank as certainly the first and one of the greatest examples of superb inter-service co-operation, and this of course is always largely a matter of personality linked with a degree of professional skill that evokes the respect of all other partners in the plan. Admiral Saunders and his officers and men, and General Wolfe and his, planned and fought as a team operating with what appears to have been extraordinary harmony and understanding. The French have seldom, if ever, attained so high a level of team-work.

Brigadier-General Murray's task in taking over Quebec was not an enviable one. Much of the town had been laid in ruins by Moncton's guns on Point Lévis. Under the administration of Vaudreuil and Ramesay the people had lost all sense of civic pride, and even of law and order. Theft, pillage and drunkenness—the stocks of liquor were abundant—were so commonplace as to have become accepted, and Murray's first need was to restore a proper discipline among the townspeople. This was done by a combination of ruthlessness, determination and tact, and it is remarkable that the citizens of Quebec soon looked on him as a friend. Other, and worse, troubles began with the coming of a really severe Canadian winter, at the beginning of December. Frostbite and scurvy became insoluble problems. Sentries became frostbitten even though they were relieved every hour, and of all the troops the Highlanders suffered worst—the kilt offering little protection in such conditions—until they were provided with long woollen stockings knitted for them by the nuns of various Orders in the town. By Christmas there were over 150 cases of frostbite and the lack of any fresh provisions so increased the number of scurvy cases that as spring approached there was hardly a single man unaffected by it.

To add to all this was the perpetual threat of an attack by de Lévis, known to be doing his utmost to collect together every available man in a force large enough to overwhelm all British resistance and retake Quebec. Murray had established two fortified outposts, one at Sainte Foy and the other at Vieille Lorette, a few miles west of Quebec, and the French occupied St Augustine, two days' march away. There were several skirmishes in these places; the French were driven from St Augustine, and it was perhaps unfortunate that the British were so consistently successful in minor actions that they began to despise the French as adversaries. Murray received frequent, accurate intelligence of de Lévis's intentions and capabilities, so he was under no illusions about the French resolve to drive him out, and on the other hand de Lévis knew exactly what was going on in Quebec. At the end of March 1760 he heard that Murray had only 3,000 men fit for duty and that 700 corpses lay in convenient snow drifts until the ground became soft enough for the digging of graves.

On 17 April Murray was told by his agents that the French preparations for an attack were now complete, and so he sent a force to the mouth of the Cap Rouge river to prevent any landing at that point. Four days later de Lévis moved against him, coming down the river, not yet entirely free of ice, with a force of 7,000 men, half of them being regular troops. Collecting the garrisons of outposts on the way, he reached St Augustine on 26 April with an army now nearly 9,000 strong. Against such numbers the small British outposts could do nothing except withdraw from Cap Rouge and Vieille Lorette upon Sainte Foy.

De Lévis followed them up, all through one fearful night of sleet and tempest, thinking to catch them and destroy them at dawn, but unknown to him a French gunner, more dead than alive, had been picked up from a drifting ice-floe in the St Lawrence by a British bank piquet and, when revived, had provided valuable information. Acting on it, Murray had come out himself with half his force to cover the withdrawal of his outposts, and so when de Lévis came up to Sainte Foy in the grey morning light of 27 April, his columns, emerging from the forest, found themselves under intense cannon fire, and he could see that every house in the settlement was a strongpoint occupied by British troops. He drew back, intending to wait until it was dark enough to move unseen round the left flank of Murray's position, for he had no mind to sacrifice men to the delaying tactics of the British, and this gave Murray an opportunity to pull all his troops back safely into Quebec.

Next day de Lévis occupied Sainte Foy and pushed a small force over to his right, to Sillery. Murray was now in a very awkward situation. It had not been possible in the short time between the capture of Quebec and the onset of winter to do very much to repair the walls of the town, and they were in no condition to withstand the battering of French artillery. The ground was frozen to such a depth that it was not practicable even to attempt the construction of the defence works outside the walls which Murray had long regarded as essential, and he was uncomfortably certain what would happen if he tried to hold the town, in its present condition, against a siege.

There was only one alternative: to go out, meet de Lévis in the open, and fight him at odds of one against three. Fired by the example of his dead commander, Wolfe, Murray did not apparently find the decision very difficult. At half-past six on the morning of 28 April he marched out of Quebec with every man he could muster—just under 3,000—taking with him three howitzers and twenty field pieces, and drew up his order of battle on the same ground Montcalm had occupied just over seven months before.

Going forward himself to reconnoitre, Murray saw that de Lévis's army was not yet in position although the location of troops already on the ground indicated what his line would be. Murray at once brought his whole army forward until it was in Wolfe's position on the day of the previous battle, and his guns brought down so destructive a fire on French columns de-bouching from a wood that de Lévis had to order them to fall back. This caused considerable confusion, and Murray launched his attack on the positions already occupied by the French. All went well until it was found impossible because of the state of the ground to move either the guns or the ammunition limbers. The advance of 3,000 men through snow everywhere soft and mushy with rain had turned everything into a sea of mud, but where the ground was broken in folds or ridges there were deep snow drifts, not recognizable as such until it was too late. It was in these that the limbers stuck fast and consequently the once furious and devastating fire of the guns ceased altogether.

The French were now able to turn both Murray's flanks, and his position became hopeless. Yet the fight went on with what Fortescue describes as 'indomitable stubbornness'. The English were, as Murray said in a letter to Pitt, 'in the habit of beating the enemy', and the French, with all the confidence inspired by numerical superiority, were determined to regain Quebec. The British troops certainly were prepared to fight to a finish and when Murray gave the order to 'fall back' they were furious; but they obeyed and withdrew in such good order that de Lévis prudently refrained from pursuit.

This action at Sainte Foy lasted only two hours but it cost Murray one-third of his men, about 1,000 killed and wounded, against de Lévis's casualties of about 800. It had not solved any of the problems and had only succeeded in making things much worse for the British. Murray was now enclosed by the inadequate defences of Quebec held by 2,400 men, reduced, in the words of one of their officers, to 'half-starved scorbutic skeletons', but it was in this dangerous situation that he proved his real worth. A sudden outbreak of drunken indiscipline was checked at once by the hanging of the ringleader and the staving in of all the rum barrels owned by the commissariat department, and it may well have been this drastic action which really impressed on the troops the seriousness of their plight. At all events, it had a salutary effect on the garrison because every single man now set to work to strengthen the defences. The example came—as it always should but seldom did in those days—from the officers, who took up picks and shovels, harnessed themselves to cannon to drag them into position, and so inspired their men that in a matter of a few days 150 cannon had been mounted on the walls and brought into action against the French on the plateau. They, unable yet to bring any artillery across ground thawing out into a morass, had to content themselves by keeping under cover in waterlogged trenches.

Yet it was clear that the ceaseless toil, bad food and mounting sickness rate were having their effect on the garrison, and it was also clear that the future of Quebec, and Canada, really depended on which nation would be the first to send a fleet up the St Lawrence when the ice melted. The French had promised all possible aid to de Lévis; England, having mourned the death of Wolfe, was aware of Murray's difficulties. At length, on 9 May, the topmasts of a frigate could be seen from the walls, but there was no flag at her peak. After a period of what must have been nerve-snapping suspense the English flag was hoisted. The frigate announced that she was the *Lowestoft* and that a squadron now in the Gulf of St Lawrence would arrive in a few days. The sight of her must have taken all the heart out of the French, for had de Lévis chosen this moment to storm the town the garrison was in no condition to resist him.

On 15 May two British men-of-war arrived, and on the following day two frigates sailed up the river beyond the town and destroyed all the boats which had brought de Lévis's troops down from Montreal, together with all his supplies and reserve ammunition. That same evening de Lévis raised the siege and retreated at full speed, leaving behind all his sick and wounded (who were well cared for by the nuns of Quebec), forty pieces of artillery and all the material he had collected for the siege.

At dawn next day Murray went after him, intending to fall upon what he felt must now be a beaten and demoralized enemy, but though he picked up large numbers of stragglers the main body moved too fast for him.

The capture of Quebec had been consolidated and now, in the spring sunshine and with the arrival of fresh rations, Murray's 'skeletons' rapidly became once again fit for active service.

During the long winter, General Jeffrey Amherst, that methodical, painstaking and unfailingly successful soldier, had been planning the final campaign. His objective was Montreal, and he proposed to attack it simultaneously from east, south and west. He himself was to come with the main army down the St Lawrence from Lake Ontario, from the east; Brigadier Haviland was to move by way of Lake Champlain and the Richelieu river from the south, and Murray was to bring his army west from Quebec up the St Lawrence.

Bearing in mind the vast distances involved, the total lack of communications—a message could only be carried by a man on foot or in a canoe—the absence of any roads, and therefore the inability of one force to make contact with another once it had moved from its base, it seems almost incredible that plans so ambitious as those devised by Pitt and Amherst for the campaigns in North America could even have been conceived. The boldness and breadth of vision of the men who built Britain's empire is not always appreciated.

The essence of Amherst's plan was that his advance down the St Lawrence from the Great Lakes would cut off any attempt by the French to escape to the west, and would force them back upon Montreal where they would be destroyed by Haviland and Murray. The boldness of the plan lay in the timing. Although each of the separate columns had to start from points hundreds of miles apart, and remain out of contact, they had to converge at the same moment or the French might be able to destroy the smaller columns led by Haviland and Murray in detail.

Brigadier-General Murray moved first. His garrison in Quebec had recovered from the winter and he was able to muster a force of 2,200 men and still leave 1,700 to protect the town. He and his men embarked in thirty-two vessels of various kinds on 14 July 1760, to rendezvous with Amherst and Haviland on 29 August. He travelled slowly, cleaning up small pockets of the enemy at nightly staging posts and disarming all the local inhabitants as he went up the river. He reached Three Rivers on 4 August and saw a detachment of the French army there. Having no time to waste he ignored it, went on and at the French outpost of Sorel, guarding the eastern approach to Montreal, found 4,000 men under Generals Bourlamaque and Dumas entrenched on both banks. They got up and moved with the fleet of boats, keeping pace with them, and so the opposing forces fell back and advanced together towards the main French army under de Lévis in Montreal. What seems quite extraordinary is that during this peculiar progress up the river Murray managed to persuade about half Bourlamaque's militia to hand their weapons to him and sign a pledge of neutrality. On 24 August Murray was within twenty-seven miles of Montreal and he sent out a party to make contact with Haviland. He then moved to Île St Thérèse just below Montreal and camped there to wait for the others.

Haviland had left his base at Crown Point on 18 August with a force of Provincials, Indians and two battalions of regular troops, making a total of 3,400 men. His first objective was the Île aux Noix at the head of Lake Champlain, now held by Bougainville who had taken over responsibility for the southern approach to Montreal from Bourlamaque during the winter. Haviland landed on the island, constructed batteries for his field guns and opened fire on the fort while a force of his rangers manhandled three guns round to the rear of the fort and began to shoot with great accuracy at Bougainville's armed sloops lying at anchor close by. The sloops got under way in a panic and ran themselves aground on the first bend in the river—thus cutting off all Bougainville's contact with the outer world, and in particular with the fort at St John's down the Richelieu river. This, as Amherst had foreseen and noted in his plan, forced Bougainville to abandon the island. Only after the greatest difficulty in what must have been a nightmare of a night march was he able to fall back on St John's, where he joined M. Roquemaure, and they both withdrew, through Chambly, until they found Bourlamaque and what was left of his force on the banks of the St Lawrence. Here they halted, and their forces dwindled every day as the men deserted.

On 28 August Haviland reached the destination appointed in the plan, made contact with Murray and waited for Amherst.

Amherst himself set out from Oswego where the main army had been gathering since July. The last of the units did not come in until the first week in August, but when they had all assembled they amounted to about 11,000 men. Of these, 6,000 were British, in eight under-strength battalions, 4,500 were Provincials and 700 Indians. Their transport consisted of nearly 800 boats escorted by the gunboats built in the previous year, and the expedition set off on 10 August, making for the French outpost of La Galette at the head of the rapids on the St Lawrence. Arriving there on 15 August the gunboats attacked and captured a 10-gun French brig, the post surrendered and the fleet of little boats threaded its way among the Thousand Islands. On a small island at the entrance to the rapids stood Fort Lévis garrisoned by 300 men, and Amherst, with his usual caution and care, spent four days in capturing it and then repairing its defences and his damaged gunboats. Not until 31 August, two days after the rendezvous date, did he begin the most hazardous part of his journey, the shooting of the St Lawrence rapids.

On 4 September he came to the really dangerous section—which he later told Pitt 'was more frightful than dangerous'—and on that day sixty boats were either wrecked or damaged and eighty-four men drowned. Large numbers of Canadians stood on the banks and watched the army pass without making any attempt to interfere. The whole of 5 September was spent in making repairs. On the following day the last of the rapids was negotiated in safety and the fleet glided down to La Chine on the west bank of the St Lawrence, only nine miles from Montreal, where the troops disembarked and marched unopposed into camp almost under the walls on the eastern side of Montreal.

Had Amherst been content merely to ignore Fort Lévis, knowing its garrison could do nothing while his army was operating between it and Montreal, he would have reached his destination, like his other two column commanders, punctual to the day.

The French were now in a sad state. Bourlamaque, Bougainville and Roquemaure had all crossed the river and entered Montreal, taking with them a handful only of their original forces. Their militia had all gone home and many of the regulars had deserted. The army de Lévis now commanded amounted to barely 2,500 men and it was surrounded by a British force of 17,000 troops who, like the hounds after a long and wearisome run, knew they were in at the death. The fortifications were only intended to keep the Indians out, Amherst's artillery was now coming up from La Chine and there was no hope of escape or relief.

At a Council of War called by Vaudreuil it was unanimously decided that resistance was out of the question. Articles of capitulation were drawn up and taken to Amherst by General Bougainville on 7 September. They laid great stress on the garrison being allowed to march out with the honours of war.

This was flatly refused by Amherst. He was determined there would be no question of 'honour' where the French surrender was concerned. He regarded their form of warfare in North America as barbarous and revolting in its inhumanity. He had not forgotten the broken pledges, the slaughter of sleeping villagers, the massacre of the surrendered garrison of Fort William Henry, the torturing and slaughter of captives and wounded men after Braddock's defeat on the Monongahela and Abercromby's repulse at Ticonderoga. A whole century of wrongs, treachery and double-dealing lay behind his refusal. Despite French pleas for easier terms and despite the passionate reproaches of de Lévis, the amended terms were signed. The

French troops laid down their arms and undertook not to serve again while the war lasted. The conflict in Canada was over and England had gained half a continent for her empire.

Amherst, having achieved what no other general had ever approached during the struggle for Canada and Acadia, the steady and consistent attainment of all his objectives, then began to tidy everything up. Robert Rogers and his rangers were entrusted with the occupation of the posts of Detroit, Miamis and Michillimackinac, where the Bourbon flag was lowered for ever. The administration of the country was set in order and General Murray became the new Governor. In a General Order, Amherst appealed to his troops not to disgrace their victory by their subsequent behaviour and their conduct was a great surprise to the Canadians. Within a month Canadian peasants and British troops were sharing provisions and messing together while the soldiers helped to bring in the harvest. When Amherst issued orders that troops billeted in widely scattered Canadian households should be brought together in unit camps the local inhabitants protested and asked to be allowed to continue as hosts. If all this sounds rather too good to be true it should be remembered that when the thirteen American colonies declared their independence and went to war with England, they were quite unable to influence the allegiance of Canada.

For all this, and indeed for the conquest of Canada, Jeffrey Amherst must be given the credit. Perhaps it is because the greatest campaign of his career gained all its objectives without a great battle, and almost without bloodshed, that he is so little appreciated for what he was. Pitt took him from Germany, the home of classic, conventional war, and set him down in the 'wilderness of leaves' to take command of troops who had lost heart, to obtain most of what he needed from colonists who often enough took pride in being obstructive and difficult, and to fight a savage enemy in an unknown land. From the welter of problems and disappointments, with patience and tactful tenacity, he organized victory. To some it may seem there is a great gap in military administrative genius between the Dukes of Marlborough and Wellington; it is filled by Jeffrey Amherst.

In India, apart from the saving of Madras and Forde's success at Masulipatam, operations during the latter part of the Year of Victories were somewhat confused, disordered and indecisive. They were hardly operations so much as a grim game, exhausting for the troops involved, a sort of catch-as-catch-can among the fortresses of the Carnatic. There were continual moves and threats involving Trichinopoly, Arcot, Wandiwash, Conjeveram, Trivatore and others, and the principal players were, on one side, Lally, Bussy, Soupire and Crillon, and on the other, Eyre Coote, who had relieved the elderly Stringer Lawrence, Major Brereton, who took over from Colonel Draper when he was invalided home, and Major Monson. At sea, Admiral d'Aché never really recovered his fighting spirit after his third engagement and defeat at the hands of Admiral Pocock on 10 September 1759. He took his battered ships first to Pondicherry and then, ignoring all protests, to Mauritius. Though a brave man himself and not in the least afraid of meeting the British in battle, he refused to be associated with any more failures. This was a serious blow to Lally who was having trouble enough with his ground forces. In August his own regiment had mutinied while acting as garrison of the fort at Chittapett. The men had marched out announcing their intention to join the British. Running up and down beside the column in a most undignified way their officers had managed to stop the majority by promising to give them their pay that was several months overdue, but sixty men had had enough of the French army and deserted to Madras.

The morale of Lally's army had not been improved by an exchange of prisoners which restored to him 500 Frenchmen who, for the past five years, had been leading a comfortable and idle life with the British, and were now in no mood to return to the rigours of active service. Furthermore, the failure at Madras had greatly disheartened the French and encouraged the English. It was now the intention of the English to consolidate their success by gaining complete control of the territory round Madras, and this entailed the acquisition of such forts as the one at Wandiwash, the most valuable of the French stations between Pondicherry and Madras. Major Brereton had failed in an attempt on Wandiwash in September 1759, and it was here that Lally was faced with another mutiny in October. It was quelled by giving the men six months' arrears of pay, but the general situation in Lally's forces was by no means one to inspire confidence.

On 21 November 1759 Colonel Eyre Coote arrived at the British camp at Conjeveram and two days later he was joined by his own regiment, 1,000 strong, which had come out from England with him. He was compelled to send a detachment of 200 men off at once to Colonel Forde, now returned to Bengal, to meet a new threat from the Dutch who were seeking to assert themselves, but the strength of British forces in the Carnatic was now adequate for his main purpose—the taking of Wandiwash.

Three days later, Brereton took Trivatore, advanced on Wandiwash and drove in its outposts while Coote moved against Arcot. Hearing that Brereton was erecting batteries at Wandiwash, Coote marched there with all speed and the fort surrendered on 29 November, the day on which the batteries opened fire.

Lally began to concentrate his troops in Arcot while Bussy's irregular cavalry, operating from there, began a reign of terror almost comparable with that of the Canadian Indians in the Ohio valley. The unhappy villagers in the plains as far as Madras abandoned their possessions and sought safety in the hills.

The Dutch threat, which Lally hoped would draw British troops away from the Carnatic and into Bengal, was handled extremely competently by Colonel Forde in two decisive engagements, one outside Chandernagore and the other near the village of Bandara on the following day. The entire force of Dutch and Malays, which had been mounted in Batavia, was put out of action, every man being either killed or captured, and the Dutch settlements in Bengal, based on Chinsura, were forced to ask for mercy and protection. It was a strange episode, connected with the Anglo-French struggle only in that it momentarily deflected the plans of Clive in Bengal and Coote in south India. In Europe, England and Holland were in alliance, and when the Dutch at home heard about it they paid full compensation for the activities of the unauthorized expedition—which had apparently hoped to seize Bengal.

Clive used the advantage of Forde's victories to ensure that the Dutch could never again challenge British supremacy in

India, and in fact their expedition was of no help to Lally and only succeeded in establishing even more firmly the power and influence of the British. Thus one potential rival was removed and Coote now gave all his attention to disposing of the other.

At the beginning of January 1760 Lally divided his force at Arcot into two columns. One he placed under Bussy's command with orders to hold Trivatore while he led the other himself against Conjeveram. Coote knew nothing of this until he received a message from the garrison commander in Conjeveram, whereupon he marched at once to save the fort. When he arrived he found that Lally had merely plundered the native town and then gone off to join Bussy at Trivatore.

On 14 January, with 500 Europeans, 1,000 sepoys and 650 French and Mahratta cavalry, Lally left Trivatore and marched to attack Wandiwash, which had really been his main objective ever since Coote had taken it two months before. Coote heard of this move, and of Lally's intentions, on the evening of the 14th, and next morning he set off on the direct road to the same place. Lally, also well-informed, hastened to capture the fort before Coote got there, and on the morning of 15 February he fought a sharp little action against a British piquet in the southern suburb and at length succeeded in driving it back into the fort. He at once began to set up batteries to cannonade the walls. On 17 January he was joined by Bussy and his force from Trivatore and learned that Coote was now at Outramalore, about fifteen miles to the north-east.

Coote halted there to wait until Lally was fully committed to his siege of the fort before moving up to give battle, and because the progress of the French was so slow he had to wait for three days. At length, on 20 January, Lally's batteries opened fire and on the following day Coote advanced to within seven miles of the fort.

At first light on 22 January Coote rode forward, taking his cavalry and two field guns with him, to plan his attack on Lally's camp, and he told the rest of his army to follow him. At about seven o'clock in the morning his leading troops were seen by a vedette (outlying mounted sentries) of Bussy's Mahratta cavalry who galloped back to the French camp, and in a short while about 3,000 enemy horsemen came charging across the open plain with the dust clouds boiling up behind

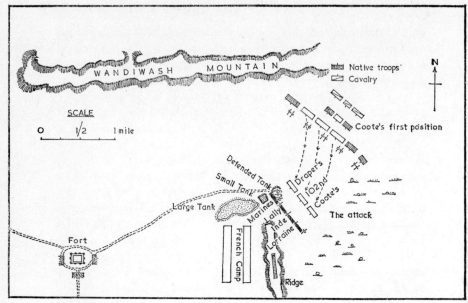

Wandiwash   22 January 1760

them. Greatly out-numbering Coote's small mounted force, they
came straight for it with wild shouts, the points of their lances
flashing in the sun; an awe-inspiring sight which left Coote quite
unmoved for he coolly wheeled his squadrons to the right and
left, revealing the two guns they had been screening. The guns
opened fire at close range, with grape, into the spate of men and
horses, and did so much damage that the Mahrattas swung
round and fled, and refused to take any further part in the
battle.

Coote then went on to take a close look at Lally's position.
The French camp was laid out in two parallel lines facing east,
about two miles to the east of the fort. The left flank was covered
by a large *jheel* (water tank) and on the left front were two
smaller *jheels*, one of which had been turned into a battery
position to cover the plain in front and, if necessary, take any
frontal attack on the camp in enfilade.

Coote's plan was to move his army round the flank of Lally's
camp, under the lee of Wandiwash mountain to the north until
he could form his line with his left flank protected by the
mountain and his right covered by the fire of the fort. He would

then have linked up with the besieged garrison and would be facing Lally's rear and left flank. Had he succeeded in carrying out the manœuvre Lally would have been in grave difficulties, with everything in his camp pointing the wrong way. He obviously realized what Coote was going to do and moved quickly to check him. Bringing his whole army out of the camp he disposed it in a single line with the fortified *jheel* as the pivotal position on his left. This position, containing four guns, was manned by French marines and sailors, and the second small *jheel*, between it and the much larger tank to the rear, was held by 400 sepoys. Another 700 sepoys were aligned on a ridge in front of the camp. The French army amounted to 2,250 Europeans, in the three *régiments de Lally*, *de Lorraine* and *de l'Inde*, and about 300 French Hussars as well as 1,300 sepoys. Three guns were placed in each interval between battalions, making a total of sixteen, and a mixed force of about 500 men remained in the batteries facing Wandiwash fort. The Mahratta cavalry, put to flight by Coote's two field guns, had disappeared.

The British force was drawn up in three lines with the British regiments in front—Draper's, Coote's and the 102nd Foot— deployed in four weak battalions and a battalion of 900 sepoys on each flank. In the second line were 300 European grenadiers in the centre and companies of 200 sepoys each on either side, and in the rear line were the cavalry, eighty Europeans in the centre and natives on either flank. Sixteen field guns were deployed between battalions and ranks. The force consisted of 1,980 Europeans, 2,100 sepoys and 1,250 native cavalry.

In this order the British force advanced to meet the enemy, and before it came within range of the guns Lally led his Hussars in a sweeping charge upon the cavalry in the British rear. The native cavalry broke as soon as they realized they were the target but the eighty Europeans stood firm and the sepoy division on the threatened flank wheeled to meet the attack in line. But before the charge came in, Captain Barker brought two detached guns into action in the nick of time and cut down about fifteen horses and men with the first rounds of grape. This shattered the Hussars who galloped away far to the rear, ignoring all Lally's efforts to rally them.

The whole British force had halted to meet this attack and

they moved on again while the guns in the French position, still far out of range even of solid shot, opened a ragged and completely ineffective fire. This was a clear indication that the guns were not being worked by regular artillerymen. Coote advanced steadily until his guns had the range and then opened a most destructive fire against the French regiments in the open. Lally ordered them to advance—which at least was better than standing still to be shot at—whereupon Coote ordered all his sepoys to stand fast while he led the British units of his first and second lines to meet the oncoming enemy. He was staking everything on the ability of the British soldier to defeat his French counterpart in a set-piece battle.

It was about one o'clock in the afternoon when both sides came within musket range and the firing became general all along the line. Coote's Regiment had only fired two volleys when Lally formed the *régiment de Lorraine* into a column twelve men wide and told them to charge the thin British line with the bayonet. Coote, who had taken up his station with his own regiment, held their fire until the charging enemy were within fifty yards and then blasted the leading files and the flanks with a devastating volley.* But the French came on, stumbling and leaping over the bodies of the fallen, and a moment later, by sheer weight, had plunged through the British line which at once closed in on the flanks of the column, gripping the enemy formation in desperate and bloody hand-to-hand fighting. This was not what the French had expected—to break the enemy line was usually the prelude to victory—and the merciless onslaught of British soldiers who had lost their temper was too much for them. They faltered, and turned, and fled back towards their camp, hotly pursued, and many died face downwards in the dust. Having re-formed his regiment after all this excitement, Coote galloped through the smoke to see how Draper's Regiment was faring on the right, and as he went, there was a sudden flash, a column of smoke and then the roar of an explosion from the *jheel* held by the French marines. A shot from one of the British guns had blown

---

* A very interesting anticipation of the French and English tactics at the Battle of Maida, in southern Italy, in 1806, which so influenced Wellington in the Peninsular War.

up an ammunition limber, killing the battery commander and either killing or wounding eighty of his men.

The men holding the *jheel* at once abandoned it and were joined in their flight by the sepoys from the small *jheel* just behind it. Coote immediately ordered Draper's Regiment to occupy the deserted battery position, but Bussy brought Lally's Regiment up to take them in the flank as they advanced. This forced Draper's regiment to wheel away and swing out round to their right to come up to the *jheel* from the north, and so Bussy had just enough time to push two platoons on to the banks of the *jheel*, with orders to hold it. Brereton, leading Draper's Regiment, moved too fast for him to do anything more, and the regiment came up the north bank with the bayonet and swept the French away. At this point Major Brereton fell, mortally wounded, while his officers and men stormed on. The battle was at its height of smoke and dust, din and confusion and it hinged on the *jheel* position. Bussy wheeled Lally's Regiment round at right angles to face the fire coming from its left and detached two platoons against the western bank of the *jheel*. But the men would not face the British musketry and made no attempt to close with the enemy. Two of the guns allotted to Draper's Regiment then came up and raked Lally's Regiment in enfilade. In desperation Bussy put himself at the head of the troops he could see were on the point of breaking, to lead them in a decisive charge against the south bank. He went forward, his horse was shot under him and as he rose from the fall he saw that only twenty men had followed him. The rest were about to run away when two platoons of Draper's Regiment doubled round and cut them off. Major Monson, coming up with a detachment of grenadiers in support of the attack on the *jheel*, took Bussy and his small party prisoner and most of Lally's Regiment was captured. The defeat of this unit as well as the *régiment de Lorraine* left *l'Inde* with its flanks open, and so this battalion turned about and withdrew in good order. Lally tried to deploy the sepoys on the ridge in front of the camp but they had seen quite enough and would not move. All he now had left was a handful of cavalry and a few men of *Lorraine* and they, limbering up three field guns, covered the French retreat. The British cavalry were too weak in numbers to charge the confused remnants of Lally's army, and Coote's native cavalry, like

Lally's sepoys on the ridge, refused to advance. Lally was thus able to set fire to his camp, gather up the men from the batteries round Wandiwash fort and make a reasonably orderly retreat. Even so, he had been decisively defeated.

The battle had been a straight confrontation between the British and the French, and the native troops on either side hardly played any part in it at all. Lally lost a total of 600 Europeans—200 lay dead on the battlefield—as well as twenty-four guns and all the tents and stores in his camp that were not burnt. Coote's casualties were sixty-three killed and 124 wounded, Draper's Regiment being the one which suffered most. The turning point of the battle was the explosion in the *jheel* battery but there is little doubt that even without the lucky—or unlucky—shot which caused it the outcome would have been the same. Bussy had begged Lally to abandon the siege of the fort when he heard of Coote's approach, and to meet the enemy with every available man, but Lally seldom listened to good advice unless it confirmed his own opinions. He was a brave, determined, obstinate and consistently unlucky man, but he almost invariably brought his troubles upon himself.

On the following day, 23 January, he fell back to Chittapett and then to Gingee to cover what he felt must soon follow: a British attack on Pondicherry, but Coote was in no haste to rush upon his final objective until he had dealt with the French outposts. The last to fall in the south was Karical, on 5 April, and this was the one station of real importance to Pondicherry, for it was the main outlet of the wealthy state of Tanjore and the supplier of provisions to Pondicherry.

On 7 April Coote began to close in on the city, but his force was too small to undertake a formal siege and he had to be satisfied at first with a mere blockade, in conjunction with Admiral Cornish, until reinforcements arrived. They came on 2 September, and with them were three men-of-war which increased Cornish's squadron to seventeen ships.

A few days later Lally made a desperate attempt against the English camp but, as so often before, things went wrong and he was repulsed with heavy losses. The civilian authorities in Pondicherry gave him nothing but opposition and disloyalty but he was determined to hold on, to wait and pray for some relief. For a brief moment it seemed as if his prayers had been answered, for on 31 December 1760 a sudden fearful hurricane swept down on the city. Three of the blockading ships were lost with all hands, three were driven ashore and all the defence works destroyed. But it was no longer possible to take advantage of the British misfortunes. The ships came back, the fieldworks were repaired and on 15 January 1761, at the point of starvation, the garrison surrendered. In the next few weeks the last remaining forts and factories held by the French were captured, and the last French flag in India was lowered on 5 April.

Lally, having fought to the limits of his ability and endurance on behalf of his country and to the exclusion of all private interests, was taken back to France and, as had happened to la Bourdonnais, was immediately sent to the Bastille. Finally, on 9 May 1766, after a long imprisonment, he was led out to the Place de Grève and publicly beheaded for having betrayed Pondicherry to the English—the nation he really hated in the very depths of his being. His execution on so infamous a charge makes that of Admiral Byng* seem almost reasonable.

Thus, of the four principal characters in the French struggle for India—Dupleix, la Bourdonnais, Bussy and Lally—the marquis de Bussy was the only one to escape disgrace, and he was never rewarded except by his own efforts. It is a strange fact, and another of the differences between the French and the English apparent throughout the story of empires, that not one of the great French administrators, in any part of their empire, although possessing apparently unlimited skill, energy and power, ever succeeded in winning the support of their compatriots. They were always alone, committed to a solitary struggle against the English and their own subordinates, and often enough, their own government at home. Even Dupleix was thwarted at every turn and finally dismissed. This may well be because in the national character there is some element which renders Frenchmen in high station conceited and

---

* On the tombstone of the Admiral, judicially murdered on the quarter-deck of the *Monarch* on 14 March 1757, is the inscription: 'To the perpetual disgrace of public Justice, the Honourable John Byng, Admiral of the Blue, fell a martyr to political persecution at a time when courage and loyalty were insufficient guarantees of the honour and lives of naval officers.' Exactly the same could be said of the unfortunate comte de Lally.

autocratic, and makes Frenchmen in subordinate positions jealous and resentful.

On the other hand great men from the British Isles often achieved their greatness through the loyal support of their subordinates, and their ability to inspire trust and affection.

Thus, in the battle for empire, two of the great areas of conflict drop out of the story long before the end of Pitt's 'first world war'. After the capitulation in Montreal on 8 September 1760 and the lowering of the Bourbon flag in India on 5 April 1761, the French never again threatened British supremacy in North America or the sub-continent of India. In these two vast countries the struggle was over. In the West Indies, the third area, there was a compromise, but before that was reached, Pitt had resigned.

King George II, who had become completely reconciled to Pitt, trusted him and gave him full authority, died suddenly in October 1760. He was succeeded by his son George III who at first showed signs of continuing in his father's policies and attitudes, but the autocratic Pitt had made many enemies who now conspired with the new King to bring about the downfall of the man who really ruled England. It was achieved in the end, ironically enough, more by the diplomatic skill of the duc de Choiseul, who had become the leading figure in Louis XV's government at the end of 1758, than by any direct action on the part of Pitt's enemies in London.

At the beginning of 1761, with a line now drawn through the problem of Canada, Pitt could concentrate on Europe. He launched another raid against the coast of France and scored his greatest success in adventures of this type when the island of Belle Île was taken. Captured by a force of 8,000 men under General Hodgson, escorted by Admiral Keppel and ten warships, the operation lasted two months, but on 7 June the island became a watering place, vegetable garden and recreation area for ships' companies blockading the French coast. It was a success which showed how strongly the tide of war was running in Britain's favour, and Choiseul set out to stem that tide.

He knew that the recently crowned and comparatively vigorous King of Spain, Charles III, had no love for England

and would welcome an opportunity to pick up the disputes—
particularly those in connection with the West Indies trade—
which had been left on the table at Aix-la-Chapelle. Choiseul
therefore opened tentative negotiations for peace with England,
making demands he knew Pitt would never countenance and at
the same time involving Spain in the discussions. By under-
lining the utterly unreasonable attitude Pitt was adopting he
persuaded Charles III to renew the old Family Compact, and
this was signed, for the third time, at Idlefonso on 15 August
1761. Spain was now France's ally and had undertaken to
declare war on England by 1762 if no general peace had been
arranged by then. Having succeeded in thus involving Spain,
and setting at nought the achievement Newcastle had been so
proud of at the beginning of the war, Choiseul then adopted so
hectoring a tone in his peace talks with England that they were
broken off in September 1761.

Pitt's whole attitude to France caused considerable alarm
among the more timid politicians at Westminster. His aim was
the total destruction of French sea power, and it had very
nearly been achieved. Britain was within measurable distance
of gaining global control of the sea and this, argued Pitt's
enemies, would set the whole world in arms against her. A
particular aspect of Britain's control of the sea became apparent when France, thrown out of North America, appealed
for fishing rights in Newfoundland waters. On this Pitt would
not give in. He was perfectly well aware that the smooth,
persuasive Choiseul who asked so reasonably, *'Donnez-nous de la
pêche'* was really seeking a share in the best training ground for
seamen: seamen to man the ships of the line, not fishing
vessels. Pitt had his way but only after violent argument and his
furious exposure of Choiseul's double-dealing over the so-called
'peace negotiations' which were not meant to succeed.

On the next problem, concerned with Spain's alliance with
France, he was not so convincing. Everyone knew that Spain
was preparing for war and would enter it as soon as her treasure
fleet arrived from the Spanish Main. To Pitt, after the signing
of the third Family Compact, there was only one common
enemy, the Bourbons. England was at war with France and
therefore she was also at war with Spain. There was no time to
be lost. Spain must be attacked instantly. No one agreed with

him except Lord Temple and all appealed to the King. George III's decision for the majority was the equivalent of Pitt's dismissal. At least, that was the way Pitt looked at it. There was much pressure on him to continue in office until the end of the war but his view was expressed in the well-known remark, 'I will be responsible for nothing that I do not direct', and he resigned on 5 October 1761.

The Earl of Bute, George III's favourite minister, took over and at once tried to pick up the threads of the peace negotiations abandoned in the previous month. The real irony in the situation lies in the fact that Pitt the hawk, replaced by Bute the dove, had predicted that Spain, as soon as she was ready, would come into the war no matter how hard England tried to prevent her. It so happened that having made her arrangements Spain became so offensive that on 4 January 1762, to his chagrin and disgust, Bute had to declare war on her himself.

Pitt's resignation did not have any immediate effect on the conduct of the war because his plans for 1762 had been made and the means for putting them into effect had been prepared. As far back as January 1761 he had written to Amherst in Canada stating that some of the troops now unemployed after the fall of Montreal were to be used to capture the French islands of Dominica, St Lucia and Martinique. Accordingly, at the beginning of June 1761, transports carried 2,000 troops from Halifax to Guadeloupe, taken in the Year of Victories, and the force to be commanded by Lord Rollo was collected there. The expedition, escorted by the squadron under Admiral Sir James Douglas, arrived off Roseau in the island of Dominica on 6 June. Summoned to surrender, the French manned their batteries and trenches, whereupon Lord Rollo landed, attacked, drove out the French with much confusion to them and little loss to himself, and the island was surrendered on the following day. This ended the operations in the West Indies for that year, but behind the scenes intensive preparations were being made for an attack on Martinique—preparations which soon became known to the French. They, however, felt reasonably secure in the extremely difficult mountains and forests of their island, defended by 1,200 regular troops, 7,000 local militia and 4,000 hired 'privateersmen', successors of the buccaneers.

On Christmas Eve 1761 the main body of the British invasion force arrived from North America, led by General Moncton, recovered from the wound received at Quebec, and this brought the total strength up to 8,000 men. The fleet of transports, escorted by Admiral Rodney, sailed on 5 January 1762 and anchored in St Ann's Bay in the extreme south-west of Martinique. Fort Royal—now Fort de France—fell on 3 February after a series of actions as the troops worked their way across the island. The rest of the island was reduced during the next nine days and on 12 February General Moncton had completed his mission. He at once sent off detachments to take St Lucia, Grenada and St Vincent, and all these islands surrendered without resistance. He would have moved on, against Tobago, but news came of the declaration of war against Spain, and his force was diverted to a successful attack against Havana in Cuba—an operation which was not a part of the Anglo-French contest.

It was in 1762 that the fundamental miscalculation at the base of all Choiseul's crafty diplomacy became evident. Spain, for all the bombast of her bellicose monarch, was no prop to France. Too weak to defend her own possessions, she was incapable of offensive action, and far from saving France, she lost practically everything she had. France and Spain stood side by side in the Family Compact and watched, powerless to affect the course of events, while practically all the ships and islands under the Bourbon flag were taken away by an apparently invincible Britain. In the West Indies only Hispaniola remained unconquered.

Havana was taken, and with it one-fifth of the Spanish navy that was in the harbour, on 14 August; meanwhile, on the other side of the world a joint force under the command of Admiral Cornish and General Draper (cured of the illness which had forced him to leave India in the spring of 1759) had sailed from Calcutta on 1 August to attack the Spanish colony of Manila in the Philippines. At dawn on 6 October Draper's Regiment and a party of sailors stormed the breach battered in the fortifications, and the city of Manila, the island of Luzon and all its dependencies thereupon became British.

Everywhere, in all the areas of conflict and dispute, British arms were triumphant; but whereas Pitt, the great architect of

293

conquest, delighted in the news of each fresh victory, the timorous Bute, fearful of world opinion, cowered as if beaten by the blows of Fate. He was determined to make peace. George III wanted above all to stop the war in Germany, and there were many people, whose spokesman was the Duke of Bedford, who were fearful of some terrible retribution; though who would enact it, or how, they could not say. England had reached a pinnacle of success higher than even Pitt had ever contemplated and her people were filled, paradoxically, with nameless fears for the future. Pitt had a foreboding too, but quite a different one. He was convinced that security, now and in the future, depended on taking every colony from France and making it impossible for her ever to take her revenge by seaborne expeditions. He was, of course, overruled, and the Peace of Paris was signed on 10 February 1763. Under its terms France ceded to Britain all Canada, Nova Scotia and Cape Breton Island in North America, and the whole of India except for the stations of Pondicherry and Chandernagore, on condition that they would be open, undefended towns. Britain also received the islands of Minorca in the Mediterranean, and Grenada, St Vincent, Tobago and Dominica in the Caribbean. To all this was added Senegal on the West Coast of Africa.

Britain restored to France the fishing rights on the Newfoundland Banks and in the Gulf of St Lawrence, with the little islands of Miquelon and St Pierre as fishing stations. France also recovered Belle Île, Goree ('as an essential slaving station'), Guadeloupe, Martinique and St Lucia. One cannot help wondering about the feelings of men crippled by wounds and who had seen their comrades killed in the capture of these places.

Spain handed Florida over to Britain in exchange for Cuba, gave Britain the logwood concession in Honduras and abandoned her fishing rights off Newfoundland. There was no mention of Manila or Luzon in the treaty because news of the capture arrived after it had been signed.

France completed her withdrawal from America by handing Louisiana over to Spain as compensation for Spain's losses on her behalf.

It all seemed very neat and tidy, and perhaps the only discordant voice—among the politicians—was that of Pitt who, with his usual insight and accuracy, forecast a host of troubles to come. To him the treaty was but a prelude to more disasters and fresh slaughter because, as he said himself, but with slight exaggeration, 'It restored to France her former glory.'

Britain had won the battle for empire. The treaty signed in Paris on that February day in 1763 marked the end of the relentless and unremitting competition for sea power and colonies, and the wealth that both ensured; for deep down, below all the talk of power and glory, honour and might, lay the root of all the trouble: money. There was nothing very noble about the real issue for which thousands died under the hatchets of Indians, in great storms and battles at sea, of the black vomit, dysentery and wounds, on battlefields and on lonely freezing vigils in winter nights. In terms of courage, self-sacrifice and endurance the cost of winning the empire can never be measured. Nor is much thought ever given to the men who really won it: not the great men, the leaders, like Clive and Amherst, Saunders and Keppel and Boscawen, but the seamen and the soldiers, the sepoys and the militiamen, the rank and file, the ordinary people caught up in the mesh of war. They did their duty, lived and died, were slid into the sea or rolled into an unmarked grave, and their names were obliterated as the incoming tide smooths away a footprint in the sand. Yet it was through them that Britain gained her empire—and France lost hers.

Epilogue

Pitt was right, of course. The Peace of Paris certainly ended the battle for empire but it could not expunge in a few well-ordered clauses the enmity of seven centuries. France, humbled by the long series of disasters in the Seven Years' War, saw her opportunity for revenge when the American colonies rebelled.

Pitt, so great a prophet in many other ways, actively discounted what he called colonial disloyalty. Yet during the negotiations before the signing of the Peace of Paris the possibility of a revolt in the thirteen American colonies was widely discussed and acknowledged.

In America the seeds of rebellion had germinated long ago and sprouted in every Colonial Assembly whose members, to assert their independence, were wont to devote much time and trouble to the business of thwarting their Governors—often to their own disadvantage—simply because the Governor represented the British Crown. Yet there was no sign at all of any concerted action in the colonies; the rivalries and jealousies seemed far too bitter to allow any spirit of unity to link the separate states in any sort of confederation against the British. The link, when it came, was money. The energetic George Grenville of the British Treasury tried to shift some of the burden of expense for the French and Indian War on to the American colonies, and between 1764 and 1767 a series of new taxes was levied—all designed to raise revenue by import duties—and this, for the first time, provided an issue on which the colonies were united. In October 1765 the unenforceable Stamp Act was passed and a 'Stamp Act Congress' met in New York to decide on a programme of resistance, non-co-operation, and the boycotting of British goods. Although from that moment the path of rebellion did not necessarily run smooth it ran comparatively straight, to that unfortunate business in the grey light of the morning of 19 April 1775 on the village green at Lexington.

Paris fêted Benjamin Franklin when he came to ask for help and the French provided money, weapons and material of war; they also encouraged volunteers, like the fickle Marie Joseph, marquis de Lafayette, to aid the colonies in their 'struggle for freedom'. Yet, for a while, French aid was clandestine. Not until Benedict Arnold* had defeated 'Gentleman Johnny' Burgoyne at Saratoga in October 1777, and thus proved that the colonies were capable of waging war effectively, did the French come out into the open. On 6 February 1778 Benjamin Franklin signed commercial and political treaties in Paris under which the French recognized the independence of the American colonies and undertook to make war against the British until this independence became a reality. France provided an army under Rochambeau and a fleet under de Grasse, and it was Admiral de Grasse's temporary command of the waters of Chesapeake Bay and his defeat of a British squadron under Admiral Graves that compelled Cornwallis to surrender at Yorktown. England lost her American colonies and France got her revenge—but she never recovered, economically or politically, from the cost of supporting the colonists. The Treaty of Versailles was signed in 1783 and six years later France was torn by her own Revolution. As always, vast social upheavals throw up spectacular characters, and in the ruins of France an obscure Corsican gunner subaltern rose, by his own genius, to be an Emperor who conquered all Europe save Britain and Russia. And so the centuries-old conflict between England and France went on, until the rainy evening of 18 June 1815, when the remnants of the *Grande Armée* left the battlefield of Waterloo and France lost everything.

She then dropped out of the colonial competition, content to maintain her interests in Africa, the Indian Ocean, the Far East and the Caribbean. England, in the reign of Victoria, went on to build an even greater empire covering a quarter of

---

* Most accounts give the credit to Horatio Gates, but this is because Benedict Arnold turned traitor in 1780 and tried to sell the key stronghold of West Point to the British commander Sir Henry Clinton for cash. It is the evil that men do that lives after them.

the globe, and creating, among many different peoples, peace, prosperity and the rule of law. Great Britain's colonial record has been much abused by her enemies, internal as well as external, but it can be summed up by the poignant remark of an old Indian shopkeeper in the city of Peshawar at the time of the Partition of India in 1947:

'Sahib, when the British go, who will protect us from the dangers of the night?'

Bibliography

BEESTON, SIR W., *A Narrative of the Descent in Jamaica by the French*, 1694
BERRIEDALE, KEITH A., *The Constitutional History of India*, London, 1936
BRADLEY, A. G., *Fight with France for North America*, London, 1900
BRIDGES, THE REV. GEORGE WILSON, *The Annals of Jamaica*, 1827
BRYANT, SIR ARTHUR, *The Years of Endurance*, London, 1942
                     The Age of Chivalry, London, 1963
CAMERON, IAN, *Lodestone and Evening Star*, London, 1965
CANNON, R., *Historical Records of the Queen's Regiment of Foot*, London, 1883
CARRINGTON, C. E., *The British Overseas*, Cambridge, 1968
CHURCHILL, SIR WINSTON, *A History of the English-Speaking Peoples*, London, 1958
CLARKE, THE REV. J. S., *The Life of James II*, London, 1813
CORBETT, SIR J. S., *England in the Seven Years' War*, London, 1908
CRONIN, VINCENT, *Louis XIV*, London, 1964
CUNDALL, FRANK, *Historic Jamaica*, London, 1915
                     Lady Nugent's Journal, London, 1939
Dictionary of National Biography
EGGENBERGER, DAVID, *A Dictionary of Battles*, London, 1968
FORREST, SIR G. W., *Life of Clive*, London, 1919
FORTESCUE, HON. J. W., *History of the British Army*, London, 1899
GARCIA, A., *History of the West Indies*, London, 1965
GLOVER, MICHAEL, *An Assemblage of Indian Army Soldiers & Uniforms*, London, 1973
GREEN, V. H. H., *Renaissance and Reformation*, London, 1952
HERTZ, G. B., *British Imperialism in the Eighteenth Century*, London, 1908
KEITH, A. B., *Constitutional History of the First British Empire*, Cambridge, 1930
LONG, *History of Jamaica*, 1774
MALLESON, COL. G. B., *History of the French in India*, Edinburgh, 1909
MAUROIS, ANDRÉ, *A History of France*, London, 1949
MITFORD, NANCY, *Madame de Pompadour*, London, 1954
MOOREHEAD, ALAN, *The Fatal Impact*, London, 1966
MORDAL, JACQUES, *Twenty-five Centuries of Sea Warfare*, London, 1959
PARES, R., *War and Trade in the West Indies, 1739–1763*, Oxford, 1936

PARKMAN, FRANCIS, *A Half-Century of Conflict*, London, 1899

PARRY, J. H., & SHERLOCK, P. M., *A Short History of the West Indies*, London, 1956

ROBERTS, CHARLES G. D., *A History of Canada*, London, 1898

ROBINSON, CAREY, *The Fighting Maroons of Jamaica*, Kingston, 1969

ROMIER, LUCIEN, *A History of France*, London, 1953

ROWSE, A. L., *Bosworth Field & the Wars of the Roses*, London, 1966

SEELEY, SIR J. R., *Expansion of England*, London, 1883

THOMSON, THE REV. THOMAS, *The Comprehensive History of England*, London, 1861

VILLIERS, ALAN, *Captain Cook*, London, 1967

WHITE, FREDA, *Three Rivers of France*, London, 1952

WILLIAMS, B., *Life of Pitt*, London, 1913

WILLIAMSON, JAMES A., *A Short History of British Expansion*, London, 1945

Index

Abercromby, General James: replaces Loudoun, 234; his attack on Ticonderoga, 236–42; relieved of command, 242; 243, 279

Acadia: definition of, 29; French established in, 31; brought under English flag, 38; contest for control of, 168–9

Aché, Admiral d': arrives in India, 222–3; defeated, 224; defeated again, 227; and again, 261; never recovers fighting spirit, 281

'Aeterni Regis' (Papal Bull), 50

Agincourt, battle of, 2, 7

Aix-la-Chapelle, Treaty of, 126, 157, 158, 164, 166–7, 191

Akbar, Mogul Emperor, 84

Albuera, battle of, 2

Alcáçovas, Treaty of, 50

Alexander VI, Pope, 12, 15

Alexander, Sir William, 35

Alivardi Khan, 205–6, 231

Almanza, battle of, 139

Almonde, van, Admiral, 75

America, naming of, 12n

Amherst, General Jeffrey, 188; sent to America, 234; takes Louisbourg, 235–6; sets out to join Abercromby, 243; task for 1759, 261–3; advances towards Quebec, 266; campaign against Montreal, 276–80; insists on surrender, 279; his achievements, 280

Amore, battle of, 113

Andros, Sir Edmund, 45, 46, 129, 132

Annapolis Royal (Port Royal), 139; abortive French attack on, 145–6

Anne, Queen, 138, 139

Anson, Admiral Sir George, 156, 176, 200, 233

Anunderaj, 232–3

Anville, duc d', 153, 155, 156

Anwar-u-din: declares neutrality, 100; fooled by Dupleix, 102; sends help to English, 107; makes peace with Dupleix, 108; killed at Amore, 113

Appanages, system of, 3

Apraksin, Marshal Count Stepan, 203

Arawaks, 47, 50, 59; cultivate Barbados, 63; in Jamaica, 68

Arcot, siege of, 120–1

Ardent, 146

Argall, Captain Samuel, 32–3, 35

Armagnacs, 3

Arni, battle of the, 122

Arnold, Benedict, 297, 297n

Artillery: Indian, performance of, 105; at Louisbourg, 149

Asiento, the (Contract), 159, 161

Augsburg, League of, 72

Aurungzebe, Mogul Emperor, 84–5; death of, 90

Auteuil, M. d', 124

Aztecs, 52

Babar, Mogul Emperor, 84, 92

Bantry Bay, battle of, 73

Barbados, annexation of, 63

Barber, Charles, 78

Barfleur, battle of, 75

Barrington, Colonel, captures Guadeloupe, 250–1

Bart, Jean (pirate), 74

Beachy Head, battle of, 74–5

Beaujeu, Capitaine, 180, 182

Beauséjour, Fort, capture by Moncton, 187

Beckford, Colonel, 77

Bedford, John, Duke of, 4

Beeston, Sir William, 77–81

Belle Île: naval battle off, 156; capture of, 290

Bellefonde, Marshal de, 75

Benbow, Admiral, 159–60

Bengal: operations of Clive and Watson in, 210–21

Berry, dukes of, 3

Berryer, M., 252

Berwick, James Fitzjames, Duke of, 138–9

Best, Captain, 87

Béveziers, battle of, 74–5

Biencourt, Governor, 33

Bienville, Céloron de, 170

Black Hole of Calcutta, 208

'Black vomit', the (yellow fever), 70